PRAISE F[...]
EDWARD M. HALL[...]
and CONNECT

"A real boost toward building a lifelong support system; this has the overall feel of a long, comfortable chat with a trusted friend."

—*Kirkus Reviews*

"Hallowell's style is easy and will be especially appealing to baby boomers searching for meaning and balance. . . . He may not be the first to identify the missing ingredient in many lives, but he can claim authority of a splendid articulation in this book."

—*Publishers Weekly*

"Aware of the pain and anxiety of life that is integral in the discovery process, Hallowell provides techniques and insights on how to achieve happiness in spite of what life throws in your path."

—*Cape Cod Times* (MA)

"There is a treasure on every page—a story, a quote, a snippet of a conversation and the reflections it sparked in Hallowell's own mind."

—*NAPRA ReView*

"Useful for those who feel disconnected, disconcerted, and discontent in a world where personal achievement has replaced personal relationships."

—*Library Journal*

BOOKS BY EDWARD M. HALLOWELL, M.D.

Worry: Controlling It and Using It Wisely

When You Worry About the Child You Love:
Emotional and Learning Problems in Children

What Are You Worth? (with William Grace)

Finding the Heart of the Child:
Essays on Children, Families, and Schools
(with Michael Thompson, Ph.D.)

Driven to Distraction (with John J. Ratey, M.D.)

Connect: 12 Vital Ties That Open Your Heart,
Lengthen Your Life, and Deepen Your Soul

Answers to Distraction (with John J. Ratey, M.D.)

CONNECT

12 Vital Ties that Open Your Heart, Lengthen Your Life, and Deepen Your Soul

Edward M. Hallowell, M.D.

POCKET BOOKS

New York   London   Toronto   Sydney   Singapore

POCKET BOOKS, a division of Simon & Schuster, Inc.
1230 Avenue of the Americas, New York, NY 10020

ISBN: 0-7434-0621-4

First Pocket Books trade paperback printing April 2001

10   9   8   7   6   5   4   3

Printed in the U.S.A.

To my mother and father
and
to the many people who offered their
personal stories for this book

Only connect . . .

Think where man's glory most begins and ends,
And say my glory was I had such friends.

Mutual empathy is the great unsung human gift.

With somebody to love, even the
most severely afflicted can make it.

CONTENTS

Introduction: What Counts Most in Life?   xi

PART ONE: THE POWER OF HEARTFELT CONNECTIONS   I

1: In the Human Moment   3
2: Speaking Personally: Connection Saved My Life   22
3: Me and Mr. S: A Miracle of Connection   37

PART TWO: CREATING CONNECTIONS   51

4: You Are Already Rich in Connections   53
5: Family: What Strings Our Hearts,
   and Unstrings Them, Too   64
6: Children: The Agony and the Ecstasy   80
7: Intimacy: The Example of One Marriage   84
8: Friends   103
9: Work, Part I: Creating Good Chemistry   112
10: Work, Part II: The Value of the Human Moment   124
11: Beauty   141
12: The Past   147
13: Nature and Special Places   156
14: Pets and Other Animals   161
15: Ideas and Information   165

16: Institutions and Organizations:
A Connected Man in a Connected Place 171

17: Creating a Connected School: Shady Hill 182

18: Mission amid the Rubble: One Connected Institution 191

19: Finding Your God: Connecting to What Is Beyond 199

20: A Good Place for You to Grow:
Your Connection to Yourself, Part I 205

21: Tapping Your Creative Side:
Your Connection to Yourself, Part II 215

PART THREE: HOPES AND FEARS:
CONNECTION AND DISCONNECTION 223

22: If Connection Is So Good, Why Is It in
Such Short Supply? 225

23: The Community of Good People 239

24: A Murder Next Door 243

25: Be a Hero, or a Star? Which Do You
Want for Your Children? 253

26: Breaking a Connection 260

27: When the Worst Happens: The Death of a Child 269

PART FOUR: SELF-ASSESSMENT AND PRACTICAL TIPS 283

28: How Connected Is Your Life? A Self-Assessment Quiz 285

29: Practically Speaking: Tips on Creating a
More Connected Life 291

PART FIVE: FINDING THE HEART OF YOUR LIFE 301

30: "If You Want to Be Happy . . ." 303

Acknowledgments 312

Index 315

INTRODUCTION

What Counts Most in Life?

"I ALMOST DIDN'T make it," a man said to me. "I don't know how I survived." He had just weathered bankruptcy and major surgery, both in the same year.

"How *did* you make it?" I asked.

He thought for a moment, then replied, "It was other people. My friends, my family, and thinking about what my dad would have done. That's what saved me."

I hear comments like this in my professional practice and in my private life every day. The connections we make are what pull us through the hard times and give meaning to the good.

Simply put, we need one another. We need connections that matter, connections that are heartfelt. We need to connect—or reconnect—to our friends, our families, our neighbors, our communities. We also need to connect—or reconnect—to our pasts, our traditions, and our ideals.

The way this can be done most naturally is in person through what I call the *human moment*. A human moment occurs anytime two or more people are together, paying attention to one another.

These connections are the key to what counts in life, from a happy family to a successful business to a sense of inner peace, even to physical health and longevity. But these interpersonal bridges are breaking down. Just as our highway system needs repair, the interpersonal infrastructure of America is weakening. We're losing human contact with one another, even though we don't mean to. We're busy. We're otherwise engaged. We're *somewhere else.*

More and more of us ache inside, yearning to connect but wondering how to. If you feel this way, don't feel alone. You are in the company of millions.

It is time for us to find one another once again. It is time to reconnect in this busy, disconnected world.

For most people, the two most powerful experiences in life are achieving and connecting. Almost everything that counts is directed toward one of these two goals. The peaks of life for most people are falling in love (connecting) and reaching a hard-won goal (achieving).

While we are doing well at achieving, we're not doing well at connecting. This book is about connecting, especially connecting with other people, live, in the human moment.

There are many kinds of connections people make. You can connect with your family, your friends, your pets; you can connect with your neighborhood, your political party, your baseball team; you can connect with your job, your garden, a part of the city you love, a favorite piece of music; you can connect with nature, the house you used to live in, your past; and you can connect with whatever is beyond knowledge—with the transcendent, with whatever you call God.

Strong connections make life feel satisfying and secure. But many of us have started to neglect the life of connection, giving most of our time to achievement and daily chores. This is a dangerous trend. It is time to make connecting a top priority again, because *both our health and our happiness depend upon it.*

Maybe you feel powerless; you think disconnection is a sign of the times. Life has grown too busy, you say, and you have all you can do just to stay afloat. Maybe you feel you don't have much control. But you have more control than you may think. Let me give an example of one woman's grassroots attempt to deal with the problem of weakening connections.

Christine Mitchell was upset because the people in her neighborhood didn't talk to one another. She lived in a perfectly pleasant suburb of Boston. The problem was that most people came home each day, closed their doors, got up the next day, went to work, then came home and closed their doors again. Few people knew one another. Now and then someone would walk outside to see what the siren and flashing lights were all about if an ambulance went by, and once in a while Christine would see two people actually standing on the sidewalk conversing. But that was rare.

Many people around the country are in such a situation. Most of us feel we are too busy to do anything about it, or we feel powerless or simply shy. Christine, however, decided to take action in her own small way. She went down to city hall and for ten dollars bought a booklet that listed all the phone numbers in her town by street address, followed by the name of the person who lived there. She then wrote a list of all the people who lived in her neighborhood. Eight hundred names.

I'll bring these people together, face-to-face, she said to herself. *I'll set it up so they'll have to talk to one another.* Her idea was simple. She decided to organize a neighborhood block party, inviting all the people on her list of eight hundred.

She had never organized a big event before, but she pushed ahead anyway, with her husband's enthusiastic encouragement. "Let's bring these people out of hiding!" he said to her.

"If this is a flop, I don't know what I'll do," she said back to him.

"It won't be a flop," he said.

How does he know? Christine thought to herself, but she went on with it anyway.

Many people said they'd come, but Christine was still worried. We've all seen people act enthusiastic about showing up somewhere, then opt out at the last minute for a million different reasons. It has become the modern style! Say *yes,* but do *no.* Still, Christine ordered refreshments for four hundred, a disc jockey, and some clowns and a magician to entertain the kids. Her work completed, she went to sleep wondering what she'd do if only a handful of people came.

The day arrived, the sun blessedly came out, and Christine got busy. The police arrived, as promised, and cordoned off the street. The DJ showed up early, as Christine and her husband put out tubs of Coke and tables of cookies and brownies.

Then there was a moment when all was ready but no one had come.

But that lasted only a moment. People started opening their

doors and walking out of their houses, ambling up the hill with their kids, and coming around the corners with their friends. Before long, the street was full of neighbors. People came in droves. In fact, 90 percent of the people Christine had contacted actually came. They talked, danced, sat on porches and ate, skateboarded down the street, and in general had fun together. A community began to take shape that afternoon.

After the party, this old neighborhood that had lain moribund for about three decades took on a whole new life. In the weeks and months that followed, there wasn't perfect harmony, of course, but at least there were signs of community where there hadn't been before. People started to stop and chat, they waved hello, and now that they actually *knew* some names, they called to people by their names. Neighbors started extending invitations to one another, taking the first steps out of anonymity. They began to share human moments. People started to connect.

Connection is an essential vitamin. You can't live without it.

Yet we are letting connections vanish. We see them disappearing like a coastline slowly eroding, but we don't know what to do about it. So we watch, and hope the tides will shift before we lose too much ground.

"There's nothing I can do about it," a busy working mom says to me. "I'm a slave to my schedule. Between the kids and my job, I barely have time to brush my teeth, let alone stay connected with my friends and neighbors. I'm already burning the candle at both ends. What else can I do?"

"I'd love to spend more time with my friends and relatives, or just work in my garden, but get real, it's impossible!" a man tells me when I suggest his excessive worrying may be due to a lack of connection in his life.

"I believe what you say about connection is true," a patient tells me after I tell him his poor health may be due to his isolated life. "I believe it is the key to feeling good in life. But most people are just too busy to be bothered. What can one person do?"

Not everyone can plan a block party like Christine's, but everyone can make a number of little changes that can deepen the connections in their lives. For example, you can get in touch with a relative you have been ignoring or feuding with; you can plan a regular lunch with a friend; you can start a book group that meets once a month; you can plan a regular card game or start some form of exercise with a friend you otherwise would hardly ever see; you can communicate with your elected representatives more than you do now; you can visit a museum you have been meaning to visit for years; you can attend your high school or college reunion; you can patronize a small local store or restaurant regularly and become friendly with the people who work there; you can say hello to toll takers; you can practice civility, even if others don't; you can go back to church or synagogue, or follow whatever your belief system dictates; you can eat family dinner as often as possible and read to your children whenever you can. These concrete steps, and others like them, can create a connected life for you. That will not only make you happier but make you live longer.

Moments of connection boost our spirits. For example, even though I may not have seen her in months, Karen, the woman behind the counter at the local florist shop, always smiles at me and says, "Hi, Ned," whenever I go in. She even remembers my wife and kids and asks after them by name! Or when my kids rush up to me when I get home, and yell, *"Daddy!!"*—at that moment it really doesn't matter what kind of day I had. The glow can last for hours. Even a connection to the past can pick up our spirits. On a wall in my office I have a photograph of Ted Williams. Many times have I sat back and gazed at Ted, who is frozen in the photograph at the end of his swing, and for some strange reason I have felt better about life for having looked at him.

Maybe Karen smiles just because it is good business to smile, and maybe my kids rush to greet me just because they want something from me, and maybe my feeling for the photograph of Ted Williams is just sentimental nonsense. But I think we all know there's more to it than that. All these ordinary kinds of connections—and thousands more—make ordinary life extraordinary, if we let them.

As a psychiatrist I can always tell when my patients are starting to get better, because they start to increase their connections. They see more of their friends, or they deepen their relationships at work, or they rediscover an old interest like gardening or sailing, or they start going to religious services, or they get closer to their extended family, or they start having more fun with their immediate family.

Far more telling than financial gains or other kinds of trophies, increased connection reflects improved emotional health. It also creates it.

What is connection, or what I sometimes call *connectedness*? It is a feeling of being a part of something larger than yourself. The something may be a friendship, a marriage, a team, a school, a company, an activity you love, a country, even a set of ideals, like the Bill of Rights, or a belief system, like a religion.

People know instinctively what connectedness is. A New York cabdriver didn't use the word "connectedness," but he evoked the feeling of it when he told me about his old neighborhood. "I grew up in this city, in L'll I'ly," he said (his pronunciation of "Little Italy" omitted the *t*s). "The candy stores had jukeboxes. I met my wife at one when she was seventeen and I was eighteen. We danced in the store. Old men played pinochle at card tables on the sidewalk. All that is gone now. But I'm still married. To the same woman, too!" A connected family, a connected neighborhood, a connected workplace all convey a special feeling, akin to being in love. That feeling of connectedness leads to health and achievement.

When you walk hand in hand with someone you love, when you pray, when you lie in bed sick and stroke your dog, who has hoisted herself up next to you knowing you're not feeling well, when you see a photograph of your high school class—all these moments connect you to something larger than yourself.

These connections, put together, form what I call *connectedness*. (I use the words "connection" and "connectedness" synonymously.) It can be a titanic force in our lives. It is as crucial to how we feel about ourselves as is our physical health or economic state. Indeed, it helps control both. What exact good does it do us? What is the price of ignoring it? What are some practical ways each of us can tap into its power in our own life more fully? These are the questions this book answers.

For evidence of the transforming power of connectedness, you don't have to look at scientific studies, although they now abound. You only have to look at your own life. Think of the number of times you have felt down and looked for a friend to pick you up. Think of feeling disappointed at work and taking solace in a long phone conversation that night. Think of the excellent work you once did when you were part of a well-run team. Or consider how much your children mean to you. These connections are our life-lines; they save our lives.

Not so fast, the skeptic objects; connections may feel good but they don't save lives. Oh yes they do. A study done in the 1980s by Dr. David Spiegel on a group of women suffering from terminal breast cancer provided a vivid example of how connection can save lives. Half the women in the study met regularly together and talked about their lives, while the other half did not. The half that met as a group lived, on average, *twice* as long as those who did not meet. The healing power of such human connection is now widely recognized by doctors, as evidence from studies like Dr. Spiegel's pours in.

Of course, it can happen the other way, too. Disconnection can hurt, even kill. The bit of criticism at just the wrong moment, or the one rejection too many, or the phone that doesn't ring can make you miserable. Disconnection can be devastating. Nothing hurts more. This is why the ancients feared banishment as a punishment worse than death. Indeed, we have scientific evidence now that so-cial isolation leads to death.

Not only do individuals thrive on the power of connection; busi-nesses and other institutions do, too. Businesses today more and more are trying to hold on to their good people, and a chief means of doing this is to create a connected atmosphere in the workplace. This does not require touchy-feely encounter sessions, it just re-quires tapping into the invisible force of connection. You do this by talking to people, and treating them with respect. The connected employee stays with the company, works harder, and is more apt to be creative.

As a psychiatrist for the past twenty years, I have seen thousands of individuals in my private office, as well as families, couples, and groups. Outside the office, I have consulted to schools across the country, to businesses, to churches and support organizations, as well as to other groups. As a member of the faculty of the Harvard Medical School I have taught medical students, residents, and fel-lows. I have worked across the socioeconomic spectrum, treating low-income patients in state hospitals as well as the very well-to-do. I have treated the seriously mentally ill and the mildly upset. I have treated children as young as two and adults as old as eighty-two. I have treated people from all lines of work, from bus drivers to doctors to professors to actors to people the world calls bums.

Many of their stories appear in this book. The stories and anecdotes in this book are true, with the exception of a few that are composites of several true stories.

The most important lesson I learned from all these people is the power of connection.

The aim of this book is to convince you to make time for connectedness, even if it involves aggravation—and it usually does! The aim of this book is not just to convince you that connectedness is healing—although information will be provided to show you it is much more powerful in healing than you ever imagined. It is also to show you that connectedness is attainable, and once attained, enduring.

A poignant example of just how enduring and powerful a connection between two people can be was given to me by a woman whose parents were in a nursing home: "Almost a year ago my dad had a stroke during a surgical procedure. After two weeks in intensive care, he was transferred to the nursing home where my mother was already a resident, suffering from Alzheimer's. Dad's language now was made up of mostly nonsense syllables. But even with Mom in her own world, suffering from Alzheimer's, and Dad coping with his stroke, each one found ways to continue to look after the other and get help when it was needed. For example, Mom alerted the nurse when Dad had a grand mal seizure, even though she often doesn't recognize us! The way Mom and Dad look at each other, touch each other, and just stay beside each other holding hands is a testimony to their deep connection. This year, on October first, they will celebrate their fifty-ninth anniversary."

The ability to connect with others is built into us, like sight or touch. The chance to connect is open to us all for as long as we live.

But many people, especially us men, go through life rarely opening up, always playing our cards close to the vest. "When it comes right down to it," we say defensively, "it's a dog-eat-dog world." Or, "I ask no quarter and give no quarter." Or my uncle's favorite, "Trust no one and you'll never get disappointed." Aphorisms like these can justify a lifetime of being guarded. The statement "We are all fundamentally alone" becomes self-fulfilling prophecy. There are legions of people who trust no one.

But why not take a chance? Sure, we are alone in some basic ways, and sure, people can let you down. But connections always beckon, like lights flickering along the shoreline. They're there, if only we'll respond.

Everywhere I go I see the same problem screaming out at me. It is the problem of not being sufficiently connected—to a person, to a job, to a peer group, to anything that can give meaning to your life.

It's gone too far. If a surgeon came upon a man in the street whose leg was severed in two, he would instantly rush to offer help. All his training would propel him to the injured man's side, no matter what else was going on. As a psychiatrist, I find that human disconnection today screams out at me with the urgency of a body hemorrhaging in the street. I want to apply tourniquets, stop the bleeding, put a pillow under the victim's head, make sure the airway is clear and the heartbeat is strong.

It is one thing to attend to a bleeding body. But how do you attend to emotions? How do you put a tourniquet on time? How do you say to people, "Slow down, talk to one another, reconnect with what matters"? How do you say, "Your life depends upon it"? How do you say this and be heard?

I say it the only way I can, simply and plainly. The human heart is hungry and there is sustenance all around, free. It is called connectedness.

Rebuilding connection in your life does not mean you have to attend a love-in, or that you should want to. And it does not mean you must adopt some mindless, naïve view of human nature. One of my teachers used to caution me, "It is impossible to overestimate how selfish people are." His is a point of view we all have shared, I suppose, but we all have also found, now and then, that given the right opportunity, people do go the other way, if not *against* their self-interest, then *toward* the interest of another person. Maybe the trick is to find out how to make those two dovetail: self-interest and other-interest. This can be done, because as much as self-interest rules us, the desire to connect and to help others also runs deep within most people. Ask an average person what they would do if they won the lottery. Soon after saying they'd quit their job and fly to Hawaii, they usually think of some person or some organization they'd give some money to. People are not so selfish. They just need to find the right way to connect.

Connectedness can work for you, but it is far from simple. It can be dangerous, arduous, miserable, or simply boring. Cultivating connectedness requires determination and patience, much like cultivating a garden, only this is the garden of your connections.

But the rewards of making this garden grow can be nothing less than all that matters.

I

The

POWER

of

HEARTFELT

CONNECTIONS

~~~⁀~~~

ONE

In the Human Moment

LIFE IS LOSS. For all we gain, we also lose—a friend, a day, a chance, finally life itself. To oppose the pain of loss, we use a human glue, the force of love. The force of love creates our many different connections. This is what saves us all.

If you think about what you live for, what really matters to you, you usually think of some person or group of people—maybe your spouse and your children, maybe a friend. Or you might think of an institution you give your all to, or your work, or a set of ideals.

These are all different kinds of connection. To thrive, indeed just to survive, we need warmhearted contact with other people. The close-to-the-vest, standoffish life is bad for your body and your soul. Like a vitamin deficiency, a human contact deficiency weakens the body, the mind, and the spirit. Its ravages can be severe (depression, physical illness, early death) or they can be mild (underachievement, fatigue, loneliness), but they are certain to set in. Just as we need vitamin C each day, we also need a dose of the human moment—positive contact with other people.

We know we need food, we know we need vitamins and minerals, we know we need water and air, clothing and shelter. Most of us even know we need sunshine. But most people *don't* know that a major other factor belongs on our list of essentials: one another. This is not a warm-and-fuzzy proclamation. It is as scientifically proven as is our need for vitamin C. Only here the C stands for "connection."

Don't confuse connection—feeling a part of something larger than yourself, feeling close to another person or group, feeling welcomed and understood—with contacts. Don't confuse connecting with networking. Sure, every businessperson benefits from many contacts and a full Rolodex. And sure, networking is a good way to develop opportunities.

But at the same time, contacts can overrun your life like wildflowers; they may be pretty, but they can suffocate important growth. Networking can distract you from your primary goal, as "opportunities" these days pop up like weeds, everywhere you look. The Internet is full of opportunities, all vying for your time. You can spend so much time networking, contacting, and surfing the Net that you forget what you're networking, contacting, and surfing for. One deep connection to a person and one properly executed business strategy are worth much more than a bevy of contacts and a frenzy of networking and surfing.

Luckily, the kind of positive connection we really need is available in all our lives. My experience as a psychiatrist, the experience of physicians in all medical specialties, and an abundance of solid scientific data all prove the enormous benefits of connection in daily life. But many things get in the way of people reaping these benefits, stumbling blocks like too many daily obligations, or shyness, or time, or fear.

You can step past those obstacles and strengthen your connections in a variety of practical ways, which this book explores. The benefits of connection will repay you many times over. Meaning, satisfaction, intensity, pleasure, ease from pain—the benefits we yearn for—are all to be found in various forms of connection.

I see the need to connect frustrated everywhere I go. Traveling the country as a lecturer or traveling the aisles of the local supermarket as a shopper, I feel people's desire to connect, as well as the pressures that prevent them from doing so. "I'll catch you later, OK?" "We *have* to get together sometime!" "I can't believe how long it's been!" People want to connect, but they are just so busy. People want to reach out, but they feel too hurried to do so, or too scared.

And yet their lives depend upon it.

It is only recently that researchers have proved the lifesaving value of connection. Among those who gathered the quantitative scientific evidence that now confirms the importance of connection, Dr. Lisa Berkman stands out. Before her studies, skeptics insisted that connections might be "nice" but were not powerful enough to affect basic biology.

Dr. Berkman showed otherwise. Now chair of the Department of Health and Social Behavior at the Harvard School of Public Health, she was the author of the groundbreaking Alameda County Study, published in 1979. This study followed the lives of some seven thousand people in Alameda County, California, for nine years.

To measure the effect of connection quantitatively, Dr. Berkman and her team surveyed the people to find out the specifics of how they were connected or not connected. They found out whether the people were married or lived alone, what kind of contact they had with friends and relatives, whether or not they belonged to a church or other religious organization, and how much they participated in voluntary organizations and groups.

Armed with this information, Dr. Berkman then looked at the people's risk of dying over a nine-year period. She found that the most isolated people were *three times* more likely to die in that nine-year period than those with stronger social ties. Never before had death itself been proved to be linked to social isolation or lack of connection.

The protective value of connection showed, under statistical multivariate analysis, to be present at all ages. The people surveyed in the study were of ages thirty to sixty-nine; a statistical advantage of living longer was enjoyed by the highly connected group at every age. Even in the presence of health hazards such as smoking, obesity, alcohol use, poverty, poor use of health services, and poor health at the start of the study, people who had strong social ties lived *significantly longer* than those who did not.

To gain the benefits of connection, it didn't matter what kind of connection a person had. For example, you could live alone, but have frequent contact with friends or relatives, and be protected. Or you could belong to various voluntary organizations, but not participate in any religious activity, and still be protected. Or your connection could come from church and family, but not from any volunteer organization, and you would still be protected. The key to gaining the benefits of connection was to have several kinds of connection, but the kinds could vary from person to person.

The people who were in the most danger of dying were the 10–15 percent who were most isolated. This study has been replicated about fifteen times now in other parts of the United States and around the world, including Sweden, England, and Finland.

On a smaller scale, I looked at the power of connection in a different group of people—high school students—by going back to my old high school, the Phillips Exeter Academy. Exeter is a prep school in New Hampshire, an academically rigorous, competitive boarding school.

In 1989, the woman who was then principal, Kendra O'Donnell, asked the school's psychologist, Dr. Michael Diamonti, and me to systematically examine Exeter—the students, parents, and faculty— and try to find out which factors predicted success and happiness.

Contrary to stereotype, Exeter is not just for the wealthy. Its large endowment allows 35 percent of the students to receive financial aid. Its student body, from forty-four states and twenty-seven foreign countries, is geographically and racially diverse.

Mike Diamonti and I interviewed hundreds of students, parents, and faculty. These people also filled out questionnaires assessing a wide range of variables, including basic demographics like race, religion, and income, and other variables, like self-esteem, feelings about the future, drug use, and depression.

From the huge amount of data, one factor emerged as the most telling: connectedness. Those students who did well had it, while those who didn't lacked it.

We defined connectedness as a feeling of being a part of something larger than yourself. We assessed it, on questionnaires, from responses to statements like "My friends can get me through anything" and "There are groups for whom I would make great sacrifices" and "I feel a strong commitment to my family." Students who agreed with these statements and others like them were considered connected, those who disagreed were considered disconnected. About 80 percent of the students fell into the connected category, about 20 percent into the disconnected.

On every measure of mental health and happiness that we used, as well as every measure of achievement, the students who did the best were the connected students. Those who were in distress were the disconnected.

Specifically, the connected students were the least depressed, had the highest self-esteem, felt most comfortable with their families, were most positive about their education, used the least drugs or alcohol, felt the least stress, and had the highest grade point averages.

Now, almost ten years after the study at Exeter was completed, the value of connection has been confirmed by a large national study. Michael Resnick, from the University of Minnesota, teamed up with others around the country on the National Longitudinal Study on Adolescent Health. They studied some twelve thousand adolescents in grades seven through twelve and came up with some powerful findings, which they published in the *Journal of the American Medical Association* in 1997.

Like the Exeter study, this study set out to determine which were the most significant risk factors as well as protective factors in adolescents' lives. The interviewers asked the students about emotional distress, suicidal thoughts or actions, violent behavior, the use of cigarettes, alcohol, or marijuana, and early sexual intercourse or pregnancy.

The study then looked at dozens of variables in these students' lives, searching for what mattered most, both positively and negatively.

The study found two conditions most protective, and these findings were remarkably similar to our findings in the Exeter study.

The first protective factor was parent-family connectedness. This was defined in the Minnesota study as "closeness to mother and/or father, perceived caring by mother and/or father, satisfaction with relationship with mother and/or father, and feeling loved and wanted by family members."

The second protective factor was similar to the first. It was connectedness at school. This was defined as the student's feeling that people are treated fairly at school, that he is close to people at school, and that he feels part of his school.

In assessing connectedness, what mattered was the adolescent's perception, not some concrete prescription of what makes for a connected family or school. There was no unique formula for creating feelings of connectedness. Both parents did not have to live in the same home, nor did the family have to eat dinner together. The family simply had to do *whatever it needed to do* to create the *feeling of connectedness* in the family. Different families did this in different ways. All that mattered was that they did it. The same applied at school. No one kind of school was best. All that mattered was that the student *felt connected.*

The study showed that when the feeling of connectedness to family and school was present, the children were protected, but when such feelings of connectedness were absent, the children were at much higher risk for emotional distress, violent behavior, suicidal thoughts and actions, and substance abuse.

As we parents wonder, sometimes with a feeling of helplessness, if there is *anything* we can do to reduce the chances of our children getting into bad straits, it is good to know that, yes, there is something that can be done. It takes effort and creativity, but a determined effort to create connectedness at home and at school will help—more than anything else.

The protective force of connection applies not just to children. The MacArthur Foundation Study on Aging (published in 1998) showed that the two most powerful predictors of well-being in old age are (1) frequency of visits with friends and (2) frequency of attendance at meetings of organizations. This study, like the Minnesota study, was carefully designed and conducted over a wide sample of individuals nationally. Again, it is useful to know that two simple steps can protect you as you age, and that these two steps are actually fun! Just keep up with your friends and go to meetings of organizations you believe in.

We have data, then, showing the positive effects of connection in the old and the young. How about the middle aged? A study done by Sheldon Cohen and also published in the *Journal of the American Medical Association* (June 25, 1997) looked at people in the middle of life, ages eighteen to fifty-five. Cohen wanted to test the hypothesis that ties to family, friends, work, and community could alter the body's ability to fight off infections.

He found 276 volunteers and asked them about twelve different types of social ties, such as to spouse, friend, workmate, and parent.

Then he infected all the volunteers with one of two different viruses known to produce the common cold.

He found that the more connected people did better in fighting off the virus. Specifically, "those with more types of social ties were less susceptible to common colds, produced less mucus, were more effective in ciliary clearance of their nasal passages, and shed less virus." Those who had six or more social ties did *four times better* than those who had less than four social ties.

So what matters is not only the presence of connection but the diversity of it as well.

These studies are not minor footnotes in some obscure journal, but major findings, of enormous significance. It is time for the message to make its way from the medical and scientific journals into the minds of us all. Connectedness is essential for emotional and physical health at all ages.

As a practicing psychiatrist, I learned about the power of connectedness at the start of my career. Back in the early 1980s, as I was finishing up my training, there was a spike in the incidence of depression among young adults nationwide. This was a new trend. The highest levels of depression had previously appeared among old people, people who were dealing with distressing issues of sickness, loss, and death.

But now many young people, in the eighteen-to-thirty-five age group, were feeling depressed, as well as many people in middle age. The once upbeat baby boomer generation, as it came of age and achieved success, was not glorying in its achievements but rather was feeling dissatisfied, cynical, and disconnected. As much as it had achieved, its achievements were not leading to happiness.

Many of the young people who sought treatment for depression had achieved high levels of material success but felt depressed because they had not connected in a significant way to anything larger than themselves. Although they had succeeded professionally, they were depressed because they had failed to connect—to one another, to a loved one, to an ideal, or to a purpose or group they believed in. Although they loved independence and freedom, life was becoming too much of a one-man or one-woman show.

As the years have passed, I have seen the trend only deepen. People are increasingly working at home or working in isolation at their jobs, spending time marketing themselves, coming up with creative ways of reinventing themselves according to the prevailing needs of the new, knowledge-based economy, but all the while feeling more and more insecure, cynical, worried, and finally, isolated.

Let me offer an example from my practice in those years. In the 1980s a twenty-six-year-old man—Mr. G—came to see me because, as he put it, "I don't love anyone."

The externals of Mr. G's life sounded almost ideal. He was in perfect health and looked great. He still played basketball twice a week and looked as if old age would never overtake him. He had built a successful business from the ground up, relying on hard work and intuition to make it thrive. Now, only five years out of college, his business was in good shape and he was doing well, having started with nothing. He was married to a beautiful woman who loved him, he was welcomed in many clubs and organizations, and he had friends who liked him. So, why was he unhappy?

Because he had never learned how to make loving connections. He had grown up disconnected, with parents who never showed him how to take pleasure in other people or in himself. As we looked at his externally successful life, we found that he took real pleasure in almost none of it. For example, he told me about his business in about thirty seconds, as if it were no achievement for a man to go from nothing to owning his own successful business in five years. "It's no big deal," he said. "Anyone with half a brain can do it. All you have to do is get an idea and put in the hours. It means almost nothing to me. Millions of people have done better."

I asked him if he enjoyed his basketball. Even that was becoming a trial, he said, because he pushed himself so hard. As for his friends, he saw them mostly as "just acquaintances—people I have to network with to make a business grow."

When I asked about his wife, he said, "I feel sorry for her. I really do. I feel very little toward her, and she deserves better than that."

Growing up, he got little from his parents, both of whom had to work hard to make ends meet. They were not abusive to him, but they were not loving, either. "My father was basically a stiff. He still is. He told me he didn't amount to anything, and I would never amount to anything either. As far as I'm concerned, he was right." Speaking in a tense, slightly sarcastic way, he then asked, "Is there a cure for someone like me?"

As the therapy progressed, we began to see a pattern in Mr. G's life. Whenever he felt bad, his solution was to try to *achieve more,* whether in school, college, or work. In fact, success became his only cure. He had no lasting ties. When he was a child, his family moved around a lot, so he never made strong bonds anywhere. He never attended church, and he never got involved in any club or group like Boy Scouts or YMCA. "I thought those things were for dweebs," he said.

His only means to make himself feel better was to achieve. He developed this strategy over years, starting in about eighth grade, and it continued right into the present. The fact that it didn't work only made him try harder. He figured that someday, if he made enough money or grew his business big enough, he would feel happy inside. His entire life was based on that assumption. As he was growing up, no one told him or showed him any different, and as an adult he found no other route. So success became his mantra.

He was a proud man, and not about to reach out when he felt lonely or sad. Work hard, however, he could do. So the pattern continued: pain followed by hard work, followed by more pain, followed by more hard work. It was amazing, really, that he came to see me. He did so only because his family physician had insisted. "I went out and got all the things I was supposed to get, the pretty wife, the business, the house. Now, you tell me—where did I go wrong?"

His appreciation of the irony of his situation—having it all but enjoying none of it—deepened as the therapy progressed, leading him to bitter condemnations of himself, and pretty soon of me. "I'm a loser," he would say. "I'm just another guy with an OK business." Then, "Don't you have any solutions? What a racket you have!" At the same time that he was beating up on himself and on me, he decided he wanted to meet with me more frequently.

I was basically treating a vitamin deficiency in this man, only the vitamin was human connection. At last, with me, he got a chance to be himself, for no gain other than the gain of connection. He could complain, be as cynical as he wanted, feel sorry for himself, ridicule me, put up no pretenses at all, and still find me wondering what he was really all about.

As we met more often he began to devalue me and the psychotherapy even more. "Nice work if you can get it" became his mocking refrain for the job of being a psychotherapist. He also began to criticize the way I dressed, the appearance of my office, and my casual demeanor. "You'd get eaten alive in the business world," he chided. "Do you even *own* a suit? I just can't see you closing a major deal." At the same time, he started to feel better.

His self-condemnation began to subside as his anger found a target other than himself—me! One day he made the following interpretation: "You know, coming in here and getting down on you feels a lot like what my father did to me and what I do to myself every day. It makes me feel good, getting it off me and onto you." He then thought of his wife and his mother and began to feel sad for having "dumped on them" even though they had both been good to him.

I then reminded Mr. G that "Nice work if you can get it" was a refrain from a love song.

He agreed that he had dismissed love, the way he had dismissed me.

"Well, that *is* interesting," I said. "You used to say you had never felt love at all."

He was discovering in his sessions with me a new aspect of life. While Mr. G had started off in therapy as driven, self-absorbed, unable to love, and feeling empty, he now was becoming filled—with anger and sadness. More and more a genuine person was emerging from the steel beams he'd lived within.

As true feelings emerged, he also began to joke around with me. Instead of just insulting me, he would tell me humorous stories from work, or jokes he'd heard on the radio. The cynicism in the room subsided, and the warmth began to increase. Mr. G began to relax as he started to trust me.

He also began to welcome his wife into the new world of emotion he was discovering. He began to joke around with her. "She's got a great sense of humor," he said. "I just have never tuned in to that."

"Probably because you kept her at such a distance," I replied.

He started to want to hear about the details of his wife's day, about her life, not out of obligation but because he really wanted to hear. "Her day is more interesting than mine, why shouldn't I want to hear about it?" he asked rhetorically, as if he had to justify an interest in his wife. She was a teacher. "I love hearing her stories about those kids. I don't know why I didn't get into this sooner," he exclaimed to me. "My wife is in fact very cool!" Soon she asked him if they could have a child, and he agreed to start trying. Not long after that his wife became pregnant, and Mr. G began to think of what he would do for his child that had not been done for him. He also became more of an interactive manager at work, delegating more, setting up others for success.

All these changes happened gradually, and many details have had to be omitted here to condense the story. The unifying theme, though, was always the opening up of Mr. G's capacity to connect. That capacity had been there all along; it was simply never developed. He learned the basics of connectedness with me, and it started to grow in his sessions with me, then quickly it spread to all other aspects of his life. This is the way with the feeling of genuine connection: once you have it in one place, you want to feel it everywhere.

When I looked at depression in the successful adults I treated in the eighties, I would see the themes of Mr. G over and over again. No matter how much success people had, they felt alone. That kind of isolation breeds depression.

A popular—and excellent—book that had come out shortly before that time (in 1979) was Christopher Lasch's *The Culture of Narcissism.* Lasch looked at the same phenomenon I would be seeing in my practice and dubbed it narcissism—a generation and culture preoccupied with itself.

I took a different slant. In treating successful but depressed adults, I found that the solution to the pain they felt was for them to forge connections that mattered. A true narcissist is so self-absorbed that he can't do this, but I did not find most of these people to be truly narcissistic. This is because, like Mr. G, they wanted to connect, given the chance and some encouragement. But they were caught in a culture that didn't easily offer connections. The problem was not so much within the mind—that is, a narcissistic personality—as within the changing world. Community had broken down during the decades of this generation's coming of age, starting in the 1960s.

The trend has only become more pronounced in the years since I first started thinking about it. This breakdown in the structures of community has led to what *looks like* widespread selfishness and narcissism but really is only the logical outcome of people's not feeling connected to something larger than themselves. When the center of your world is yourself, you look pretty selfish.

But selfishness is the effect, not the cause. While it may look as if an increase in selfishness is the cause of the breakdown in community, it is actually the other way around. The selfishness that now appears to be rampant is actually emotional isolation.

Just look at Mr. G. He was never introduced to the kinds of connections that could have sustained him, so he turned with single-mindedness to success and achievement, neglecting his capacity to love. The real enemy was emotional isolation, from childhood on up. You can be the person in charge—as was Mr. G, as an adult—and still be emotionally isolated. Such people can *look* selfish and narcissistic. But unlike the true narcissist, they still carry the capacity to love, waiting, ready to be activated within them. They just need to learn how to connect, and then make time to do it.

The sources of connection the previous generation relied on have been trimmed way back. The family unit is in flux. Extended families are so extended that regular contact is rare. Politics, since the Vietnam War and Watergate, have spawned a hugely alienating cynicism that persists to this day.

Neighborhoods lack the cohesion they used to have. There is such mobility in our society that people come and go all the time. Mr. G experienced this as a child and suffered for it, in that he developed no lasting roots. While it is a great blessing that we all have the chance to improve our lives and get better jobs, one of the unfortunate consequences, sometimes, is that we do not put the time and effort into getting to know the neighborhood we move into. Why should we? We'll be gone in a few years. Why set ourselves up for more losses than we have to? Our "neighborhood" then becomes the ersatz one of TV and the Net.

Churches, synagogues, and other places of worship try to make up for what's missing. More and more, places of worship attract members not because of theology but because of the community programs they offer, the drama or reading group, the teen program. Or they may offer nonreligious services, like day care, grief counseling, and marriage counseling. People often "shop" for their place of worship not based upon denomination but upon these other, nonreligious factors. While God is still part of the message, human connection is often the more powerful drawing card. As Louise Conant, associate rector of Christ Church in Cambridge, Massachusetts, said to me, "It used to be that people came together in church on Sunday morning to celebrate the community that they had the rest of the week, and now they come to church on Sunday morning to find the community that they don't have the rest of the week."

Schools also have taken on much of the burden of trying to fill the connectedness gap, but they can't do it all. I consult to many schools around the country, both elementary schools and high schools, and I hear of the same dilemma every place I go. The schools are being asked to do more than they can do. They are being asked to give children everything from values and table manners to organizational skills to friendships and clubs, as well as academic skills—not to mention self-esteem! We have to find more creative solutions than transferring the demands of the connectedness gap back onto the few institutions, like schools, that have survived.

The personal freedom this generation—my generation—worked so hard to achieve has exacted its price. The price is disconnection. You want the freedom to get divorced and leave a painful marriage? Fine. You want the freedom to stay away from church because of all the hypocrisy you see infecting it? Fine. You want to flee neighborhoods because they're stultifying, or because you can make more money by moving? Fine. You want to postpone or avoid having children so you can develop your career and avoid making the same mistakes your parents made? Fine. You want to disconnect yourself from politics because you think it's so corrupt? Fine. You want to put a wall up against members of the opposite sex because you don't trust them? Fine. You want to stay away from your parents and other extended family members because they hurt or bore you so much when you see them? Fine.

But in exchange for the freedom to disconnect in all these ways, you will have to live with the voids you create.

Not only do I see the problem of disconnection in my practice, but I see evidence of it in the press every day, often in unlikely places—for example, the fashion pages of the *New York Times*. On March 24, 1998, Amy Spindler wrote, "Everyone watched the Academy Awards last night. Everyone has seen 'Titanic.' Everyone is on the Internet. Everyone wears the same 15 or so designer labels. So why is it that the more consumers have in common, the more isolated they feel and the more disconnected they feel from the culture and from one another?" She goes on to comment how Steven Meisel's photography for a Calvin Klein advertising campaign "tapped into the latest spirit of the times: disconnection. . . . images depicting the height of isolation, figures in close proximity but with eyes never meeting."

Eyes never meeting. We walk down the sidewalk and we look above, beyond, or away from the people who pass us by. There isn't the familiarity or trust to offer a smile, so instead the gaze averts. Like figures in the Calvin Klein ad campaign, we stand near one another but we feel no connection. It bespeaks a massive problem, a problem that I have been seeing grow over the past twenty years. The problem that started as an increase in depression in young adults has billowed into widespread disconnection throughout our society. Old people talk of feeling cut off or isolated, as well as young people. Almost everyone recognizes a decline in civility, or that they get bad service more and more, or that their doctor doesn't talk to them; or they recognize simply the disappearance of what I call the *human moment:* people talking to one another in person with interest.

We must work creatively to regain the company of one another. As one of my patients said to me, "We have to learn how to hang out together again."

The patients I see now, at the end of the 1990s—as opposed to someone like Mr. G, from the 1980s—complain not so much of depression as of insecurity and worry. They are incredibly well connected electronically, but they feel overwhelmed with all they are connected to. They feel overwhelmed with the need to keep up, to pursue new opportunities while taking care of current business— the need to be ready for change, indeed to *anticipate* change, while staying on top of each day's demands.

They worry they will not be able to make next year what they made this year, or they worry their business will get taken over, or they worry that they are becoming obsolete, even if they are not. Their real problem is that they have no stabilizing network of human connections to help them keep perspective.

What makes life so hard now is precisely what is making it so easy. The very tools that have opened up the economy—the tools of technology—are the tools that have made everyone feel vulnerable. As the advertisement says, the rules have changed. In this knowledge-based, global, speeded-up economy, I hear my patients who work in business, law, and even medicine tell me all the time, "The only constant is change." Frenzy and worry have overtaken depression. You have no time to be depressed. You might lose your job!

One woman, Dr. L, came to see me to help her deal with insecurity in her job situation. A principal investigator (PI, for short) of a research team at a major hospital, this physician/scientist appeared to be on top of her profession. Indeed, she was. She had grants that would carry her research for two more years, she had a clinical practice that she enjoyed, and she had a happy marriage with two children. Another Mr. G—someone who seemed to have it all but wasn't happy.

However, her reasons were different. Unlike Mr. G, she knew how to connect. Her problem was that the fast-changing world was becoming too much for her emotionally. Too much insecurity, too many bureaucratic demands, too many people depending on her, not enough downtime. It all added up to a woman who was doing extremely well but who felt she might collapse at any moment. "I am a living house of cards," she said to me.

She lacked the stabilizing connections she needed, she lacked moorings in the rough sea of modern life—moorings like a sage mentor, or a belief in God, or just the security that she would have grant money for more than two more years!

"I run the lab, I'm the PI, so I am everyone else's mentor. I don't have a mentor anymore, only competitors. I go to these conferences in Washington where I am feted along with the other PIs, and we all congratulate each other, but the subtext is that we're eyeing each other all the time, trying to see who is getting what. My research is good, so I know that a lot of them would love to see me fail. And I could deal with that, if all I had to do was research. But that is the least of my problems. I love doing research, but I hardly have any time to do research at all. Writing grant proposals is a full-time job in itself. Not to mention seeing my patients, and once in a while spending an evening with my family. Everything is out of balance, but for the life of me I can't see how to fix it."

This is the common dilemma now: so many obligations that it is hard to balance them all, but not enough security to cut back on any.

I wasn't able to give Dr. L a solution, but in spending an hour with me now and then she started to calm down inside. It is amazing how powerful worrying out loud with another person can be. Indeed, my first law of worry control is simply "Never worry alone." Dr. L worried with me. In the process she started to feel less vulnerable, more in control, less frantic. Perhaps I served as the mentor she no longer had, although I was not teaching her or directing her research. I filled a role in her life, and I gave her a time and a place where she could tend to herself.

I provided a stabilizing connection for Dr. L. This was more important than any solution I could have come up with. She was better at solutions than I was, anyway. She knew her life better than I did. But what I could offer was the time, place, and structure to connect. She took strength from our discussions. She also had a place to relax and laugh. Laughter is a good sign that a connection is strong.

Both Mr. G and Dr. L needed help in securing stronger connections: Mr. G to other people, and Dr. L to herself. In both cases, sitting down with another person—in this case, me—made a big difference.

The essence of making connection is the human moment, two people sitting together, talking, or even just sharing each other's silent presence, but with concern for the other person. This certainly does not have to involve a psychotherapist, just any interested other person. But the human moment is disappearing from modern life as technology makes contact in person unnecessary and as the hurried pace makes it impossible.

A vast irony surrounds the current crisis of disconnection. It is that—electronically—never in human history have we been as connected as we are today. Indeed, the technological explosion of various forms of connection and communication in the past two decades may be *the story* of the twentieth century.

Technology has indeed worked miracles of connection. E-mail, faxes, FedEx, answering machines, cell phones, televisions, teleconferences, the Internet, and so on have put us in touch with one another in ways we've never been able to be before. Indeed, we are *instantly* reachable, anywhere, all the time.

The irony is that as electronic communication has grown, human connections have declined. We are close electronically. Yet we are far from one another personally. Our technology can separate us even as it is putting us in touch with people far away.

For example, my patients often pull a ringing cell phone out of their briefcases or pocketbooks during a session with me, all the while complaining of how they hate interruptions!

What is missing in the lives of most people is not electronic communication—indeed, that abounds!—but human connection, the feeling that you are an important part of something that matters. You can feel connected sitting quietly by a lake in Maine, and totally disconnected sitting with hundreds of people on a crowded subway or chatting with millions of people over the Internet.

I have worked with many couples whose relationship was on the rocks precisely because of an inability to regulate technology. How much TV to watch, how many hours to spend on the computer, how long to talk on the telephone—once humorous questions, now these are marriage-breaking dilemmas. One of my patients calls her husband's computer "his plastic mistress."

In working with patients who have attention deficit disorder (ADD), I often see how their bottom-line, cut-to-the-chase style proves advantageous in the business world, helping them get a lot done in a short period of time, while it proves a major hindrance in their intimate relationships. There, you must linger. It is distancing, for example, to state impatiently, "OK, so you love me, now what's your next point?"

The hurried approach has caught on with everyone, everywhere, not just with patients who have ADD. Indeed, it is so common our whole culture looks like it has ADD, a condition I call pseudo-ADD, or socially induced ADD. If you don't have ADD when you wake up in the morning in New York City, you have it by the time you go to bed.

I am not a Luddite wishing to turn back the clock. Modern life is exciting! The changes we have seen in the past fifty years are truly

marvelous, but as with any massive change, unexpected consequences have occurred. As we've gained speed, we seem to have lost
one another.

We don't talk to one another face-to-face as much as we used to.
Instead we leave a message, send an E-mail or fax.

Yes, we can contact more people in a shorter amount of time
through the wizardry of technology, but these contacts are not
building heartfelt connections. An astonishing study out of Carnegie Mellon University followed people for two years after they
gained access to the Internet for the first time. Expecting to find
evidence of how the Internet had improved connection in these people's lives, the authors found just the opposite! "Greater use of the
Internet," they reported, "was associated with declines in participants' communications with family members in the household,
declines in the size of their social circle, and increases in their depression and loneliness."*

Technology can be wonderful, indeed a godsend, and, used properly, a major ally of connectedness. We just have to learn how to use
it right. Used right, technology does not impede human connectedness, it improves it. The mother who stays in touch with her son
at college through E-mail, the shy person who meets people over
the Internet, the business manager who improves service to customers through a Web page and an E-mail address, the physician
who saves paperwork through a new computer system that allows
him to spend more time talking to patients face-to-face—these are
just a few examples of how technology strengthens the human
connection.

But if we want to connect in a meaningful way, we have to slow
down now and then. We have to listen. We have to make time for
the human moment.

It may be that you have to turn off the TV now and then, or set
aside chunks of time for just hanging out, or take on a responsibility you don't want. This is not easy. But it isn't impossible. For
example, Orthodox Jews have a wonderful observance: from sundown Friday to sundown Saturday they can *do no work.* They can't
drive, they can't talk on the telephone, they can't go shopping. So,

* Robert Kraut et al., *American Psychologist* 53, no. 9 (Sept. 1998): 1017.

on that day they interact with one another, or they pray. They talk to the neighbors, they talk to their families, they go for walks. Their religion forces them to make time to connect—with one another, with their community, with God. Furthermore, as a group, Orthodox Jews are a high-achieving people, which gives the lie to the notion that so much down time leads to low productivity.

The challenge of today's world is this: how do we hold on to both the cell phone and the day of rest? We have to figure out how to hold on to the technology *and* the human moment. It is a bad solution to get rid of either one. We can't—and shouldn't—turn back the clock and dismantle or throw away our technology. On the other hand, we shouldn't let go of the personal connections we need with one another. We need to hold on to the human moment, either through a tradition such as Orthodox Jews have, or through family, neighborhood, or workplace habits and rituals that we invent. Given our powers of innovation and the human need for personal connection, I am confident we can do it.

TWO

Speaking Personally

CONNECTION SAVED MY LIFE

I AM WRITING this book not only as a professional but as an individual who has felt firsthand the power of connection. If it hadn't been for certain people at certain times—my wife, my cousins, many teachers, many friends—I would never have survived.

I am a fifty-year-old man, married ten years, a father of three young children, a writer, a psychiatrist. Those are my basic demographics. But who I really am and why I care so fervently about connection are questions that evoke a deeper response. My passion for connecting grows out of my life.

Ever since I was a little boy I have been seeking to find where I belong. Like many in my generation of baby boomers, I had a topsy-turvy childhood. I was born to loving but unsteady parents. Married fresh out of college, they made a bright picture on the society pages of the Boston papers. My father was a dashing young man, a good student and an all-American hockey player. My mother, the paper said, was "one of the prettiest girls in Boston." But life would bring them down, each in different ways.

My father had manic-depressive illness, which led to my parents' getting divorced when I was four, when Dad was confined to a mental hospital. My mother soon remarried an older, retired man, a sophisticated devotee of literature who was an alcoholic; he spent most of his time pouring martinis or recovering from their after-effects. His name was Noble Cathcart, and I called him Uncle Noble. (It was a custom back then to dub all sorts of people "uncle," as if to make them part of the family.) My dear old mother herself would turn out to be alcoholic, and would die of the medical complications of that condition when I was in my late thirties. Because I fought with Uncle Noble like a pit bull every day (he beat up my mother, so I hated him) and because my father's mother had enough money to subsidize my education I was sent away to a boarding school in the fifth grade. I attended boarding schools ever after. They became my home.

I remember, from as early as age eight, explicitly wondering where I was supposed to fit in. I remember wishing my father hadn't gone away to the mental hospital. I remember fearing and hating my stepfather when he was drunk (which was most of the time), and I remember praying that my mother could be happy someday.

The praying got started very young. My mother from as early as I could remember used to tell me, "God is everywhere," a line that has terrified many children through the ages but in my case was reassuring, because it gave me something to count on. When Uncle Noble abruptly moved us from our home on Cape Cod to his home in Charleston, South Carolina, taking me away from my extended family, I was sent to church for the first time. Mom and Uncle Noble rarely went with me, but I actually liked going by myself. My mother would roll over in bed and tie my necktie as she and Uncle Noble slept off their gin; then I would ride my bike down to Saint Michael's Church, where I sang in the choir.

I found church a happy place. Strange as it may sound, being in the choir became a sort of team sport for me, almost like Little League. I also liked the minister's daughter; her name was Tinka Perry. On Sunday mornings I got a glimpse of what I imagined were "normal" families. Not that I felt abnormal; I just knew I didn't have the sort of home other eight-year-olds had.

For example, the other kids would usually appear for choir accompanied by a parent or older sibling. I just showed up by myself on my red Schwinn and parked it up against the church. Other kids would talk about having gone fishing the day before with their father, while my memory of the day before was of listening to my stepfather rail against my mother while he got drunk. Other kids would talk about getting in trouble for not doing their homework, while my mother and Uncle Noble never asked me about home-work or anything else related to school.

So I started to fit myself in, as best as I could, to the "family" of the choir. The choir director, a woman named Mrs. Selby, was very organized and nice, and I was always amazed that she played the organ not only with her fingers but with her feet! When we sang, I tried to sit as close to the organ as I could so I could watch Mrs. Selby's stockinged feet softly slip across the wooden pedals. I can still see her taking off her blue high heels and putting them under the bench before she sat down to play and to conduct us in our hymns and anthems.

The choir sat in the back balcony of Saint Michael's, and for me it became like the backseat of a family car. We kids would giggle and whisper and poke and squirm as the service proceeded, Mrs. Selby doing her level best to keep us on cue and relatively calm. By the time Communion came around the balcony was usually abuzz with petty disruptions. I can remember the priest, the Right Rev-erend Dewolfe Perry, glaring up at us as he prepared the Blessed Sacrament, as if we were agents of the devil. We never received much punishment for our sins, though, and we regularly received the great reward of ham and sausage biscuits and orange juice once the service was over.

During this after-church breakfast I would see parents come in and talk to one another and to the children, sometimes even to me. They would ask me, "How's school?" I learned that was a normal-parent question. They would ask me, "Are you playing football this year?" I learned that was also a normal-parent question.

I took my place in the choir/family as a boy who was accepted and welcomed, and that felt good. Whether it was direction from Mrs. Selby, reprobation from the Reverend Perry, interest from another parent, or giggles from a chum as we poked each other, I found fragments of family life in the Saint Michael's choir that I pieced together into a warm quilt.

Since on Sunday mornings I learned the framework of the Epis-copal service, I started praying in other places. The praying hap-pened playfully, believe it or not, not out of fear or obligation. I even built a little altar at home looking out on the bay to Fort Sumter. I spread a folded pillowcase across the windowsill in my third-floor bedroom, and put leaflets from the church on it, and a prayer book, and two candles in candlesticks I took from the attic. It was not that I was deeply religious—I was too young for that. I certainly didn't go around talking to other people about God or anything like that. I think I was just bringing the choir/family home with me. I was creating a place to fit in and feel secure. My little altar was like a clubhouse, I guess.

My two older brothers were packed off by the time we moved to Charleston, both to boarding schools back up north. They stayed away from Charleston and Uncle Noble. During school vacations they would go to Dad's mother (we called her Gammy Hallowell) or to our aunt and uncle and cousins in Chatham. For a few embattled years, it was just Uncle Noble, Mom, and me at home in Charleston.

Things happened back then that shouldn't have. I remember one night Uncle Noble pulled me out of bed about 3 A.M. and brought me down to the second floor, to the master bedroom. When I got there I saw three of his friends (one of them was another "uncle") standing around the bed. Mom was asleep on the bed, naked, her back to me. I had never seen my mother naked, so that in itself was a shock.

Then Uncle Noble explained to me what was going on. He and his friends were playing dice ("Craps is the game," as he told me that night), using my mother's backside as the wall against which the dice were thrown. Once the dice bounced off her, they'd fall onto the bed, and the number would be made. Uncle Noble asked me if I'd like to play. There was a big stack of cash on one corner of the bed, and he told me I might win some of it if I joined the game. I'd never seen so much money before. It looked like a big pile of rubbish, only I knew it was real money. I told Uncle Noble I didn't want to play. He told me to stay anyway, I could learn something. As soon as I could tell he wasn't thinking about me any longer, I silently retreated back to bed. The next day, nothing was said. For all I knew, he had no memory of what he had done. But I remembered.

From then on we waged war, Uncle Noble and I. It wasn't just that incident of the dice game that set off our war. There were many other incidents just as bad. To this day I don't know exactly when or why I started to hate him. I don't think he ever knew, either. My hatred must have come as a surprise to him, because at first I had adored him. I had adopted him as my new father, and he had adopted me as the son he never had, or so he said.

I didn't piece it together back then. I didn't know that I hated him *because* of what happened that night, or the various other nights; I just knew I started to hate him. I had never hated anyone before. In fact, my mother always told me hating was against the rules in life. But I hated Uncle Noble. We fought every day. That's why I got sent away, at the age of ten.

The connections I found at my schools saved me. I found teachers at Fessenden (the boarding school I attended from fifth to eighth grade) and then at Exeter (from ninth to twelfth grade) who became my substitute parents. I even found them at Harvard, a place not known for the time its tenured professors spend with undergraduates. But I found one who took me in, so to speak. The teacher was Professor William Alfred, poet, playwright—author of *Hogan's Goat*—and Old English scholar. We met once a week for two hours, one-on-one, for two years, ostensibly to discuss English literature, but the topic was always life itself.

At Fessenden there was Mr. Cook and Mr. Gibson and Mr. Maynard and Mr. Slocum and Mr. Fitts and many others. They didn't know how much they were helping me just by being there, just by connecting with me in an ordinary, teacherlike way. I'm sure Mr. Maynard, for example, simply thought he was teaching me geography and coaching me in baseball. He didn't know that, on the day he stopped me in the corridor and slapped me on the back and told me I had scored the highest grade on the seventh-grade geography exam, I had just had a telephone conversation with my mother in which she had asked me what grade I was in now. I don't hold that against Mom in the slightest—she did the best she could against great odds—but I hold the story up in thanks to Mr. Maynard, who only thought he was passing along simple good news, not saving a child from despair.

That Mr. Maynard and many others noticed me and knew me made up for what my parents couldn't do. This is the transportability of connection. If you don't find what you need in one place, you can find it somewhere else.

For me it was my teachers, from Mrs. Selby in choir to William Alfred at Harvard, who helped me grow. They didn't know it at the time, and neither did I, but the connections we made pulled me like lifelines out of the pluff mud of Charleston onto safe ground.

The years passed after college. My life went on. I went to medical school and became a doctor, then a psychiatrist. I got married, got divorced (my ex-wife is a wonderful woman, but we weren't well matched), got married again, had three children, and began to try to tell others in writing what I had learned along the way.

One day I went back to Charleston. At age forty-nine I went back to the city where I had learned how to hate. The last time I had been there I was twelve, on Christmas vacation from Fessenden.

I went back to Charleston this time to give a lecture on learning problems. I went back as a professional, was put up in a beautiful hotel, and was paid to impart knowledge to a grateful audience.

As I flew back for this visit and drove into town with my kind-hearted hosts, I felt a schism grow inside of me. How could I find the connection—between the me of then and the me of now?

I could imagine me-then and I could see me-now, but it felt as if the divide between the two me's was unbridgeable. How could I connect the two?

The bridge has to be made, I told myself. *You are, after all, the same Ned Hallowell. You did go to school in this town thirty-seven years ago. You are that person. You have grown up and changed, but he is still you.* And yet, it felt awfully hard to connect the two of us.

The memories from me-then flooded in whenever I opened the gates. There was no problem *finding* me-then; the problem was what to do with that me. Unlike a lot of people who can't remember much about their childhoods, especially the difficult parts, I have rafts of memories. They aren't all bad memories, either. In fact, only a select few are the stuff of later scar tissue. Many are happy. I remembered them now as I returned to this city with the tender curiosity of a visitor at the museum of his own life. I peered at myself going to Citadel football games. The team played at night, so the memories were floodlit in yellow. Uncle Hugh would let me sit near the bench. I learned the rules of football by watching the Citadel. I can still see their powder blue uniforms. And I remembered going to an amusement park for the first time. I was given two dollars, a princely sum it seemed, and sent off on my Schwinn bike with Bobby Hitt, my best friend from back then. I liked the games of skill at the amusement park, like knocking over the three milk bottles with a baseball, or tossing a softball into a tilted wicker basket, even though I couldn't win any of them. I didn't know the games were crooked. I didn't know anything was crooked then.

But having me-now go to Charleston felt like a violation of some law of physics. As the airplane touched down and I was driven in, making pleasant conversation all the way, it seemed physically impossible that this adult version of me should be able to occupy the same space that the child version of me once occupied. How could that me be *here*? The me who had inhabited this city was a little boy, fighting with his alcoholic stepfather, trying to protect his sweet but sometimes clueless mother. How could the grown-up forty-nine-year-old writer/psychiatrist drive into *Charleston, South Carolina,* and check into a hotel? It felt as wrong as a cat barking.

And yet, here I was. Me-now in the city of me-then. Of course, the city had changed a lot, too. I noticed that on the way in. In the past, I had always come to Charleston on a train, so even my port of entry was new.

My hotel was off King Street, a street I remembered well, but of course King Street had changed. It hadn't changed all that much, just enough to make me feel sad. Stores were different, and the little Esso station where I used to buy Pepsi was gone. Storefronts looked polished and new. I could only try to reconcile what I recalled from then with what I saw now.

Gradually I put into place various blocks as I tried to build a bridge to the past. A movie theater here, a Rexall's drugstore there, Henny Gaud's backyard chestnut tree over there, an old boat wreck on the mudflat down that way. Gradually I filled the set of now with blocks from my memory—but all that did was superimpose the past upon the present. The past and the present could coexist, it seemed, without violating the rules of physics—but could they coexist without violating the rules of me?

How could I put the me of then into the me of now? How can anyone do it? I wasn't even sure I wanted to. I felt protective of that little boy from back then. I didn't want him to have to give up his private haunts, the altar at his bedroom window, the tree he liked to climb, the concrete basketball court where he shot foul shots for hours on end (while the others drank) until it got too dark outside to see. I didn't want him to have to explain plunging his hands into his pockets and kicking a stone in anger. I didn't want him to have to talk to anyone who was going to make everything all right. I didn't want him to give up his reality, however painful it may have been. It was his reality, after all. If he gave it up, he might disappear. I didn't want the me of then to cease to exist under the pressure of the me of now. I didn't want to bring that little boy out of the past just to tidy him up to be seen in public.

It's too bad, but I have always felt that to let him (me) be seen in public, I would have to tidy him up. I couldn't just tell the truth. I have always felt, *If people knew my story, they would think less of me.* I have always felt, at some deep unspoken level, that I was a tainted person because of what happened in Charleston, and no matter what I did, I would always be impure at the core, flawed in the eyes of others, if they knew. Somehow the taint upon that time—the strange goings-on—had tainted me, at least in my imagination, and set me apart. All the normalcy I missed became a kind of deficit I could never make up. Perhaps that's why, over time, a gap widened within me as I distanced myself from my life back then and the little boy of those years long ago.

But now I reminded myself, *He still is you.* Whoever you now are grew out of him. There is no disconnection between then and now (even though it feels that way to you) because time never stopped. Like Ole Man River, it just kept rolling along. Time skipped no hours, no days. No years were omitted. Nor did you have a brain transplant. The boy who learned state capitals in third grade from Miss Poulnott in Charleston and the boy who learned the personal pronoun chart from Mr. Houck in the fourth grade in Charleston is the same person as the man who just flew into town to give a lecture, and is the same person as the boy who mixed martinis for his stepfather, and learned the difference between a dry martini and a Gibson before he knew what fly-fishing was, and watched his mother's bare backside be used as part of a craps table.

The fact is, we have all had experiences we wish hadn't happened, but that did. We have all had bad times. Many of us have felt tainted by those times, and we have felt the need to cut those parts of ourselves off from the rest of us. But this is a mistake. It is a mistake to disconnect yourself from who you were and where you've been. It's better to reconcile.

After I checked into the hotel I went for a walk, to try to reconcile, I guess. My feet took me back to the Gaud School, where I'd done fourth grade. I looked in through one of the ground-floor windows and saw that now the place was not a school but an office. I saw a custodian emptying trash and placing a new plastic bag in the can. His eyes met mine. Suddenly I felt like an intruder, so I stepped away.

From there I walked the couple of hundred yards that separated the school from the building in which I had lived back then, on East Bay Street. It was a large, three-story brick building, divided vertically into three separate dwellings. Our third, number 76, was on one end.

The sight of number 76, in brass—probably the same brass as was there almost forty years ago—triggered my memory. I shot years back. As I stared at the door I could see the series of black maids whom I loved, Victoria, Georgiana, and Viola. Each of them worked in the house for as long as they could stand Uncle Noble. They were all good to me, mothering me and watching out for me with loving care.

I also recalled some of Uncle Noble's own relatives: the ancient, racist Gramps, who used to come over on Sunday afternoon with his bighearted wife, to get drunk after they'd gone to church; the Ravenel cousins, who were warm and loving and whom I wished I could have lived with; a mighty strange grown-up daughter from Uncle Noble's first marriage who detested my mother; and the true-blue Uncle Hugh, physician in chief at the Citadel, who befriended me and would come talk to me when everyone else was preoccupied with their life.

Uncle Hugh was Uncle Noble's cousin, but he couldn't have been more different. I remember one Christmas afternoon I was sitting on the ground outside the house to get away from the fights inside, when Uncle Hugh drove up in his old Plymouth. It was a cold, gray day, but Uncle Hugh always brought warmth with him. A wiry man with dark curly hair and clear-rimmed glasses, he got out of his car and said, "Hey, fella." ("Hey" is what they said in Charleston instead of the Yankee "Hi.")

"Hey, Uncle Hugh," I said, having learned the word early on down there.

"Can I sit down with you?" he asked, as he opened his trunk.

"Sure," I replied, glad that he hadn't asked why I was sitting outside on Christmas, and glad to have his company, because he was always nice.

When he closed the trunk I saw he was carrying a case of pop bottles. "A Christmas present for you," he said, putting down a case of Pepsi next to me. Twenty-four glass bottles clinked against one another as he sat the wooden box down on the ground. "Wow, thanks, Uncle Hugh," I said. He sat down and we talked, I can't remember what about.

But I do remember that case of Pepsi. I can safely say that that Pepsi, and Uncle Hugh along with it, saved that Christmas day and saved a part of me that was sinking fast.

Through the power of connection—or Pepsi—I have found my way to a pretty good place in life. I am lucky enough to have now the stable family I never had as a child.

These many years later, standing in front of the brass number 76, I could see exactly where on the ground I had been sitting that day, and where Uncle Hugh had put the Pepsi. Uncle Hugh was long dead, but I cast a look out at the street as if I might catch a glimpse of him driving up right then.

He wasn't there in person, but I felt his presence.

I stood still, listening to the past. I could hear the happy-sounding woman who would push her cart full of fresh shrimp down the street early every morning, singing out as she walked, "Shrimpy, raw, raw, raw." I often waked to her voice. She had probably passed away by now, as well.

Dozens of images swirled into my mind, one after another, filling me with who I was and where I'd been. There were the movie theaters, the Garden and the Riviera on King Street, where I'd go and see movies for a dime, escaping into the world of John Wayne; there was the fort I built out toward the harbor; and around it all there was the then-quiet city of Charleston in the 1950s, before so much in this country, and in me, started to change.

While the front door was closed tight, the door on the side of the house was open, leaving only a screen door for me to knock on. The screen door rattled when I rapped on it. "Yes, yes, I'll be right there," I heard a man say, and then he appeared, wiping his hands on a dish towel, telling me he was off to Italy tomorrow with his wife, I had caught him just in time.

"I used to live here," I said.

"Well, isn't that something? Please do come in." He immediately swung open the screen door and stood aside. "Will you sign my guest book?" He pointed to an open book on a table beneath a mirror in the front hall. "I have a book for all new visitors. I'm a retired Episcopal priest. Having people sign the book is probably a remnant of soliciting new parishioners. But it adds something, don't you think? When did you live here?" He was so congenial. It felt to me that he made this conversation just to put me at ease.

"In the late nineteen fifties," I replied.

"Oh, my," this nice man exclaimed, "you do go back a ways. The widow Smith was still alive."

"You mean she died?" I said, and felt as if a large book had just been dropped to the floor.

"Oh, yes, years ago."

"I played with her son, Alan," I volunteered.

"He's dead, too," the man said, almost cheerfully, as if glad to give me an update. I guess priests don't look at death with as much dread as the rest of us.

Oh, no, I said to myself. I think the man sensed I was a bit shocked, as he saw me turn around in circles taking in all I could see. "I knew his father, too," I added. "The eye doctor. Alan had bad eyes."

"That's why the widow Smith married Dr. Smith, the story goes. Dr. Smith married his own nurse. Quite the talk back then. But she needed someone to take care of her son's eyes." The man knew the whole story.

"We used to play together."

"Of course. He was your neighbor. Let me show you around." This man then took me through the whole house. It looked so much smaller now. I remembered it as being vast. The living room floor, where I used to read the comic strips, like *Dondi,* before school, while Mom and Uncle Noble slept, had always seemed to me as large as a school playground. Now it seemed no bigger than a good-sized living room, which is what it was. I could almost hear Georgiana's voice calling me, "Ned! Nay-ud! Hurry up! You'll be late for school!" And I could almost see old Gramps nodding off in his chair after his first few drinks. And I could distinctly hear Uncle Noble in his drunken slur, bellowing, "If you don't like it, shove off!" I looked at the corner of the room where the table that held the liquor used to be. Now there was a green vine. Under my breath, I spoke a few words to Uncle Noble's ghost.

We headed up the stairs I remembered so well—I would stomp up those stairs after being told to go to my room —only to find that the bedrooms on the second floor had shrunk, too. But the contours were the same. I could hear Uncle Noble's hacking smoker's cough from the bathroom as if he were in there now, clearing out his chest as he did every morning. My host must have thought I was in a trance. I guess I was.

Then we hit the third floor, where my room had been. My host's wife was in "my" room, packing for their trip. "Sorry to interrupt you," I said.

"This man used to live here," my host said.

"Oh, really," his wife said cheerily. "I'm so glad you stopped by. I wish we could offer you more hospitality."

"Oh, please," I said, "it is very nice of you just to let me look around. What memories. This was my bedroom."

"Really?" the lady said.

I looked at where I used to have my altar, and I took in the view of the harbor from the window. That hadn't changed much. As I turned around, I noticed a fireplace in the corner. "Oh, so you added a fireplace to this room?" I asked.

"Actually, we didn't add it," the man responded. "It was here when you lived here. It's been here since the house was built. You don't remember it?"

"No, I don't remember it at all."

"Well, it had to have been here. Funny what we remember and what we forget, isn't it?"

"It sure is," I replied, shaking my head. A fireplace that I didn't remember, in a room I thought I remembered so well.

I stood in the room for an extra moment, knowing that it was time to leave, that this family had packing to do, but I wanted to absorb from the room as much as I could. My play had closed. The stage was the same, but the sets had changed. The room had been washed clean. It belonged to these players now. The old cues were only in my mind.

As the man and I walked downstairs it finally occurred to me to introduce myself. "I'm Ned Hallowell," I said. "I'm sorry I didn't introduce myself sooner."

"Of course," the man replied, "we both got caught up in this trip down memory lane. I'm Frank McClain."

"I can't tell you how much this has meant to me," I said, shaking his hand good-bye at the door.

"I can imagine," he replied. "Come back anytime."

Outside, I started to walk away, but then I turned around for another look. It was just a big brick house next to a little playground. Most of what I had seen on my tour was in my mind. What I had seen had happened long ago, and was long gone, brought back only by my memory, my imagination, and the connection I made to this place all those years ago.

I took a walk after that. I went down to the Battery, looked out at Fort Sumter, and strolled past what used to be the Fort Sumter Hotel (which Uncle Noble once won, then lost, in a craps game at the annual meeting of the yacht club). It was now a condo complex. I then looped around and walked down the other side of East Bay Street, along the pastel row of houses made famous in *Porgy and Bess,* and across a few more streets, until I found myself coming upon the women weaving baskets on the sidewalk outside Saint Michael's Church. This was where I was baptized, where I sang in the choir, where I was an acolyte.

I went into the church. It, too, was much smaller than I remembered. I had thought it was a vast cathedral then. In fact, it is not very large, as churches go. But it is beautiful, especially the stained glass window behind the altar. It depicts Saint Michael slaying the dragon.

The pews have little gates. I opened one and took a seat on the padded bench. Then I knelt and said a prayer. I prayed for my family now and for my family then. I thanked God for Uncle Hugh. And I thanked God for bringing me back to this city, to reconnect.

I can't tell you exactly how it happened, but over the few days I spent in Charleston I bridged the gap between the me of then and the me of now. It happened at the level of feelings, not the level of thought. I simply came to feel more comfortable with what had happened in my life back then and who I had been. I started to stop feeling ashamed.

Although I still carry with me (and I imagine I always will) a font of sadness and worry from my childhood, I think even my connections to the hard parts of my past sustain me now, and help me understand other people's suffering better. Most of us, after all, have suffered through some bad times. The bad times can actually become useful especially if you don't have to hide them.

To begin to bridge the gap between me-then and me-now, I took concrete steps. I walked through my old house, saw my old school, prayed in my old church, and came away feeling more whole. There was no roll of drums. It all happened quietly. It happened as the current world was moving right along, as it always does—as a custodian was emptying a trash can, as the McClains were getting ready for Italy, and as women were weaving baskets on the sidewalk outside Saint Michael's.

Not more than a month after my visit to Charleston, as chance would have it, I received a telephone call from Charlie Terry, one of my teachers at my old high school, Exeter. He told me that Fred Tremallo had just been diagnosed with lung cancer and had only a few weeks to live.

As much as Uncle Noble had been a person who made my life hard, Fred Tremallo was one of the people who had made my life good. He was like a good father to me while I was at Exeter.

He taught me English, but more than that, he told me I was worth the time of day. He set it in my mind that I could write, but more than that, he told me that what mattered in life was not how good I was but how much good I did.

When I heard that he was dying I got into my car and drove up to New Hampshire.

I found him in his hospital bed, with his wife, Ellie, at his side. He had his laptop computer set up in front of him so he could finish writing up his college recommendations. "I only have a few weeks to live. Gotta finish these before I die!" he said with a chuckle.

A line of students was forming outside his room, so I had only a few minutes. Again as chance would have it, I had recently written an essay about my old teachers, entitled "I Am Here Because They Were There." I had brought the essay along with me because it was mostly about Fred. I hadn't been sure if I would be able to read it, but once I got to his bedside I felt it was one gift I had to give him, after all the gifts he had given me. So I read it out loud, as Fred and Ellie listened.

When I finished there was a brief silence, which Fred soon broke. "Well," he said, clearing his throat, "my own feelings aside, that is an excellent piece of writing."

Right up to the last possible moment, Fred was giving me and many others encouragement. As he lay dying, he was writing college recommendations and teaching students. We talked philosophy a little before I said good-bye. He told me his thinking now was summed up in three words: "focus," "flow," and "faith." "Focus on the moment," he said. "Get into the task, into flow. And then you must have faith. I'm learning about faith from physics." Fred was a lapsed Catholic, so I knew his faith would not be of the Christian kind. But up to the last he was exploring, and sharing his explorations with his students. That was his life, helping students.

I hugged him as best you can hug someone who is lying in bed, and I kissed the top of his head, impulsively, not knowing where exactly to kiss but wanting very much to kiss him somewhere. Then I hugged Ellie and I said good-bye. Fred died about a month later.

I went back and spoke at his memorial service. How remarkable—in the space of just weeks I had spoken to the spirit of my demon, Uncle Noble, and then to the spirit of my teacher/father, Fred Tremallo. What struck me driving home from Fred's memorial service, and what made me cry in the car at last, was that Fred would have urged me to "explore" the character of Uncle Noble. He would have gently urged me to let go of the hatred, if I could. "It clouds your vision," he would have said, "and a writer must see clearly." He would have put it in terms of what a *writer* should do, knowing that would grab me, but his real message would have been one of love, a word he never would have mentioned at all.

THREE

Me and Mr. S

A MIRACLE OF CONNECTION

DURING MY FIRST few months as a resident in psychiatry at the Massachusetts Mental Health Center, a young man was admitted to the hospital who opened my eyes as no one had before.

At that point in my training I had no idea how utterly disconnected a person could be. I had no idea how cut off and removed from reality one mind could become. Nor had I seen someone who was terribly cut off make a meaningful connection. But Mr. S showed me. Even though we breathed the same air and spent many hours in each other's presence, Mr S lived in a world utterly different from mine; yet his world ended up influencing mine forever.

Our two years together—I as his doctor and he as my patient—taught me the power of connection. It was as if Mr. S took me up in an airplane for my first ride ever and said, "Look down!" Mr. S revealed to me a new landscape of human connection. He gave me a perspective on the mind that I had never seen, or even imagined, before I met him.

Mr. S suffered from schizophrenia—essentially, a disease of disconnection, hardwired into the brain. The schizophrenic patient, it is said, cannot make friends with other people.

When Mr. S was admitted to the hospital he refused to speak. Instead he handed the admitting psychiatrist the following poem:

> I am imprisoned inside an hourglass,
> Beneath me is the ebbing sand, alas;
> The sand gives, and terror lives;
> I plummet downward toward acid
> And spikes, cobra spears,
> Tiger-hunting forks, and the like.
> I am impaled upon a dozen blades;
> Darkness weaves with many shades.

When I met him on the ward the next day, he would not speak, just as he had refused to speak the night before. He looked at me briefly, then looked away, chuckling to himself. He looked like many of the young men admitted to Mass. Mental; he looked like a street person. Mass. Mental was a state hospital, a place for poor people who suffered from severe mental illness, and so the attire of most patients was shabby at best. But Mr. S added color and variety to his shabby attire. A red sash, a plaid shirt, maroon baggy trousers, old motorcycle boots, and a bandanna around his head gave him a dashing look, like a pirate.

He looked extremely fit. Indeed, as I was to find out, he was a bodybuilder, committed to strengthening his muscles for a specific, and as it turned out, sad reason. He was swarthy, with deep dark eyes and a mass of curly black hair sprouting from his scalp like rough underbrush. In another setting he could have been mistaken for a rock star.

But he wasn't a rock star. He was, at age twenty-four, a chronic mental patient. This was his eighth admission to the hospital. Every time he got discharged, something bad happened to bring him back. This time he had attacked his half brother with a fork when his half brother tried to change the TV station from the professional wrestling Mr. S was watching.

Since Mr. S wouldn't talk to me that morning, I decided to read about him from his chart, which was very thick. I plunged into it like a mystery novel, reading the reports written by other young doctors, residents in psychiatry like me, who had treated Mr. S from the day of his first admission, at age sixteen, to his last discharge, a year ago. I actually knew the doctor who had treated him last. He was a year ahead of me in the training program. All of us in training learned from the same patients because they came back to the hospital year after year. The teachers at Mass. Mental were as much these long-term patients as the senior psychiatrists who oversaw our work. Mr. S was to teach me about the miracle of connection.

We started off slowly. After meeting him and reading his chart, I thought it was about as likely that he and I could converse in a useful way as for me to chat with a post. Although his IQ had been tested very high—140—his intelligence was often hidden under crazy thinking.

As I read on in his chart, I discovered that his life, like the lives of so many of the patients we saw at Mass. Mental, was sad beyond what most of us ever imagine. His mother had been schizophrenic like him. A hugely obese woman, she spent Mr. S's childhood and adolescence in and out of Mass. Mental herself. One afternoon when both she and the then sixteen-year-old Mr. S were at home, she called to him from her bedroom. When Mr. S got to her room he found her climbing out the seventh-story window. He ran to her, grabbed her wrists, pushed his feet against the wall beneath the window, and strained to haul his mother back to safety. But she was too heavy for him. He called for help, but no one was within earshot. Finally he couldn't hold her any longer, and she slipped out of his grasp, dying when she hit the pavement. That was when Mr. S committed himself to making himself superstrong. It was also when he began to go crazy.

He started his long series of admissions to Mass. Mental. At first, doctors resisted the diagnosis of schizophrenia, hoping that his deranged state was caused only by the death of his mother, not by the inherited biological brain disease called schizophrenia. Some people, after all, do go crazy after a parent's suicide, but later get better. Everyone was hoping that this brilliant young man would be one of the lucky offspring of a schizophrenic parent who did not inherit the disease.

But it wouldn't turn out that way. Instead of getting better, Mr. S got worse. Doctors became less hopeful. One of them noted in the chart that Mr. S had warned him, "All my doctors think I have so much potential." The doctor agreed he did have lots of potential, but began to doubt it could ever be developed.

As his condition worsened, he became more and more

psychotic—the term simply means cut off from ordinary reality. He turned to bodybuilding with a vengeance, and he began spending most of his other time watching professional wrestling on TV or reading comic books about superheroes. It seems he himself wanted to become a superhero, maybe one who could save a person from jumping out a window.

Earlier on, he did talk to his doctors, but only once, briefly, about his mother's death. All the efforts on the part of the various people treating him to get him to open up on this topic failed.

Rather than talk about how he felt, he did once give gruesome evidence of feeling guilty, or at least of wanting to hurt himself. During one of his periods out of the hospital he jumped out of a taxicab, smashing his face on the pavement. The impact knocked out several of his teeth. As he lay on the street, as best anyone could figure, he tore out the rest of his teeth on his own, because when he was brought into the emergency room he had only a couple of teeth left. The dental people said it was unlikely the fall alone could have done that. After that fall he refused dentures. Instead he developed the habit of talking with his hand cupped over his mouth.

By the time we met, even though Mr. S was only twenty-four, the consensus was that he would remain a chronic patient for the rest of his life. I was given the chance to try to make contact with him, but my supervisors told me there was little chance he would change. "Sit with him," they told me, "and see what happens."

Sit with him. This is the bare bones of connecting: sit with someone and see what happens. Boiled down to the basics, this is how to connect. Sit—next to someone on a plane, next to someone at a party, across from someone at dinner, or in the extreme case of Mr. S and me, in an office on a ward of a state mental hospital.

After a few days he started to communicate with me a little bit, mainly by chuckling and grunting. Now and then he'd make a statement, but not allow any conversation. Once he remarked, "They said I am a hopeless case." But he said no more.

Of the many different medications he had tried in the past, none had worked very well. This was the late nineteen seventies, and we didn't have the new, dramatically effective antipsychotic medications like clozapine that we have today. The medications we had, like Haldol, helped Mr. S somewhat, but he still remained more in a world of his own than in the world of other people.

I sat with Mr. S. At first there wasn't much to report. He would chuckle and look at me. I would wonder what to say next. If I hadn't known his history I would have thought he was playing a game with me, but I knew he wasn't faking. This was just the way he was. So I wondered, *What do you say to someone who is not responding?* In real life, you ask what's wrong. So I tried that. "What's wrong, Mr. S?" I asked, like a dummy. No reply. "You've been hurt in life. It's hard to talk." Still no response. "Maybe you need to get to know me better?" No acknowledgment. In real life there are other responses you might have: you might walk away, or get angry maybe, or plead. None of those seemed appropriate here. My supervisors urged me just to hang in there, sit, and see what developed, while warning me that nothing might develop.

Never before, personally or professionally, had I tried to connect with someone and met with such a nonresponse. Like a Zen master, Mr. S was teaching me the first lesson of connection: patience.

The second lesson, I learned, was persistence. This was urged upon me by my job, by my supervisors. I would have walked away from Mr. S and tried to find someone who wanted to talk to me, but I was told instead to sit and wait. It was like fishing—sooner or later I might get a bite. I was also told that it was probably a waste of time, but I should try anyway. I began to wonder if my supervisors were Zen masters, too. In any case, we sat, Mr. S and I, waiting to see what we could see.

Week after week, we sat. Then one day I thought of the poem Mr. S had given to the doctor who admitted him. I wondered if maybe Mr. S and I could write a poem of our own together. I asked him if he wanted to. He chuckled, as usual. But I went ahead and I wrote a line. I handed the piece of paper to him and gave him my pen. He looked at the line I had written, stroked his chin, picked the paper up, put it back down, and then he wrote a line himself. After that, he pushed the paper back to me. I read what he had written, added a line of my own, and pushed the paper back to him.

Me:	They said I am a hopeless case
Mr. S:	Not I, a member of the human race, in disgrace
Me:	I wish they wouldn't say that
Mr. S:	In a nonjoking way
Me:	It makes me

Mr. S:	Suspicious
Me:	And angry and sad
Mr. S:	Which aren't the strongest emotions I've had
Me:	The strongest are
Mr. S:	Composed of these
Me:	Combined into
Mr. S:	Something I don't want to feel
Me:	Something like
Mr. S:	Rage, but not quite
Me:	Also like
Mr. S:	An intense feeling

I was astonished. Here was a conversation. Here he was, telling me what he was feeling, while warning me he didn't want to feel it.

These written interchanges, which Mr. S and I called poems, continued for the next year and a half. All told, we wrote about thirty of them. He usually would begin them—simply by picking up the pen I always set down next to him—and he usually would end them, simply by writing, "The End," when he thought the poem was done.

We can see him struggle with emotion in the next poem, while alluding to his mother's death:

Mr. S:	Nothing lasts forever
Me:	No one lives that long
Mr. S:	Not on earth
Me:	Sometimes I want to get away
Mr. S:	Into the body of a robot
Me:	No feelings there. Just safe steel
Mr. S:	No way to get hurt or die
Me:	Sometimes I want to die
Mr. S:	To live in heaven forever
Me:	Where people stay with you
Mr. S:	And never leave
Me:	Leave, leave, leave
Mr. S:	I wish my feelings would leave sometimes
Me:	But they stay
Mr. S:	And haunt

The End

Similar themes enter the next poem:

Mr. S:	I love to watch movies
Me:	There I'm alone
Mr. S:	In my world where people live happily ever after
Me:	It's hard to get in or out
Mr. S:	Why would someone want to get out?
Me:	Why would someone want to get in?
Mr. S:	To escape
Me:	The boredom and loneliness
Mr. S:	And be free
Me:	To be
Mr. S:	Happy

The End

His question in this poem was essentially the first question he had ever asked me. In answering it with a question, I risked putting him off, but he answered directly, essentially the first time he had done that as well. In fact, every line of each poem constituted a kind of question, in that a response was presumed, but within the context of the poem, the questions were not felt as threatening.

The next poem continues our voyage.

Mr. S:	I hope we have a good supper
Me:	There's nothing much to count on
Mr. S:	Except the cheeseburgers and hot pastrami
Me:	Full of grease, good grease
Mr. S:	To straighten the hair from the inside
Me:	Pull it out so hard it hurts
Mr. S:	It hurts to want people to like you
Me:	Because when you try you feel
Mr. S:	Like a fool
Me:	A greasy cheeseburger
Mr. S:	Won't betray you
Me:	It slithers down and gets digested
Mr. S:	But feelings can't
Me:	Digest so freely, only
Mr. S:	Hide

The End

Things were getting stirred up. Mr. S was talking to me now, as well as writing the poems. Of course, he always talked with his hand cupped over his mouth.

The next time we met he told me he had dreamed about his mother crying. He then gave me the pen and asked me to write the first line, a departure from our usual procedure.

Me:	When she cried I felt
Mr. S:	So sad
Me:	That I
Mr. S:	Was too ashamed to cry
Me:	Afraid
Mr. S:	Of people thinking I was weak
Me:	It made me sad to see her cry
Mr S:	But I had to stay strong and not cry
Me:	Or
Mr. S:	People would pick on the weakling. So I make people think I avoid them
Me:	But really
Mr. S:	I want to hit them with lightning so they will think I'm irresistible
Me:	But all I've got
Mr. S:	Is charisma
Me:	My mother
Mr. S:	Was emotional
Me:	And she left me to
Mr. S:	Live life without her

The End

The last two lines summed up much of his dilemma. Even as he had been unable to make useful emotional contact with his mother in her lifetime, he could not be rid of her now that she was gone. In a sense the physical weight of his mother's body, which he could not hold at the window, was continuing to pull him down.

Just as we began to get into the whole subject of his mother, Mr. S implied in the next poem that he was suspicious as to what I might be up to:

Mr. S: A leaf begins to grow I think on a tree in Hades
Me: It is black
Mr. S: And an evil tree
Me: Whose roots descend
Mr. S: To the heart of the unnamable one
Me: No name, but owning a heart he is
Mr. S: Vulnerable
Me: He
Mr. S: Should be wary
Me: Of all things black and hairy
Mr. S: And deceptively good
                        The End

I got the clear impression that I was the one who might be "deceptively good." But he let us go on.

Mr. S: I like cloudy days
Me: They block out harmful rays
Mr. S: Like a dog's third eyelid
Me: Or a hand held over the mouth
Mr. S: It does keep flies out
Me: And feelings in
Mr. S: Dangerous feelings
Me: About people that leave
Mr. S: And broken hearts
Me: Sad, red hearts
Mr. S: That might not be mended
Me: By a doctor
Mr. S: Or witch doctor
Me: Or
Mr. S: Anybody at all
                        The End

From now on, Mr. S talked more and more with me directly, writing fewer and fewer poems. However, he did still write at times.

Mr. S:	I remember my mother singing when she felt happy
Me:	Her voice filled up my world
Mr. S:	A world of emotions
Me:	Since she died I
Mr. S:	Think of the future
Me:	Rather than the past
Mr. S:	People learn from the past
Me:	But I can't believe she's dead
Mr. S:	With no afterlife
Me:	No song
Mr. S:	No needs, no wants
Me:	She always needed so much
Mr. S:	Attention
Me:	She made me feel
Mr. S:	Unindependent sometimes
Me:	Wrapped up in her
Mr. S:	Maternal needs
Me:	She gave me
Mr. S:	Worry

The End

Shortly after that poem, Mr. S took his hand away from over his mouth during our sessions. He started to talk openly and freely, with sadness as well as anger, about his mother and about his life. The need to write poems was less frequent, but occasionally he wanted to, especially when strong feelings came up.

Mr. S:	I heard a new song today
Me:	Tomorrow another new song
Mr. S:	That I might remember
Me:	Long enough
Mr. S:	To judge
Me:	How long it's been
Mr. S:	Since a song reminded me of someone

The End

As he took up his sadness like this and really felt it with me, a more hopeful tone entered the poems:

Mr. S: I think I have a way with imagination
Me: A world of fascination
Mr. S: And impossible things
Me: Silver shuttlecocks and boomerangs
Mr. S: And eternal victory for myself

And later:

Me: Shadows long and dark cast by
Mr. S: Forbidden monsters and prophets
Me: Fearful, unpredictable
Mr. S: But not unconquerable
Me: I have begun to fight
Mr. S: The evil ones with the help of the good ones
             The End

As he began to let go of the weight of his mother, he became more playful. I felt it too, writing a whimsical line like "Silver shuttlecocks and boomerangs" after he had announced, "I think I have a way with imagination."

He began to put it all into perspective as he began to get ready to leave the hospital. One of our last poems harkened back to the poem he had given the admitting psychiatrist:

Me: The hourglass is falling still
Mr. S: My actions are meaning nil
Me: I won't let them mean
Mr. S: More than my feelings
Me: My feelings now are like
Mr. S: Something more controlled
Me: Something like a spring, slowly unwinding
Mr. S: Or a lion stalking its prey
Me: Coming in on padded feet
Mr. S: With more experience than instinct
Me: Circling, watching, eyeing, smelling
Mr. S: Because instincts are too predictable
Me: But my feelings are
Mr. S: More controlled because they are stronger

Me: I feel
Mr. S: More instinctual and inner peace
                    The End

After Mr. S was discharged, he came to see me as an outpatient. In our first appointment, he asked to write a poem. This was the last poem we wrote:

Me: Now that I'm home I
Mr. S: Am happier
Me: Than I was before. But sometimes
Mr. S: I'm sad
Me: When I think of
Mr. S: My mother
Me: I think of her
Mr. S: Very rarely
Me: Now
Mr. S: I learned to live without her
Me: I learned
Mr. S: We all have to die sometime
Me: We all
Mr. S: Are mortal
Me: For now I
Mr. S: Feel healthy
Me: My hope is
Mr. S: To go to heaven
                    The End

I wish I could say Mr. S was cured, but he wasn't. As of yet, we have no cure for schizophrenia. I moved on out of training, and Mr. S moved on to yet another doctor. He did stay out of the hospital for a few years, but then he came back in, psychotic again, in need of help. I am told that he has been put on clozapine and is doing well outside the hospital, living within his schizophrenia.

During our time together he grieved the loss of his mother. This was helpful to him. And for my part, I learned about connection in a way I never could have done from a theory or a lecture. I learned that connection is possible, even when it seems impossible. Mr. S is with me still, informing my work with my current patients, deepening my understanding of human nature and of life, and most of all raising my hopes and giving me a deep inner smile whenever his face comes into my mind. We connected, and the connection endures.

I I

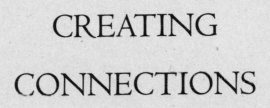

CREATING

CONNECTIONS

FOUR

You Are Already Rich in Connections

MOST PEOPLE HAVE no idea how rich they are in connections, or at least potential connections. Looking up a good friend you've lost touch with, or reconciling with the sister you're at odds with, or going back to that regular night out with your spouse—these are just a few concrete ways connections can be strengthened.

Sometimes I imagine all the connections we make in life like a garden we are always growing. One plant dies, another grows up, some get weeded out, while now and then we transplant. The garden is constantly changing, but certain parts last from year to year, like the old crab apple tree in the corner or the elm we swung from as children. Certain people stay with us always. Even after they die, our connection to them does not break. These are the constants in our garden.

I see my garden of connections with a rosebush here, a cauliflower there, a lemon tree, and maybe some herbs, a rotund pumpkin, a deeply purple eggplant, and a climbing vine of beans. My old friend Joe Kublicki, whom I haven't seen since we waited tables together on Cape Cod in the 1970s, would be the cauliflower. Solid, strong, unpretentious. My mom, God rest her soul, would be a lily of the valley. My brother John would be the pumpkin, don't ask me why. And my wife, Sue, would have to be the rose. Play the game yourself. Imagine your connections, growing all around you.

The garden varies from person to person, as gardens do. There is a huge variety in what we can grow there. But like all gardens, it requires our faithful attention to make it flourish. If we neglect it, it will overgrow with weeds and gradually turn into nothing more than what the wind brings in. But if we tend it, water it, weed it, fertilize it, protect it in bad weather, and generally fuss over it as we would over a garden we love, then it will grow gloriously from year to year, and bring us joy and strength.

I imagine the different kinds of connections we make as fitting into twelve broad categories, which I will outline here. There is no hierarchy in this list. By putting one kind of connection before another, I do not mean to imply that it is more important or more valuable, any more than one flower in the garden is superior to any other.

If I would recommend anything, it would be to develop a balance between them, trying to keep alive as many different kinds of connection as you can, not overvaluing one, expecting it to meet all your hopes and needs. For example, don't expect your marriage to do it all for you, or your job, or your kids, or your friends, or golf. While some people can find happiness and satisfaction from just one source of connection, most of us do better with many, just as most gardens thrive on variety.

THE TWELVE POINTS OF CONNECTION

FAMILY OF ORIGIN First is the connection we are given at birth. As we grow up, the people who raise us enter our lives and imaginations to stay forever, be they our biological parents or adoptive or foster parents. We develop similarly powerful connections to other family members, like siblings or grandparents.

If you are adopted—and a large percentage of Americans are either adopted or raised in foster homes—the connection to your biological parents continues throughout your life, even if you never meet them. You develop a crucial connection to them, even if only in your mind.

If you are raised by your biological parents, after you leave home and even after your parents pass away, your connection to them lives on forever.

This connection explains who you are, in many ways. It includes our biological parents and the people who raise us, as well as siblings and extended family.

These primary connections give us our genes and our earliest memories. They cause great pain at times, but also create our bedrock, for better or worse.

IMMEDIATE FAMILY The connection we make to the family we create when we grow up includes the connection to our most intimate other, be it a spouse, a partner, a best friend, sometimes even a pet. We think of this person as our main ally, the person we rely on most consistently. In addition, this connection may include children (biological, foster, or adopted).

Falling in love is the driving force behind this kind of connection. We all do it differently. I think of the couple from whom my family rents a house each summer. A surgeon and his wife, married and in love for over fifty years, they are never out of each other's thoughts. They have quite different personalities—she a formidable matriarch, he an unassuming, old-fashioned doctor—but you can almost reach out and touch the bond of love between them when they're together. It isn't all hearts and flowers. No, it is much stronger than that.

Love that lasts is made out of something so strong that it endures the constant pressure of self-interest that beats within each of us. Love is made of an alloy that even human selfishness can't tarnish.

While love may reach its peak with people who are "in love," love in its various forms waters all that grows in the garden of connections. Without love, no good connection lasts. While a bad connection may be built on fear or hatred, it is love that makes a connection good. To your pet, to your favorite painting, to your friend, to the company to which you've given all these years there is no positive connection without some kind of love. And the more love, the stronger the connection.

FRIENDS AND COMMUNITY The positive connections we make to our friends or our neighborhood or town make us feel good about life. As the poet William Butler Yeats wrote, "Think where man's glory most begins and ends,/ And say my glory was I had such friends."

The connection to friends and community is a connection we choose. If we nurture it, it pays us back as few investments can. Unfortunately, it is neglected in our busy lives these days. But if they are made a priority, friends and community can become as powerful as family, and sometimes better, because you can choose your friends, whereas you can't choose your family! I have known many people—friends of mine as well as patients—whose lives have been dramatically changed for the better, or even saved, by friends or by a community that cared.

WORK, MISSION, ACTIVITY Your connection to work, to a goal or mission, or even to a loved pastime or hobby can sustain you every day. Work is the most important connection of all in many adults' lives. A nonwork activity, like fishing or skiing, can also become a person's most passionate connection, or simply an additional important source of positive energy. A love of gardening may be deeply sustaining. Volunteer work, like Meals on Wheels or a reading-aloud program, can connect you to a whole new realm.

Feeling a sense of mission in what you do for a living can make you want to go to work. For example, a teacher who makes little money can become rich from the satisfaction the job may provide. Or a start-up entrepreneur can live off hot dogs and beans, feeding himself another kind of food with his dream of what his company might turn into. Even a connection to a game can feed the soul. Although we may joke about it, the fact is that some people connect so deeply to the game of golf that when they are playing it they feel more at peace with the world than at any other time. If you feel a sense of mission at work, or take deep pleasure from a game or some activity, those connections can strengthen you and lengthen your life.

BEAUTY The connection we make to beauty—music, art, literature, whatever we find beautiful—becomes as powerful in our lives as we let it. For some people this connection carries no power at all, because they do not allow it to develop. For others it means everything. We may sit in a museum in front of a painting for an hour carrying on a kind of conversation with that painting and develop a special relationship with it as we look at it. It is said that Henry Clay Frick, the famous industrialist who put together one of the greatest private collections of art ever assembled, used to get up in the middle of the night and go down and sit alone in one of the large rooms where his old masters hung. He would look at these works and listen to the paintings as they spoke to him silently. One of the paintings was a Rembrandt self-portrait, full of sadness and pain. The image of Henry Clay Frick, a ruler of the world in his day, sitting alone before Rembrandt at midnight speaks to me of how art and beauty can connect with the human spirit as nothing else can. I imagine Rembrandt told Frick things no one else would, and evoked in him feelings nothing else did.

THE PAST The connection we feel to the past is not just a knowledge of history; indeed, you can be rich in historical connection without knowing much schoolbook history. What I mean by connecting to the past is having an awareness of where you came from, instead of feeling as if time started when you were born. You can acquire historical connection by talking to your grandparents, or by learning something about your ancestors (what work they did, what struggles they faced, why they came to this country or the region you live in, what dreams they had for their descendants—you) and by considering how you have fulfilled their dreams, or how and why you have altered them. Studying history in school gives you a certain kind of historical connection, but learning your personal history at home fills it out, usually in more emotional terms.

This is valuable because the past can become your invisible companion. You can feel, as you drive down the highway to work, that you are here by the grace of your grandfather, who worked an extra job to help pay for your dad to go to college, who then made your education possible. Or you can appreciate the changing status of people in your area who share your ethnic background, and wonder what life must have been like for your great-grandparents. The historically connected person thinks back to the past often, now and then visits places from the past, and maybe discovers an old forgotten friend. Memory can create historical connection as well, as we remember where we've been and what we've seen. At best, the past prods us and guides us, a sage spirit at our side.

NATURE AND SPECIAL PLACES For some people, their connection to nature is so profound as to become a kind of religion. Particular places also draw deeply upon our souls. We connect to the essence of certain places—what is called the *genius loci,* or spirit of the place. The house we lived in at age six, a special bench in a certain park, a favorite corner store, a room where we love to read, a secluded spot on a beach we love—each may speak to us in a language no other place or person can, giving us comfort every time we visit or even think of the place. The place enters into a dialogue with us, speaking to us even when we are not there. For example, if you have a favorite place to go away to on vacation, often just imagining that place puts you in a good mood even though vacation is months away.

PETS AND OTHER ANIMALS The connection we make to pets and other animals, and even to inanimate objects like teddy bears when we are young, can go deeper than words. The psychoanalyst D. W. Winnicott called objects like teddy bears *transitional objects,* and he explained how essential they can be in growing up:

> There may emerge some thing . . . perhaps a bundle of wool or the corner of a blanket . . . that becomes vitally important . . . and is a defense against anxiety, especially anxiety of the depressive type. . . . This then becomes what I am calling a *transitional object.* The object goes on being important. The parents get to know its value and carry it round when travelling. The mother lets it get dirty and even smelly, knowing that by washing it she introduces a break in continuity . . . that may destroy the meaning and value of the object.*

Basically, a child connects with the teddy bear to help uplift his spirits as he makes the transition from subjective fantasy to cold reality, and from childhood to adulthood.

Pets similarly lift the spirits of us all, child and adult alike. So deep run the feelings people have for their pets that many people make arrangements for their pets in their wills. We had collies when I was a child. Bessie, Ike, Mike—these were a few of them. We also had a mutt named Rusty. I loved them all, and can vividly re-

*D. W. Winnicott, "Transitional Objects and Transitional Phenomena," in *Playing and Reality,* first published in 1971 by Tavistock Publications Ltd, reprinted by Routledge (New York, 1989).

member falling asleep in front of the fire using Ike's chest as a pillow many times. I can almost feel his rhythmic breathing now. Our connections to pets, and even inanimate objects, provide some of the earliest and most powerful lessons of love, loss, and restoration that we ever learn.

Furthermore, we can learn about the pleasures of caretaking from our pets. They give us such unconditional love that we *want* to provide their food and shelter. Children learn the responsibilities of caretaking from pets, for they know that pets depend on them for sustenance just as they themselves depend on their parents. For older people, getting up to walk or feed the dog may be the only tug that gets them out of bed, the only pull that brings them out of themselves.

The depth of these connections also proves that profound connection need not depend upon language. A dog and its owner or a child and his teddy communicate in a rich and complex fashion without the dog or teddy ever speaking a word in English, although they speak a host of imagined ones! We can *commune* with a pet —as I do often with our dog, Pippy —in a unique way. I'll sit and talk to Pippy just as if she were a person, and she will look up at me with inquiring eyes, and I will imagine she is talking back to me. Funny thing, though, we never argue!

IDEAS AND INFORMATION The connection we make to ideas and information can be a supreme pleasure, as well as our livelihood. Never before has the old saying "Knowledge is power" proved as true as it does today. Our modern era makes forging the connection to knowledge easier for us than it has ever been in human history. We are awash in ideas and information every day. Connecting to them requires not that we dig them up so much as that we choose among the millions we are offered.

Your thoughts are free. You are free to turn over any idea you like, and in this country at least, you are free to speak and write about it however you want. The pleasure of the world of ideas is a pleasure we usually take for granted, until we meet some old friend from whom it has been taken, as by Alzheimer's.

We all think, so we all connect with information and ideas somewhat, but we probably know a few people who have really delved deeply into the pleasures of thought. Just as we've known great gourmets, we've enjoyed the company of a true thinker, someone who loves thought, not to show off but for the sheer joy of the connection. I remember my college roommate Phil Green saying his greatest pleasure in life was simply to sit and think, or better still, lie down and think! He was as humble a guy as I've ever met, but he was a true genius. Many times I would come back to our room, see Phil on the bed, say, "Hi, whatcha doing?" only to have him reply (sounding slightly annoyed at being interrupted), "I'm thinking."

While few of us go as deeply into the pleasure of ideas as Phil Green, still we can all enjoy thought. We develop the pleasure of the connection with ideas in many ways. For example, we befriend certain people because they always have some new idea or something interesting to say. Or we open up the newspaper every morning and go straight to a favorite columnist's page, as I used to do to Frank Rich's in the *New York Times.* (My second stop is sports in the *Boston Globe.* I guess that bespeaks my pleasure in my connection with a certain body of information!) Or we may subscribe to a certain magazine and look forward to each issue because we know it will feed our connection to ideas in a way we enjoy.

Whatever our areas of interest, we enrich that area by the give-and-take of opinion, the satisfaction of finding agreement, the stimulation of encountering disagreement, and the excitement of breaking new ground in how we think—developing new ideas, based on new information.

Never before has the world of information and ideas been so open to everyone. Never before have we known as much as we do today. And never before has access to a wide range of ideas been more convenient. From our favorite columnist to the talk show host we love to hate, to our growing connection to a new information-management skill like sending E-mail or finding timesaving ways to word process, to our evolving feelings about a certain philosophy or way of thinking, we all *connect* to information and ideas. For some people it is the central connection in their lives. But even for those to whom it is peripheral, it can be richly rewarding.

INSTITUTIONS AND ORGANIZATIONS The institution you connect to may be the place you work, or it may be your school. It may be a club, or a political party, or a volunteer association, or a team. It may be your country. Unfortunately, connections like these have eroded over the past several decades, as cynicism has undercut our trust in many of our institutions and organizations. In politics we seem to have lived in a haze of cynicism, from Vietnam to Watergate and Contragate to the impeachment trial. In business we live in the age of Dilbert. In professional sports, and even big-time college sports, the name of the game is personal gain, not team spirit. Indeed, team spirit has become a joke in some sports.

However, positive energy still grows strong within the human spirit, if we nurture it. Watch someone starting a business he believes in. I have had the pleasure of seeing a number of my patients do just this. The enthusiasm they feel practically lifts me off my feet—and I weigh over two hundred pounds! Sure, they also feel fear, but they tap into their positive energy and that of their cohorts to pull them through. "I remember working all night in my basement," one such man told me, "with nothing but my faith in my idea, my wife's encouragement, and my partners' cheerleading to get me through. Looking back, I don't know where we found the nerve—or the money—to survive, but we did!" That can-do attitude became the bedrock of what is now a solid organization—built on risk, hope, a good idea, and people's faith in one another.

This is what a positive connection to an institution is all about—good people putting faith in good ideas and in one another.

If you can renovate your connection to an institution you believe in, this connection can give both you and the institution renewed strength. If you can get past your understandable cynicism and pick one organization you believe in, and then invest special energy there, the rewards can be enormous. Or maybe you can start your own!

WHATEVER IS BEYOND KNOWLEDGE The conditions of life urge us to consider the questions for which we have no provable answer. "You never know what life means till you die," wrote the poet Robert Browning. "Even throughout life, 'tis death that makes life live." In developing your connection to whatever is beyond, you nourish your soul and make meaning out of life.

People give this connection various names. They may say they connect to the cosmos, or to truth, or simply to the unknown. They may even say there is nothing beyond, and so they can have no such connection. Even this is a kind of connection—to nothing. Others have a well-articulated idea of what lies beyond knowledge. Some call this God. For still others, their connection to nature constitutes their connection to the beyond.

In my own case, God is where I turn with the big questions. This connection has always been with me. Sue and I have tried to pass it along to our children. I came out of the shower the other morning and saw Tucker, my three-year-old, cuddling in bed with Sue. I said, "That is so adorable, just the two of you together." To which Tucker instantly replied, "God's here, too!" I was so glad to see that Tucker was developing a connection, in his childhood, to God—a feeling that God is with him everywhere, so he can never be totally alone. This is a great gift for a child, or anyone, to have.

YOURSELF The connection you make to yourself gives you a sense of independence and identity.

We all have a relationship with ourselves. We carry on an inner dialogue. We look at ourselves, and we judge ourselves. We have the gift—or curse—of self-awareness, and with that comes the inevitability of self-appraisal.

For some people the connection they make to themselves is harsh and self-condemning. For others it is upbeat and encouraging. No one really knows exactly why this connection can develop in such different ways, but the good news is that we do know it can be changed. Indeed, one of the best ways of changing it is to deepen some of the other eleven kinds of connection. As you improve them, it is almost certain that you will feel better in your connection to yourself.

Your connection to yourself may not be in need of healing, but rather expansion. A common example of this is a person who wants to work on developing their creative side. Many happy, successful people know they have let their creativity atrophy, and they wonder if they can reclaim it. The answer is, absolutely yes! Creativity does not die; it just gets ignored.

A healthy connection to yourself does not mean that you have to think you are perfect; indeed, people who think that are in big trouble. Nor does it mean you have to have fully developed all your talents. No one ever has.

A healthy connection to yourself simply means you offer yourself a good place to grow. You don't hold yourself back or get in your own way, at least not too much.

The goal in connecting to yourself is to create conditions under which you can become whoever you are meant to be and feel proud of who you are. The goal is for you to be as much at ease within yourself as an ancient elm.

All these kinds of connection entwine to create a connected life. You do not need to connect to the fullest in each of the twelve ways—don't turn connecting into another job or achievement! Just try to make connections matter. Most people find that their happiness depends more upon connection than on anything else. To achieve it, do what seems right for you. Hold hands as you walk with your child, get to know your neighbors, line up to give blood at the Red Cross in a time of disaster, dance at your prom, pray at a funeral, be part of a team performing heart surgery or part of a team playing football—however you do it, *connect*.

The rest takes care of itself. Like magic.

FIVE

Family:

WHAT STRINGS OUR HEARTS,

AND UNSTRINGS THEM, TOO

ON LABOR DAY weekend of 1998 I took my two young sons to see their grandfather's—my father's—grave. Sue was doing some desk work, Lucy was away at a friend's, so Jack and Tucker and I set out to the park to play ball. After that we decided to go for an ice cream, and after that, while driving home, we passed Mount Auburn Cemetery. That's where my father is buried. On an impulse, I turned in.

The boys didn't mind. They'd never been to Mount Auburn Cemetery before, and they seemed curious. I parked the car, and they jumped out and walked over to a grave with a marble tiger on top. "Who's buried here?" they asked.

"I don't know," I said.

"Can we sit on the tiger?" they asked.

"Well, you probably shouldn't," I said, "because someone is buried underneath that tiger, so we should treat the grave with respect."

From there we walked along the edges of the graves, making our way down to Dad's site.

Mount Auburn is a vast cemetery, beautifully landscaped, filled with all kinds of interesting trees and shrubs and plants, as well as the tombs and gravestones of some famous people, like Henry Wadsworth Longfellow, Oliver Wendell Holmes, Mary Baker Eddy, and Bernard Malamud, plus thousands of unknowns like my dad. It is said to be one of the most beautiful cemeteries in the world.

I had discovered my father's grave site myself only recently. Since attending his burial, twenty years ago, I had not visited his grave until, again on an impulse, I drove into Mount Auburn a few months before and got directions through the maze of roads and paths to where his grave lay.

Now I was able to guide my boys there. When we came to the plot, in the middle of a little gully, Tucker ran up and started knocking on the headstone, I guess to see if someone would talk back. There were two oval-shaped granite headstones side by side, one for my grandmother and her husband, the other for my father and Betty, the woman Dad married years after he divorced my mom. The boys, of course, wanted to know who each of the four names they saw inscribed on the headstones belonged to, and they wanted to know where these people were today. "In heaven," I told them. "You'll meet each one of them someday."

"Your grandad was great," I said to the boys, who were now climbing on top of his headstone. I thought of telling them to stop, but then I figured this was as close as they'd get to climbing into their grandfather's lap, so they should climb all they wanted. "He was such a nice man," I told them. "He almost *never* got angry." That's true. I can't remember one time I saw my father angry. "He taught school, and he played hockey, and he fished and sailed." The boys weren't listening, but I wanted to say the words anyway. "He loves you both very much." Then I asked the boys if we could kneel down and say a little prayer, which they agreed to do.

As we left the little gully, I had the feeling of having just walked onto a playing field long after a game was over. There had been cheering and noise and victory and defeat there once, but now there was only silence, and the beauty of the grass, growing at its own pace. Nothing was in a hurry here.

And yet, I thought, *the game still goes on.* Look at Tucker and Jack. They wouldn't be here if Dad had never lived.

I loved my dad, imperfect as he was, and I still miss him a real lot. I wish the boys could have known him. He was so good with kids. I wish he could have taken them skating and told them stories of his days playing hockey in college, and I wish he could have told them about his days as captain of a destroyer escort in World War II, and taught them how to fish and to sail—but he can't. He is gone.

Still, the family he continued lives on. I think that families never die, they just gain and lose members. I think of families as an energy source that constantly pulls people toward them, and that people are constantly trying to gain distance from. Finding the *right* distance is the challenge most people face with their families.

Too close, and you can become so entwined that you have no freedom. Too distant, and the family becomes almost a memory, losing its power for good or for bad in your life.

Alice came to see me because she was upset with her relationship with her parents, particularly her mother. Now thirty-seven, married, with children of her own, Alice couldn't shake the feeling of living under her mother's thumb. "I live in Boston," she said to me. "She lives in Charlotte. Hundreds of miles separate us, but she might as well live next door, psychologically."

Alice, a dynamic businesswoman who worked for one of Boston's most high-powered consulting firms, didn't look like someone who'd be under anyone's thumb. "But you don't know my mother!" she replied when I commented how independent she seemed. "And the pettiest things still bother me. You'd think I'd be used to the fact that my brothers are gods by now, wouldn't you? The two of them were worshipped while we were growing up, and they're worshipped today. We girls were, well, OK, and we're still just OK today. The fact that the three of us have made much better lives for ourselves than the boys doesn't matter. Mom probably doesn't even notice that."

"That doesn't seem like such a petty thing," I said.

"No, but my responses to it are," she replied. "For example, I went to Mom's home with my kids last month, and when we got there, late at night, as I was lugging our bags to our rooms I noticed that the beds in my brothers' rooms had been turned down. But when I got to my room, the bed had not been turned down. I went berserk inside. Of course, I didn't say anything. How could I without looking like a total spoiled brat, but it burned me up! It was so typical! Treat the boys like princes, and treat me like just another person."

Alice and I worked on helping her separate psychologically from her mother. In my experience as a psychiatrist, this is a delicate maneuver. Taking the bad part out of anyone's relationship with a parent is sort of like taking the chocolate out of a chocolate cake—it is pretty hard to do without taking away the whole cake.

I tried to appeal to reality. "You are a grown woman now, you are powerful and strong, more so than you say your mother ever was. You have your own family, your own friends, your own career. Why should you let her have such a hold over you? Why should you still want her praise so deeply?"

"I know," Alice said. "It is ridiculous. It is stupid. I feel ashamed even telling you about it."

So, that approach didn't help.

I tried to get angry for Alice, taking on her mother myself. "She has no right to treat you like that. What an uncaring woman. She sounds incredibly difficult." Alice missed her next two appointments after I said that. Alice did not want me putting down her mother.

So I tried another tack. I tried to interpret the psychology behind her feelings. "It is only natural that you should feel this way, having grown up in the shadow of your brothers. Now that you have achieved more than they have, you want your just due, and when it doesn't come, just as it didn't come years ago, it makes you very angry, as it did back then."

"Yes," Alice said, "that's right." The interpretation may have been right, but I don't know that it was helpful.

I then tried another angle. "Maybe you miss your mom, and feeling resentful toward her is your way of preserving your attachment. It is less painful than the ache of just missing her."

"I don't think so," Alice replied.

Round and round we went, week after week, month after month, and nothing really changed. Alice still felt her mother's judging eye over her shoulder, and still resented that she withheld praise.

What I was able to do—and this is something that psychotherapy is very good for—was be there with her in the midst of her feelings. Even though we didn't resolve or change anything, at least not dramatically, Alice kept coming back because she felt a connection, both to me and to troubled feelings she was having a hard time bearing alone.

Then one day Alice got word that her mother had cancer. She came into my office a mess. This woman who usually looked like she just stepped off the cover of a magazine had mascara streaked down all over her face, and her eyes were red from crying. The minute she sat down in my office she started to sob some more. A crusty part of me wondered inside, *What's the matter, aren't you glad your old nemesis is about to bite the dust?*—but that was not what I said. I said, "How bad is it?"

"They won't know until they operate," she replied after she blew her nose. "I'm flying out tonight. I can't believe that jerk of a doctor didn't pick this up sooner."

"What kind of cancer is it?" I asked.

"Colon," Alice said. "She had just had a complete physical six months ago. He should have picked it up then."

Two weeks later, Alice returned. She had good news. The cancer had not spread, or so it looked to the surgeon, and her mother's prognosis, with chemotherapy, was good.

That episode caused a dramatic change. Although Alice still felt resentment toward her mother, I began to hear many loving stories about her as well. Alice's descriptions of her mother and her memories of her changed from angry to fond. Her mother's brush with death seemed to spark, if not a resolution to the conflict, then a moving past it.

Alice took a supervising interest in her mother's health care, making calls to the doctors in North Carolina, getting additional opinions from the Boston medical community, and, I imagine, scaring the daylights out of some of the medical people in Charlotte. Alice was a formidable woman. I wondered if she and her mother weren't rather similar.

As she supervised her mother's care—her father and her siblings were perfectly happy to have her do this—she went home more often. She and her mother talked frequently in person, instead of just over the phone. The stories Alice told me became less and less complaining. She wanted to make good the time she had left with her mother. I imagined this was a two-way street, her mother probably reaching out and opening up in some ways, too.

None of this seemed intentional or the result of psychotherapy—which, as usual, reminded me of how humble I should be. Instead, nature or God had sent a messenger, in the form of possible death. The messenger said to both Alice and her mother, "Stop. No more time for your carrying on. Now it's time to get ready for the end."

Prompted by cancer, Alice and her mother finally found the right distance.

What happened to the critical voice of her mother that used to plague Alice, the voice that Alice imagined so frequently putting her down? The critical voice didn't fall silent completely, it just ceased being such a dominating force in Alice's life. It changed from a church bell to a little ping. The fight—for whatever it is we try to get from our parents—ended as Alice and her mom prepared to say good-bye.

I have seen time and again in families that love rears up even when you think it never will. I have treated people for years who had thoroughly convinced me that one or both of their parents were utter monsters, only to see, in a moment of crisis, love pour forth from parent and from child. More than a few times I have had the inner reaction I had with Alice: *What do you mean you're upset? I should think you'd be dancing in the street that so-and-so is sick!* But that is rarely the reaction I see.

Even without much time spent together, a family connection can be lastingly close. I know a rabbi who told me this story about himself: "Ever since I can remember, I have felt connected to my grandmother. This is so even though in my youth I lived in New York City and Los Angeles and she lived in London. I met her *only once* in my entire life, when I was twenty-two, and she died half a year later, now some thirty-two years ago! She still remains a pivotal part of my life in spite of these circumstances, although I am now fifty-four. It all began with the 'Dear Granny' letters I wrote her, from the time I was six until her death. I regularly wrote the typical sort of letter—'How are you? I am fine. I hope to hear from you soon.' And she would respond in her simple, elegant, handwritten notes filled with affection for me. In short, I loved her, and she loved me in an unambiguous manner. The one time I met her was when I traveled abroad at age twenty-two. Her mind was lucid, to the point where she questioned why I would want to be a rabbi in a world where religion causes such conflict among people. My answer was that once ordained, I would be the sort of spiritual leader who would help bring harmony among different groups. I don't think that I convinced her, but I feel that encounter was tantamount to a lifelong personal challenge and pledge, which I have done my best to meet. She died at the age of ninety-six. While I never saw her except that one time, she is still very much with me."

There is no one right way to do family. The call family answers is so strong and deep within us that family can happen under almost any conditions. Just as some wildflowers will grow through rocks, some families will thrive under the most difficult conditions.

For example, I have a patient whose parents divorced in a bitter struggle, literally kicking and screaming. In one session in court, the mom picked up her lawyer's briefcase and hurled it across the aisle at her soon-to-be-ex-husband. He caught it, emptied its contents out on his lawyer's desk, and started to throw the books and pads back at his soon-to-be-ex-wife. Enraged at this response, she picked up the pitcher of water on her lawyer's table and threw it back at him. They both had to be removed from the courtroom while the place was tidied up.

But once the divorce was completed, after a few months of settling, they each became concerned about the welfare of their two boys. Despite their hatred of each other, they began to cooperate about the details of managing joint custody. Amazing though it may seem, within a year they were having lunches together, joking about how impossible they each had been during the divorce, regretting that while they were not compatible as a married couple, they hadn't found a way to split up more amicably, and resolving to make the years ahead as good as they could not only for the children but for themselves as well.

Of course, it can go the other way, too. A family dispute can harden over time, even to the point that the participants forget why they hate one another; they just know they hate one another. I treated a man named Jay for depression. In describing his family, he told me, among other things, that he was brought up to hate his uncle. He didn't know why. When he would ask, he was just told, "Your uncle is the bad seed. Never speak to him. He is poison." One of the ways the family found unity was in excluding the forbidden uncle. He was never present at family events, like Christmases or baptisms, but he was often talked about. Family members would analyze Uncle Barry's personality, taking turns explaining why he had turned out so bad. It was a kind of group psychological exercise. As family members grew and matured, into high school, then college, their theories would grow with them, in sophistication and complexity. But no one ever spoke to Uncle Barry.

Then, while Jay was in college, his evil uncle wrote him a letter saying he'd like to meet him. Being independent minded, my patient said OK. When they met, the story Jay heard from Uncle Barry was, of course, quite different from the ones he'd heard growing up. Jay found that he liked Uncle Barry. But he didn't tell anyone about this meeting. So strong was the family instruction to exclude Uncle Barry that Jay feared he would be excluded himself if he ever let it be known that he had had lunch with Uncle Barry. And that he ended up liking him would result in banishment for sure!

Jay was able to keep up his relationship with Uncle Barry. But (at least not in the year we met together) he never dared tell anyone in his family about this reconciliation. He feared that his family would feel betrayed and react with great wrath against him.

I have treated a man who was betrayed in business by his brother and never spoke to him again. I have treated a man whose own father had an affair with his wife. I have treated a grown woman who felt so upset every time she visited her parents that she would often have to get out of her car and throw up just before arriving. The family connection taps into our most powerful feelings.

I don't think there is one formula that guarantees a happily connected family. No one structure works best. I have seen families work (and by work I mean help the members more than hurt them) where there was one parent and eight children, or four parents and one child, or parents at opposite ends of the country with the children in different boarding schools, or grandparents instead of parents, or a parent in and out of a mental hospital, or both parents recovering from drug abuse, or no parents, just substitutes. I have also seen the traditional family of a dad who works and a mom who stays at home fail miserably. I have seen enough to know there is no one formula.

What works best is simply to create the feeling of connection between all members of the family, without the feeling of imprisonment. And there are many ways to do that.

I think of my own life and how much stability I found in the boarding schools I attended and in the substitute parents I adopted among my teachers. Many kids who grow up within difficult families find a substitute family somehow. It may be the neighbors, or the grandparents, or even their baseball team.

A woman in her fifties told me the following about her childhood years: "Growing up, I felt disconnected from my family—alcoholic father; professional mother, whom I loved but who worked very hard. My connection back then came from many years at a six-week summer camp—counselors whom I loved, and fellow campers. I was also close to several teachers in high school. In addition I was very close to my wonderful, loving aunt and uncle—and still am!" Now she has reconciled with her parents and has a good relationship with them, but during the years when they weren't there for her, she managed to create another, makeshift family that got the job done.

I hear of and see these kinds of stories all the time. The call to connect runs so deep that, given a chance, people will find a way.

When I worked on a children's inpatient unit, I treated a little boy named Tibo who was admitted to the hospital after setting his mother's bed on fire. He had witnessed an attempted murder the day before, and he was in a psychotic state. Speaking nonsense, smearing his feces on the wall, swearing at whoever came into his room, this seven-year-old boy was completely deranged.

His mother loved him, but she was unable to take care of him, due to a host of problems of her own. She was a proud and angry woman who hated letting the hospital take over, so she snarled at me when we met. She held a paper cup in her hands and spit into it every few minutes, telling me she had a cold. But the real reason was clear. She wanted to spit on me and all that I was: privileged, white, male, able to help. But she cooperated. I didn't need her admiration; all I needed was her cooperation. The fact is, I admired her, but I would have got in big trouble had I told her that! She would have thought me patronizing.

Tibo found a new world for himself in the inpatient unit. The hospital was poor, but not as poor as what Tibo came from; at least it had walls and heat and food. If the paint in the inpatient unit was chipping or the food was cold or the floors were bare, this was still paradise to Tibo, compared to where he'd just come from.

The morning after his admission I walked into Tibo's room and said hello. He said to me, "I spent the night in your brain and I crawled out your nose this morning." At least he was speaking sentences. Crazy sentences, but sentences nonetheless.

Tibo stayed in the hospital two years, going home on weekends. I met with him several times a week, and the staff created what we call a *therapeutic environment.* That is a jargon term for a stable place to live. A social worker met with Tibo's mom regularly, and I joined them from time to time.

We allowed Tibo to adopt us, while we preserved his connection to his mom. We gave him a safe environment at the hospital, and gave him a chance to learn how to negotiate life without resorting to violence.

One of the ways Tibo and I did this was by playing what we called the Jesus game. A Southern Baptist, Tibo had been brought up to believe in Jesus, even if he was surrounded by violence. So we invented a game in which Tibo and I would take turns playing Jesus.

If I was playing Jesus, Tibo would ask me questions like, "OK, Jesus, what do you do if some dude disses you?"

I would reply with something like, "I tell him to stop."

"And what if he smacks you?" Tibo would ask.

"I walk away."

"Then he laughs at you," Tibo says.

"I try not to care."

Then Tibo would play Jesus, and I would ask the same questions.

Through this kind of play, and many other conversations, Tibo adopted me as a kind of substitute parent. I would remind him now and then, as I would remind myself, that I was not his real dad (his real dad was long gone) and that I could not take him home with me when he left the hospital (his mother would do that). In this way we tried to keep a handle on our expectations.

Tibo let me become a substitute father for him, just as I had done with my teachers at boarding schools. The connection we made was, to use the clinical term, *therapeutic.* Another way to say it is, we loved each other.

But it had to end, as we both knew it would. By the time I was leaving the hospital for another job, Tibo was almost ready to leave, too. But I left first.

Tibo was a changed boy. He was tall and handsome and proud, articulate, and a leader of the other kids on the ward. He knew how to talk about his feelings now—indeed, he was becoming quite a rhetorician—and he knew how to get along with others, including his mother. I could see him becoming a Baptist preacher one day!

One of the rules on the ward was that there be little or no physical contact between staff and children. I always thought this was a ridiculous rule, but its purpose was to protect children who had been abused in some way from feeling in danger. The buzzword was "inappropriate." Physical contact was deemed inappropriate.

When Tibo and I met for the last time, to say good-bye, I said to him, "Well, Tibo, I'll miss you. You and I have become pretty good friends."

"Pretty good friends?" Tibo said in derision. "*I love you!* In fact, I'd kiss you on the mouth, but that would be inappropro."

I'll never forget the word "inappropro," and I'll never forget Tibo. I don't know where he is today, but I do know that the substitute connection we made has lasted in my mind, at least.

You surely do not need to admit your child to a mental hospital or send him away to boarding school if there is trouble in the family connection. If parents can't fit the mold they imagine they should, maybe they should reexamine the mold. They need not feel guilty about failing to conform to some mythical perfect way, because there is no perfect way. What's right for one family might not be right for another. If your family works the way you're doing it, don't worry that it is different from the way you always thought it would be or the way some expert on TV says it should be. The demands of modern life are so complex that nobody can possibly prescribe one right way to make a family.

As long as you set up your family so that all the members feel connected in a positive way, then you have succeeded. And succeeded magnificently!

Whatever its structure, a family requires constant tending, like a garden. Holding families together takes effort. My generation recoiled from the negative side effects of family life—feeling controlled, losing our voice, feeling suffocated, being immersed in a struggle every day. Now, I think we are trying to construct families in a new way, without the old patterns of domination, even abuse. But we want to get back some of the good feeling that can develop around, say, the family table at dinner, or in the car on an excursion, or at a gymnastics meet our nine-year-old competes in while we watch.

The trick is to preserve the passion as you detoxify the family structure. A disconnected family may have none of the problems of the families of old, but it lacks vitality as well.

For example, I had a patient, Molly, who hardly ever saw her extended family. She was married and had one child. "My mother lives alone in San Francisco," she told me, "my father lives in Seattle with his new wife, my sister lives in New York, my brother lives in Atlanta, and I live in Boston. We never get together."

"How come?" I asked.

"Logistics. We all work, and our schedules are all different. My sister and brother both have kids, and so do I. It just never works out."

"Couldn't you make it work?" I asked.

"Sure, if there were a pressing reason to. But we never got along all that well when we were together. I think we feel we have found the right distance."

"Which is never to see each other?" I asked.

"Well, if you want to put it that way, yes," she replied.

Molly had come to see me because she was depressed. There were many reasons we could find for her feeling blue, but none of them seemed quite as strong to me as this disconnection from her family, a factor she discounted altogether. I brought up my concern.

"Well," she said, "maybe you just have some Pollyanna idea of how families are supposed to be. Maybe you are just naïve."

"Maybe," I replied. "But maybe you are overlooking a resource that is more important to you than you think."

"Why should I reach out to my family when all they will do is act bored or busy?" Molly said.

We left the topic alone for a while and focused on other aspects of her life, like her marriage to a man she got along well with, her career as a lawyer, and her son, who was a happy first-grader. The depressing feelings didn't seem to originate from those areas. Molly would simply complain, "I like my job, I love my husband and son, but I can't stand the juggling act."

Was that enough to explain her depression? I didn't think so. We did try Prozac, which was helpful, but an undercurrent of deep dissatisfaction remained.

"I have to tell you, Molly," I said after a few months of therapy, "I think the work we have left to do is with your extended family."

She rolled her eyes, as if to say, "Here we go again."

"I'm sorry," I said, "but I just don't think I'd be doing my job right if I told you that I believe the arrangement you have with your extended family is the best deal you all can work out."

"Did you come from a broken family?" Molly asked me. "Is that why you are trying to fix mine?"

"Touché," I replied. "But even if my family had been a model family—which, you are correct, it was not—I think I still would be urging you to bring yours closer."

"You're not supposed to tell me what to do," Molly said, after thinking for a moment.

"I'm giving you my humble opinion," I said. "I'm not telling you what to do. Even if I did, I know you well enough to know you will do what you decide you want to do."

She cocked her head. "Is that an insult?"

"No," I replied. "It is praise."

The seed had been planted. In Molly's mind it grew.

The upshot was that several months later her extended family all met in Seattle. Her father had the biggest house. It turned out his wife had been hoping for such a reconciliation but had felt it wasn't her place to spearhead it. However, once Molly opened the door, this woman jumped in to help make it happen.

Of course, they did not instantly become one big happy family. But anyone who saw Molly, proud, strong woman that she was, recount that reunion weekend in my office would have become a believer in the power of connections. "I missed them so much, without knowing it," she sobbed, "and they missed me." I had never seen Molly cry, even in the worst of her depression. But now, shedding tears of joy, she cried openly. "I love them," she said. "They're all screwed up, but I love them." The power of the family was there all along. It just had to be set in motion and given a chance.

Now Molly's family is in touch regularly, by phone and E-mail, and they are already planning their next get-together.

When the connection breaks, it can stay broken for a long time. The death of a grandparent or even just a geographical move by a key member can precipitate a rift that lasts a generation or two. This is one reason we should not take lightly the demands to move that companies make upon employees. The move may provide the company with what it needs and offer the person who moves a better job, but the cost to the family involved is a hidden cost no one can calculate. As Molly can tell you, the cost of prolonged separation can be high.

It seems that grandparents often are the ones who bring families together regularly. Once they're gone, they leave a void. Echoed by many are these words from one fifty-five-year-old woman: "My grandparents provided a connectedness within our family that is no longer there. We met over holidays and had large family dinners with delicious Italian food, with everyone pitching in to help out. The children in the family would often put on shows, to the delight of everyone. There was so much love and acceptance. We've tried to get together in some way without them, and the thing that seems to work best is a family reunion at a country inn. We've been able to get some of that old feeling back of being with each other."

Of course, the family connection is not an unalloyed blessing. Sometimes the family you grow up in is so close that you can't wait to get rid of it. You can't wait to get out on your own. Psychologists call this process of setting out on your own *separation and individuation*. It is important for us all to be able to separate from home and to declare our own independence, our own identity.

But sometimes separation and individuation go too far. You end up cutting off your nose to spite your face, as Molly and her siblings had done.

This question of distance comes up again and again. How close you want to be to your family and how close your family wants you to be to it combine to create an almost daily dialogue for many of us. As one woman said to me: "I am very close to my mother. I am also very close to my daughter, who is twelve years old. I know my mother, now seventy, is getting older and won't be here forever, and I am fearful that when she is gone it will be like a part of myself dying. In some ways we have a love-hate type of relationship. I love her very much, yet if we live together, as we have in the past, we fight a lot! I also love my daughter very much, yet I want to make sure that although we are very close, she can be an individual and be connected with me in a healthy way without that sense of being joined at the hip, possibly feeling she couldn't survive without me. That is what I sometimes feel like with my own mother."

The power of the connection in families is so strong that the closeness of the connection has to be watched: how close to the fire do you want to be?

It is especially given to some of us, I believe, to make families grow. Some people are born good nurturers. Others are not. Some people know deep down that they do not want children. You shouldn't feel guilty if you are not drawn toward making a family. Not everyone should have children. Your mission may be in doing something else. Children would only get in your way—and you in theirs! You can be happy and good in life and never marry and never raise a child. It is wrong to believe or to tell others that the only way to happiness is through family connection.

But for those for whom it is meant, there is nothing better.

Sometimes the people who grew up without what they needed are most motivated to try to make it better next time around. "My mother is a wonderfully compassionate person, but I'm not sure how she got that way," one woman told me. "At seventeen, she had *no teeth,* which was the result of an abusive parent. During the course of my upbringing I often learned inadvertently about the ways in which she was mistreated by her parents. As an example, when she married my dad, who was part Italian, her parents did not attend, as Irish and Italians should not have married. Despite her mistreatment as a child and as an adult, I always felt totally loved and connected to my mother. She nurtured and loved me and my siblings, all five of us. Despite her lack of nurturing from her parents, she was always able to make me feel totally loved and accepted. It is a mystery to me that my mother, who was not cared for and felt no connection to her parents or family, could have become such a totally loving, compassionate woman for me."

Love growing out of soil that had no love, a battered child becoming a tender mother, a teenager with no teeth becoming the adored mother of five children—that mystery is only part of the mystery of family and of connection.

It is a wonder that it comes, the power to transform the worst of family connections—such as a child being beaten time and again— into the best. Where it comes from no one knows for sure, but that it comes no one can deny.

I have learned from people like Tibo and Molly and Jay that if you keep your heart open, the rest usually takes care of itself. Studies have shown that some children who come from horrible child-hoods do very well in adult life, while most do not. The ones who do the best all share one characteristic: they are able to reach out. Tibo reached out to me and the staff on the ward, even though he had all kinds of reasons not to trust us. Jay reached back after his Uncle Barry reached out, even though he had been instructed not to. And Molly overcame her deep reservations and opened her heart once again.

If there is a method to making positive connections grow and last in families, I would sum it up like this: keep an open heart, always be ready to forgive, never amputate, and build on the belief that you're better off with them than without them. In other words, find a way to make it work.

If you can't, don't give up. Above all, don't give up. The power of the family to harm is surpassed only by its power to heal. Families have secret undercurrents. The unexpected happens.

If you want to hurry the unexpected, family therapists can some-times work magic, and almost always induce some improvement. The field of family therapy is one of the most sophisticated in all of mental health. To get a referral, talk to your family physician or a psychiatrist you trust.

SIX

Children

THE AGONY AND THE ECSTASY

LAST SUMMER I told my daughter, Lucy, she would have to be tutored for her learning disability during the coming school year. She started to cry, saying she didn't want to be tutored, that none of the kids she hung around with would be tutored, and that it made her feel stupid.

Normally Lucy is about as upbeat and playful as a nine-year-old can possibly be. Our first child, she brought a sunburst into our world from the moment she was born. Nicknamed Loosey-Goosey by a friend of mine, she has indeed been loosey-goosey and full of fun from day one. She lit up in Sue and me that great region of the heart called love for a child, which you never know is there until it lights up for the first time.

The problem with this kind of total love is that you feel vulnerable to all the things that might go wrong for your child. With an adult—your spouse, a friend, a relative—you may love them as deeply as your child, but you also know they are better equipped to take care of themselves than a child is. A child needs you as no one else does.

We found out about the ecstasy and the agony of parenthood almost the minute Lucy was born. As the doctor lifted her out of Sue by C-section and proclaimed, "It's a girl!" we both felt elated, I sitting next to the anesthesiologist at Sue's head, and Sue lying flat, feeling exhausted plus elated.

However, a few hours later we discovered Lucy had a rare heart condition called *situs inversus*. She was born with her heart on the right side of her chest, instead of the left. We were told she would need to have an echocardiogram to determine if she would be OK. There were two possibilities. She might have the good kind of situs inversus, in which all the organs are reversed—called *situs inversus totalis*. This is a benign condition. On the other hand, she might have the bad kind of situs inversus, in which only her heart was on the wrong side. This kind of situs inversus is associated with life-threatening or life-ending cardiac anomalies. We had to wait and see from the echocardiogram which one it was.

Fortunately, Sue was so heavily sedated that she didn't even hear the words that the doctor spoke in telling me about Lucy's problem. But I was awake. For the next twelve hours, as the test was scheduled and transportation from Beth Israel to Children's Hospital was arranged, I had to wait. I had never known worry like that in my life—nor have I known it since, thank God.

I experienced in those twelve hours what it is like to feel helpless worrying about your child. I had been a parent for only a matter of minutes, but I was already prepared to lay down my life for little Lucy. That was how I thought of her, *little Lucy*. That was how she looked in her bassinet in the pediatric ICU. I would stand by her and say a prayer as the doctors and nurses did their work. Giving her my life would do her no good. There was nothing, other than pray, that I could do to help her. I had to rely on the doctors and nurses to do all they could. In one of my prayers, I thanked God that Lucy's mother was asleep. I prayed and I took encouragement from my friends.

One of those friends, Phyllis Pollack, wife of Peter Metz, was a pediatric cardiologist who had trained at Children's Hospital. She was a godsend. Not only did she take the time to explain the whole situation to me; she also was instrumental in getting the procedure scheduled as fast as possible. She even offered to do it herself.

I will always love Phyllis for that. Parents who have been desperate, as I was, know the feeling of utter gratitude to anyone who helps them through. Phyllis will forever be enthroned in my mind as a special hero. Connections in times of crisis last a lifetime, at least in our mind.

I waited in the waiting room of the Children's Hospital cardiac intensive care unit for several hours. I spoke to other parents who were there, waiting for news, and I spoke to one set of parents who had heard the worst. One mom cried quietly—she didn't want her other infant to hear her—as she told me her baby had no chance. I held her hand until a doctor came and asked her to follow him. I didn't see her again.

I started to go through that inner dialogue most grown-ups unfortunately have suffered, of trying to bargain with God. *Please let Lucy be OK and I will do anything you want,* was the gist of the dialogue. *I'll make reparations for every bad thing I've ever done, and I'll never do another bad thing as long as I live.* These were my words inside. At that moment, I know, I would have done absolutely anything anyone could have asked of me that was in my power to do, if it would save Lucy.

Just as I was reaching my wit's end, my old friend Alan Brown strolled in. To this day I have no idea how Alan found me. He just showed up, like an angel. Alan is about six feet two and dresses like an old cobbler, but he is in fact a brilliant doctor. He is also a mensch. I stood up and he hugged me.

That he showed up—out of nowhere—at that time, on that day, still amazes me. He is another one who has a throne in my mind, along with Phyllis. He sat down and we talked. Then, with no fanfare or preparation, the cardiology fellow appeared. He looked at me and Alan. "Is one of you Mr. Hallowell?" he asked.

"I am," I said.

"Your baby is fine," he said. I have never heard four words that meant more to me. I remember my reaction, and Alan reminds me of it from to time, just in case I forget. I jumped up, went over to the unsuspecting cardiology fellow, hugged him, then got down on my knees and kissed his shoes. The agony was over.

At least for the time being.

As all parents know, it is only ever over for the time being.

That was why, when I told Lucy she needed to be tutored, I was somewhat prepared for the pain I felt, as I watched the pain she felt.

Lucy started to become quiet and uncommunicative over the next several days, complaining of an ache in her ear. We investigated that; she had no fever, there was no redness in the ear. She said she felt tired. One of her friends said she wasn't talking as much as usual. We asked Lucy if she was upset about the tutoring, and she angrily replied, "No!"

But, of course, she was. Sue's heart and my heart went out to her. All we could do was offer encouragement, reassurance, knowledge about what it means and doesn't mean to have a learning disability, and try to let her talk about how she felt. But we couldn't take the pain away. Here I was, an expert in the field of learning problems, unable to fix the problem and make everything all right.

All I could do, all Sue could do, was offer help. We could share the pain, we could try to give it different words, we could offer perspective, but we couldn't take it on ourselves and off Lucy. This is what makes the parent-child connection so difficult.

Lucy weathered that one. And so did Sue and I! I pray that we will weather the rest, along with the other kids. I think of horse jumpers trying to get around the course clean, without knocking down a single rail. It's hard to do in horse jumping. It is impossible to do in life.

So is it worth it, the pain a parent feels? Almost all of us parents would give a resounding "Yes!" What else makes the world go round?

SEVEN

Intimacy

THE EXAMPLE OF ONE MARRIAGE

INTIMACY IS THE ultimate of connection. As success may be the "drug" that motivates people to work their hardest, giving their all to achieve a goal, intimacy may be the "drug" that motivates us to put up with the conflicts inherent in connections. Indeed, true intimacy feels better than any drug.

You are on your way to being intimate with someone if neither of you has to put on airs. If you can be genuine, replete with burps and biases and selfish quirks, and the other person can also be his or her honest self with you, then you have the beginnings of intimacy with the person you're with.

But intimacy asks for more. Aside from the sexual feelings that often fuse intimacy, what makes intimacy so exciting, what gives it its rush, is the feeling of intensity two human beings experience once they reach a certain critical closeness. It is almost like a law of physics: once two human psyches get sufficiently close, some extraordinary force bursts forth. A unique kind of energy fires through the minds and bodies of both people. This energy doesn't feel completely good, because there is fear in it. As it builds, it becomes intense enough to melt our defenses.

This energy of intimacy gives us both a thrill and a sense of relief. We are thrilled to find ourselves truly discovering the depths of another person, we are thrilled we are no longer alone, and we are relieved to feel so at ease with another person, relieved to have found a kind of promised land.

Have you ever felt so close to someone you started to tremble as you spoke? Intimacy alters our physical state. It can make us shake, it can make us giddy, it can make us run the other way. Intimacy can wear us out. But it can also make us feel alive as nothing else can.

You just have to be careful. When you get that close to someone, the high energy can lead you to abandon your own self entirely. It feels ecstatic to leave the confines of your own personality and be so close to another person that you forget who and where you are. We all can get tired of being who we are.

But this can be dangerous. If you do not keep an eye on who you are and what's best for you, you may lose yourself in an intimate relationship, more than is good for you. You may spend months, even years, making sacrifices for another person that later you bitterly regret.

In the best kind of intimate relationship, you voyage out of yourself but you always come back. In other words, you have intimate meetings and intimate moments, but you do not abandon who you are and you do not stop looking out for your own safety.

Done this way, intimacy leads to growth. Intimate relationships become good for your physical as well as emotional health. Intimate relationships make you live longer.

Even better, they are fun.

Let me give an illustration of intimacy in action. Of the many couples I could offer as an example of intimacy, I choose Marie and Fred because they are so genuine, because they have gone through a lot, because they have managed to stay together, and because they are still in love. Long-term intimacy is rarely easy, and I want to show a couple that has weathered hard times, since almost every couple must weather hard times.

Marie and Fred are hardworking people, heroes in my estimation, but not celebrities. Both in their forties, they recently moved to North Carolina to start over again. They may not have a lot of money but they do have a lot of courage and heart.

I asked Marie to tell me her story, and she wrote me a long letter, parts of which I include here with my comments. Her words speak to the heart of a long-term intimate relationship—the work it entails and the pain it can cause, as well as the rewards it bestows.

"Dear Ned," Marie began, "I'm sorry that this has taken so long to get to you. Writing it has not been as easy as I thought it would be. As I sat here working on this, I often cried to think of all the things Fred and I had been through, and I laughed thinking of others." This is the essential nature of long-term intimacy. Never is it all good or all bad. When you live with another person, sharing everything from toothpaste to your bank account, it is inevitable you will cross swords.

Marie put a title at the top of the letter that she wrote to me: "Our Love Story . . ." Like every love story I have ever heard or known of, this one was composed of pain as well as joy.

> It began when I saw Fred driving up the street one day in his beautiful car. That was my first attraction, I must admit. I knew he was in the Fire Department, as were two of my older brothers, so I asked them who he was and what was his story. I knew that he liked to hang out at the local bar that we all went to, so I went there one Saturday night and waited for him. . . .
>
> We dated for three and a half years before we got married. When they say that love is blind, I never thought that meant me. I was crazy about him from the first time I met him. I never cared what anybody else thought, only that I loved him. People said he was too old for me, we were nothing alike, da-da-dah. But I was never one to listen to what other people thought. I always knew what I wanted and I was never one to let anyone stop me. Not even my parents!

The blindness Marie mentions may be a requirement for romantic love. One of my teachers of psychiatry used to say that romantic love was the only socially acceptable form of psychosis. We are all so flawed, and in love we have to make so many sacrifices, that we must be crazy to imagine the other person as worth it! Yet in love, that is what we all do, from Romeo and Juliet to Marie and Fred to you and me.

"Shortly after I met Fred," Marie's letter went on,

I moved out of my parents' house and into a house of my own. That way I could come and go as I pleased and not have to answer to anyone. This was important for me to do to prove to myself that I didn't need anyone! I did just that. I worked two jobs for a long time just to pay the bills, but it was worth it to me to be independent.

After dating for about three years, I began to feel that Fred would never make the commitment to marry me. I began thinking that I should start looking around to see what else was out there. We never had a possessive relationship. I was always able to go out with my friends or family without ever having to worry about answering questions about it later. My feelings were that if there was something I did that he didn't like, too bad! If Fred wanted things to change he had to marry me. If not, I was prepared to go my own way and let him do the same. I was twenty two at this time—I had a great job, made $25K a year. I was very self confident. Great self-esteem. I figured I had a great future ahead of me with or without Fred.

You can see Marie holding on to the connection to herself, which I mentioned before was so important to do. Even though she had fallen in love with this man she was not abandoning her own needs to be at his service. He had to put up or shut up for her to be willing to make more sacrifices.

He finally did.

We got married in December '83. We had a big church wedding and everything. Upon returning from the honeymoon I moved into Fred's three-room shack of a house. We were happy for a while . . . Then I got tired of working all day and coming home to find Fred and the dog he got me for a wedding present sleeping on the couch together! Fred was self-employed at the time, as a chimney sweep, a job he loved doing, but he had no self-motivation. If the phone didn't ring, he didn't work. He did not go out looking for business or even try to broaden his horizons to include other work associated with chimneys, like repairs, covers, follow-up leads, or advertising.

Every time I suggested trying a new area to drum up business he would just shut down. I now know that as much as I would try to help, what was really happening was he was getting more depressed and anxious. He was thirty years old and had not made his business profitable, he had no money to call his own and he couldn't see how to help himself. He was actually happy if he made enough to put gas in his car each week.

As the saying goes, the honeymoon was over. As often happens in a marriage or any long-term intimate commitment, each person has a different idea of how to live life. Marie once again held on to her idea of what was fair.

Me, being in sales, very ambitious, and self-motivated, I gave him an ultimatum after about ten months of this. Get a regular job— doing ANYTHING—or I'm out of here! We had dreams, but I could not accomplish them alone. I wanted a house before I had children, I wanted to have money in the bank so I wouldn't have to return to work right away, and I wanted some security, too. I wanted Fred to be part of the team, not just a tagalong.

And as often happens if both people are reasonably sane, the logjam broke.

Fred got a job, and things began to change. I wanted the American dream. A good job, house on a little hill with a fenced-in yard, and children. We began working together toward that goal of the American dream. We worked together like a great team.

Life went well.

Fred was again motivated. He began to get excited about our designs of the house, and he took me to see a friend of his who drew up our blueprints and made suggestions on what to change and how to make things better, e.g., putting a whirlpool tub in our master bathroom and putting in a certain type of heating system so we could add central air if we wanted it in the future. He couldn't wait to get things started. He totally demolished the house we had been living in in about two hours with his sledgehammer and chain saw.

For the next four and a half months we lived with my husband's parents until we moved into our new home. We were both working full time, but every night and every weekend we were there pounding nails and building our dream home. This was a great bonding experience for us. I knew my limitations when it came to building. I could pound nails and cut out the trim work, stain and paint, and manage the financing. I would always make sure that he had plenty to drink and would take breaks to eat.

As Marie said, they were learning how to be a team. This is the great challenge. Anyone can fall in love, but learning how to work life as a team—that takes practice.

Since they were doing well, they decided to add something to their lives.

While all of this was going on, I had been trying and finally given up on getting pregnant. I had been to the doctor's and I was quite frustrated at not being able to conceive a child. We had talked, and I didn't want to go through with all the testing. I felt that if God wanted me to be a mother, it would be when he wanted me to. We finished the house and moved in at Thanksgiving in 1985.

We found out in January that that little gift Fred gave me for my birthday at the end of November was the child that we really wanted. I was finally pregnant.

Children, if they come to a couple, bring with them both the greatest joy and the greatest worry most adults will ever know. Having a child opens up a part of yourself you never knew existed. Suddenly you discover that you love another being that you've only just met even more than you love yourself, a being that you met in a frenzy of pain and sweat, a being that you know will cost you time and money, a being that might break your heart someday—and yet, not for a moment do you consider anything but total devotion. Contrary to the self-protective person that you used to be, suddenly you have no doubt that you would cut off your arm or give up your life to protect your child. We know that there are hormones, like oxytocin, involved in this loving, bonding response. But all the rest that goes into it we don't really know. Of the many connections that we ever make, I can't think of any more powerful in causing a person to make sacrifices than this one. A parent's love for a child is the most spontaneously altruistic of all human connections.

Annie, our firstborn, was born six weeks premature. This was devastating for me. She had many problems during that first week of life. She coded on us three times. That was the scariest thing for us. To think that after all we had been through, we might actually lose her. She was only four and a half pounds when she was born and went down to about three and a half pounds. When she finally made it back up to four and a half pounds, after fifteen days I begged and pleaded with the doctors to let me take her *home*.

After all of that, and we finally got Annie home, it was time for me to go back in to see the OB/GYN for my checkup. I told him that I felt like I was pregnant, and of course he told me it was just my hormones . . . Well, I asked him to do a blood test just to be sure. I explained to him that I tried to listen to him when he told me, "NO SEX FOR SIX WEEKS." Unfortunately, he didn't tell Fred!

I was pregnant. He just looked at me, smiled, and shook his head.

Eric made his appearance in June of '87. He was the challenging one. From the time he was born, I told his doctor that there was something wrong with him. He only slept about four hours every twenty-four hours. And those were never four hours straight. They were usually fifteen-minute catnaps throughout the day. This went on forever . . . Each time I told the doctor of the things that Eric was doing; he just told me, he's a little boy . . . I told him that it was not normal for a two-year-old to climb to the top of a thirty-five-to-forty-foot tree in the backyard as Eric did all the time.

Finally one day I told Fred that if he went to work and left me home alone with Eric, I was going to kill Eric. I couldn't take any more. He was so demanding every minute of every day and night, I was just about over the edge. So I told Fred that if he went off to work, I probably wouldn't be there when he got back, and for sure Eric wouldn't be. I told him that I would be in jail, and Eric would be dead. Actually, jail sounded pretty good, if you can imagine that. No Eric to be at me every minute!

Once again, Marie is sticking up for herself, and for Eric's safety as well, with the kind of pluck and spunk that has helped her before. She always seems to know, instinctively, when to draw some kind of line. Being able to do this can save a couple from becoming so one-sided that the member who is down ends up leaving, or being psychologically ruined. It is a paradox of long-term intimacy that to make it work well you have to take care of yourself, even if it means being willing to lose the intimacy.

As he had done before, Fred responded to Marie's ultimatum.

Even after spending a regular day with Eric—Fred stayed home so I could leave and get away from it all—he still didn't see the problem. I realized that he didn't get to see Eric's true colors. The next time I didn't seem to be getting Fred to understand how frazzled I was, I decided to take a more drastic measure.

When he came home one Friday evening after work, I told him that I was going out, and good luck. I had decided this time that I was going to go out and not come back for the whole weekend. When I called on Saturday morning, Fred was concerned, but not yet frazzled. When I called on Sunday, he was frazzled! I asked him if he now understood what I had been trying to tell him. He told me that he had an idea now, and that I should come home, and we would discuss it further.

I was only at my mother's house, five miles away, so when I was home in ten minutes he was more than ready to talk. He realized that it is not only the fact that you had to keep an eye on Eric every minute, but that Annie was also a toddler and she needed attention too. When you do that day after day with little or no sleep for nights on end—actually, for me it was weeks and months on end—it can make you frazzled. We agreed to seek out someone other than the pediatrician, who kept telling us that Eric was just a little boy.

Then we met Dr. James (Jim) Kelly. Our lifesaver! I spent most of the first appointment with him crying. I explained that we were scheduled to go away for the weekend, but I couldn't bring myself to get into the car with Eric and drive more than half an hour. I began to tell Jim our story. He was very empathetic, and he understood immediately what I was describing.

A good therapist, as Jim turned out to be, can be crucial for couples. Some people still believe that you have to be crazy to see a therapist, or that going to one is a mark of weakness or shame. Often they fear that seeing a therapist is the first step toward divorce. None of these notions is true. And they are all self-defeating. In fact, going to a therapist is like going to a hairdresser or a car mechanic. Therapists have techniques to help couples, just as mechanics have techniques to help cars and hairdressers to help a head of hair.

When Jim told me that he wanted to see Eric first thing the next morning, I was surprised. He asked me if I could hold on one more day, and bring him into his office, which was thirty-five miles away. I said, "If you would help me, I can hold on for one more day."

Then came the process of diagnosing Eric. Please keep in mind that during all of this, I got NO family support! All I ever got was, "Don't be so mean to him," and, "All he really needs is a good beating." It was awful. After quite a difficult ordeal, Eric was diagnosed and was on a regimen of medication that was working. We modified his diet, and Jim taught us many strategies that helped us to maintain structure and harmony at home.

But then came the tough part. I found myself becoming very resentful of Fred. If he could see these characteristics in Eric, why couldn't he see them in himself? I spent many sessions with Jim trying to overcome my resentment. He would ask me, "Why do you stay with him?" I would always tell him, I don't know. I love him. I still get butterflies when the clock says 4:30 and I know that he'll be walking in the door any minute. It doesn't make sense but that's the way it is.

After a great deal of discussion, and almost the end of our marriage, Fred finally agreed to go and talk to Jim about himself. (Keep in mind that Fred had very low self-esteem, and if he felt like he was being attacked he would shut down.) Well, Jim had a few sessions alone with Fred and then asked me to join them. Jim wanted me to tell Fred what my issues were with him, and tried to help us communicate without the anger and resentment getting in the way. He would ask me in front of Fred, "Why don't you leave him?" I would still give him the same answers, and I would add that I didn't want the responsibility of raising the kids alone. I was also pregnant with our third child, Lilly.

I went into labor three times before I finally delivered Lilly. Fred took me into the hospital each time, and stayed right there with me. He usually even managed to find someone to watch Annie and Eric too. He was there for me each time—emotionally. This was an important part of the connection between us. He was strong for me. I knew he was scared, but not until it was all over did I know just how scared he was. He told the doctor the third time I went into the hospital that if push came to shove, he was to save me first, and the baby if possible. I had started bleeding and the doctors thought the placenta had started to separate. After a couple of days the bleeding had stopped and the monitor showed a strong heartbeat. The doctor sent me home. He told me that at the first twinge of pain I needed to get to the hospital immediately. Especially since I lived twenty-five miles away.

When I woke up on October 28 at six in the morning, Fred woke up too. He just lay there and listened to me get up and go to the bathroom, but when I came back to bed and curled up next to him, he felt puzzled. Ten minutes later I felt a pop. I got up and went to the bathroom again, and he got up too. He knew that it was time. He got up and got dressed, went out and put his coffee on, and went to start the car. (All before he even looked in on me in the bathroom!) I called him from the bathroom, and he walked in with the phone. I said, "What's that for?" He said, "To call the doctor!" I explained that I didn't have any pain yet, but within a minute I was in HARD LABOR. When we got to the hospital I jumped out of the car, grabbed a wheelchair and pushed it inside. When they wanted me to sit down to register, Fred said, "NOT RIGHT NOW—I'LL COME BACK IN AN HOUR—SHE CAN'T WAIT!" I pushed the wheelchair all the way up to the labor & delivery room, much to Fred's dismay. Lilly was born at 6:45 A.M.—within five minutes of arriving at the hospital.

The way Fred looked at me when she was born was something I'll never forget. He had love, joy, happiness, pride, and of course relief in his eyes. He was almost crying. I knew right then that he was in love again—with Lilly.

Through all of this we continued doing the counseling with Jim. Jim had a wonderful knack of cutting through all the walls and getting right to the heart of the matter. Fred wasn't always too happy that Jim could see what he was doing and make him face it. Fred had a way of being passive-aggressive. He would needle me and then try to act innocent, and would get frustrated when Jim would point out specifically what he was doing.

One of the things that Fred had a real hard time with was that I was sexually abused as a child. One of the things I found out in working with Jim was that the man who abused me always started by rubbing my back. Not knowing why, every time Fred would wake me up by rubbing my back I would feel like my skin was crawling, and I would wake up very angry. When I told him that I hated it when he did that, he couldn't understand and would continue to do it.

Jim explained to him that it didn't matter why, only that it really bothered me, so knock it off, or be a jerk and keep doing it and you'll sleep in separate beds! Fred understood, when Jim talked to him like that, that he needed to pay attention and just do it even if he didn't understand.

As time went by, the only time Fred would do that was when he was subconsciously very angry with me about something. So after I was awakened in that manner I would bring it up at the next session. Finally Fred understood that the "body memories" don't go away. Instead of rubbing my back, cuddle up, hold my hand, rub my leg, anything else, just leave my back alone!

After another year of counseling, he finally started to be able to tell me when things upset him. He never used to tell me if I ever did anything he didn't like. It turns out he always felt inferior to me, and was afraid to tell me if he didn't like something. So Jim assured him that it was all right to get mad at me. And that if I did something that he didn't like, he should speak up, and if I was being a bitch, it was important to point that out to me. When I objected, Jim told me that I can be a bitch, and Fred shouldn't be afraid to tell me!

The first time he called me a bitch—he was really mad—I laughed. I thought to myself, finally he can get mad, and he doesn't have to worry that I'll walk out the door. Fred was aware of how much he needed me. I wasn't aware of how much he needed me. I knew that I wanted him, not that I needed him. Not at that point anyway.

Their work with Jim Kelly is a good example of how therapy can help in a practical way. Marie and Fred learned skills they could really use.

But there were still other problems Marie and Fred would have to deal with.

During this time Fred started medication for his severe attention deficit disorder, which Eric had inherited from him. And in June of

1991 I had a complete hysterectomy. Recovery was slow going, but that was the least of my concerns. Therapy started to intensify with me and Jim. He wanted to get to the core of my reactions.

Control was a major issue for me. When Jim probed, I would try to keep him at bay, but he finally got through, and I opened up and revealed the horrors I'd had to bear as a child. Oftentimes I would go into his office and sit down, he would start talking to me, and the next thing I knew I would feel a chill, and he would be telling me that that was enough for today. I would say, "But we just started," and he would say it had been one and a half hours or two hours already. I would apparently disassociate as soon as he would start with the questions, and when he stopped I would come back.

This treatment brought my anxieties to a peak. I had experienced a period of about one and a half years where I didn't leave the house at all, except to go see Jim and the OB/GYN. Shortly after Jim started getting through my big wall, I started seriously falling apart. I became suicidal.

Fred brought me in to see Jim one day, and I sat there in his office for two hours and probably didn't say more than two dozen words. Jim knew that I had reached the bottom, and that I needed to be in the hospital. I was down to 103 pounds, I hadn't eaten anything for two months, and I would maybe drink six ounces of fluid a day. I felt like I was dying inside and I couldn't let anybody in to help me.

Fred was beside himself. He took me into my regular doctor's office and pulled him aside and explained that I was having a breakdown, and he wanted him to put me in the hospital to rehydrate me, and try to get me back on my medication for my colitis. Fred felt that if he could get me into the hospital for a couple of days, maybe I would eat, and then I might go into the psychiatric department to help me get through the suicidal feelings.

Fred called a very dear friend of mine, Tim, to come and help him to get me into the hospital. They literally carried me out of the house. I was too weak to walk across the room, but I fought them when they tried to take me out. Once they got me into the car, I remember thinking, Great—Tim has a gun in his glove box! But when I tried to get into the box, it was empty. He hopped into the driver's seat next to me, and he said, "Do you think I'm stupid? I love you, Marie. I left my gun at work!"

After we left the doctor's office they took me to the hospital, where they were apparently expecting me. No waiting in the ER. I ended up staying in the hospital for a little over two weeks, and then I went home and tried to put the pieces of my life back together.

This was a situation where I wasn't in control, Fred was, and he showed me by his actions that he wanted me, not just that he needed me. When push came to shove, he was going to take care of me and not let anybody hurt me ever again.

Sometimes, when one member of a couple does most of the organizing and planning, as Marie had done, that person can start to feel needed, like a maid or secretary, but not necessarily wanted. One of the several good things that came out of this difficult period was Marie's deepening sense that she could rely on Fred as well as he on her, and that he wanted to be there for her.

He also proved himself to her in another way. He showed her that he was willing to do what was best for her, even if it meant taking the risk of losing her. This is how Marie describes it.

Fred had been scared to death that if he admitted me to the psych unit I would leave him when I got out. He thought that I would be so angry with him for doing that that I would never forgive him. When he weighed it all out, he decided, better that I be alive and leave him and hate him, than be dead and never be there for the kids.

Although I was not really with it when all this was going on, I remember the voice he used with the doctor when we were in his office, strong, assured, confident, assertive. An "I MEAN BUSINESS" type of voice. No one had been there to protect me like that ever in my life! When I finally came through all of this, I remembered that tone in his voice, and I remembered feeling safe, if that was possible in that state of depression and despair.

That memory of feeling like he is protecting me from the world was the final clincher for me.

In a disagreement that we were having months later, I couldn't get Fred to open up and respond to me. When I pushed him for answers, he explained that he was afraid to tell me what he really thought for fear that I would leave him. He now knew that he wanted me, and not just that he needed me. He said he couldn't sleep if we weren't touching at night, he wanted to wake up and start each day with me, and he loved me more than anything in the world.

I explained that I remembered what he did for me. I reminded him of his actions at the doctor's office and at the hospital. I told him that after he protected me from everyone, including myself, I would never leave him. There was nothing that he could do that would make me leave for good. I might leave for an hour or two but I would never leave him forever. I truly love him and appreciate him. I make it a point to tell him on a regular basis how wonderful he is, and how smart he is. I always try to build his self-esteem, because the better he feels about himself, the better I feel. When Fred feels self-confident he is attentive, helpful, and open with the kids and me.

I have learned this much about men: we need praise. Women do, too, but they are much more at ease with this need, so they don't try to hide it, as men do. Men will often go to great lengths concealing their need for reassurance, putting out elaborate smoke screens that hide what is going on, getting irritable and curt when all they really want is a simple "You're terrific." Marie knew this instinctively.

Fred is a great dad. For the last three or four years Fred takes the three kids out every Tuesday night for kids' night out at the mall. They go out and have dinner, and go to the arcade to play until their money runs out. Eric loves to get into Dad's tools. Instead of getting mad, Fred shows him which tools to use and the importance of putting them back so they will be there the next time Eric wants to use them. He helps Eric make his little building projects, like bird-houses and gates that go to nothing. Annie is getting to the age that she only wants Daddy when she needs something—can you fix my bike, one of the wheels is bent on my Rollerblades, can you take me to my friend's house, etc. And Lilly just loves her daddy. She still likes to cuddle with both of us, and show us how well she can do things, like reading, counting, or washing the kitchen floor, vacuuming, dusting, or any other household chore that I usually have to do.

Marie and Fred continued to make a better and better life for themselves, relying on their strong connection. The next crisis came when they had to move because of a job change.

When the connection between us gets broken, both our lives become chaotic. Example: our recent move to North Carolina.

Fred has never really had to sell himself to get a job before. Employers have always come to him to offer him jobs. Until now—or so he thought. Our plan was for Fred to transfer with the company that he has worked for for the past fifteen years, Suburban Propane. Fred's hope was that when something became available with Roush Racing, he could get in. (My brother-in-law, Norman, is the boss of the Roush Racing shop here in Mooresville, North Carolina.)

Well, two weeks before we moved, Norman called and told Fred that a job was opening, and if he wanted it, he should be there the following week to talk to the boss. (We were going to North Carolina for the closing on our new house the following week anyway, so it worked out well.) Fred went for his interview and was told that Jack Roush asks his employees to get a physical and take a drug test before they start to work. That was all Fred basically took away from the interview. He wanted this job so badly. (Even though he was going to be taking a substantial cut in pay—he wanted to be able to tell Suburban Propane to "take this job and SHOVE IT!")

He decided that he didn't want them to find Dexedrine in his system [a prescription medication Fred takes to treat his attention deficit disorder] when he did his drug test. So he stopped taking his medication. I noticed a change after only a couple of days. When I asked him, he just explained it in a matter-of-fact way: "I'm not going to do anything to screw up my chances of getting this job."

Well, it started breaking our connection. He started going in too many directions at a time for me to keep up with him. When we went to move we needed two Ryder trucks instead of the one he thought. I had told him we would need two from the start, but he told me I had never moved before and I couldn't possibly know what I was talking about . . .

We worked for two straight days packing the two trucks, and even then everything didn't fit. To this day, we still have to make another trip to Connecticut to get the rest that we had to leave behind. Fred worked in such frenzy that he ended up just throwing everything into the trucks and not paying any attention to insure that the important things would fit.

We finally hit the road around 9 P.M. on Tuesday night. The trip from Connecticut to North Carolina was 875 miles; we could usually make it in about twelve hours. Fred drove one truck with our car in tow, my friend Tim drove the second truck, I drove the van with all the kids, and my friends Nancy and Peter drove their van. The two vans made it to the house finally at one on Wednesday afternoon. Fred showed up in the first truck at 3:30.

I was out in the driveway waiting. When Fred showed up without Tim, I asked him where Tim was. He said, "I don't know! I got off the highway and he didn't. I waited ten minutes for him to come back and he didn't show up, so I left." I was PISSED, to say the least. I told him, "Fred, you have to go back and find him. He doesn't know where he is or how to get here." Fred had decided to try a new route, not the one that I had written out for Tim in his instructions. Fred refused!

I finally found Tim at 7:30 that evening. He was soaked with sweat and as mad as he could be. When I saw him, I beeped the horn and jumped out of my sister's van before it even stopped rolling. I ran up to him and hugged him for the longest time. I told him I was soooooo sorry! I went into the convenience store where I found him and got him a drink and took him back to my sister's. My sister drove the Ryder back to her house and I drove her van. Tim had obviously become extremely upset when he got lost. He had been right on Fred's bumper the whole way down here from Connecticut, so Fred couldn't understand why at the last minute he didn't get off the highway.

Well, when I asked Tim what happened, he had quite a different story. He told me that he had done everything he could think of to get Fred's attention to try to get him to stop for a pee break for almost an hour! He pulled up along side of him, flashed his lights, pulled up on the passenger's side of him, and gave him hand signals, everything, but Fred never paid attention or noticed.

Then, when Fred was getting off the highway, he changed lanes suddenly, and got off immediately. Tim couldn't change lanes that fast, because an eighteen-wheeler was right next to him. He would have crashed if he had tried to exit at that point. Tim continued on down the highway to the first rest area, where he stopped and waited for Fred. His directions were for a different route, so he didn't know where to go.

Well, to make a long story short, Fred and I were on the outs for sure by this time. It was about 115 degrees when we got here. Fred was still out of control and going a hundred miles an hour. He started unloading the truck. When I told him that he needed to stop and take a break for a while, he just yelled at me to leave him alone and let him work.

For the next few days we barely spoke. Tim and I went to the store and got groceries and then started working on other projects around the house. By Sunday I was so far out in left field, I couldn't even think straight. I had only had about six hours sleep since Tuesday, I hadn't been able to eat at all, and I was pretty stressed out.

I tried one final time to make some kind of connection with Fred, and he just told me I was a problem for him. He called me a bitch because I kept bothering him. I tried to explain to him that I was drowning and I needed some help. I had anxiety attacks every time I would drive into the driveway, because of all the boxes piled to the ceiling in the carport, and I wasn't able to function like this anymore. But he was so far out there going a hundred miles an hour, he couldn't see the forest for the trees.

So I said fine, then. I told him that I was taking the van into the shop in the morning to get it fixed and tuned up, which he was supposed to have done before we left Connecticut and never did, and then I told him I was headed back to Connecticut with Tim. He said, "Are you going to take him home?" I told him that I would take him home, and I was going to stay in Connecticut, too. I couldn't survive here under these conditions, and if I didn't leave I would drown! (I still own a house in Connecticut that is on the market and should be empty any day now.)

Once again, Marie seems to know when she needs to draw a line. Although she has told Fred she'll never leave him for good, she knows that for now she has to get away, or at least threaten to.

Fred took some time that night when he went to bed and realized what I had said. It hit him then that I was going back to Connecticut, and now he would have to handle everything alone! He came out to talk to me, and I told him that I hadn't spent all that time working with him and Jim for him to just throw it away because HE didn't want the Dexedrine to show up in a drug test. I told him that I understood that this job was important, but was it more important than his family? I told him that he hadn't given us (me or the kids) the time of day since we had arrived in North Carolina except to yell at us or push us away. I also explained that there was no reason why it would be a problem for them to find the Dexedrine in his system. He takes it to treat his ADD, not as a street drug. Jim had written letters in the past for him and would gladly do it again.

I refused to discuss it any further with him. I knew I was tired and I would start lashing out at him and say things I shouldn't. I had to walk away and let him think about his choices.

He came out to greet me when I returned from the dealership's shop the next morning. Now he wanted to talk. He said he had thought about what I had said and he knew I was right. The kids were afraid to talk to him, and he was trying to do too much, so he never noticed the debris in his wake. He now could see how much of a mess he was leaving behind him. He told me that he started taking his medication, and started looking around at the disorganized mess he had made. He apologized and asked me to forgive him, which I did, of course.

Marie says, "which I did, of course." This is love. She knew, deep down, what she needed to do to get Fred to do what he needed to do; and she knew, *of course*, that she would forgive him.

Since then, we have been working side by side, emptying boxes, putting up the new pool, building the deck around the pool, shopping, and caring for the kids. The connection was made again once he could see clearly what he had been doing.

When he is acting like a hurricane he doesn't see the destruction, but when the calm comes after the storm, and the sun comes out, he can see what the fury of the storm has done.

We will be married for fifteen years in December. I still get those butterflies when I look at the clock and know that he will be coming in the door any minute now. I can forgive him almost anything that he might do. He is a good man, and I truly love him.

When Marie first saw Fred drive up in his "beautiful car" all those years ago, she didn't know what was in store for her, any more than any of us do. Over the years, this couple had to endure a lot—less than some, more than others, but certainly enough. You wonder how they did it, how anyone does it.

It began in passion, that sudden burst of energy that signals you are smitten. But that burst can't sustain a marriage forever, or at least it rarely can. That burst makes us crazy enough to give it a try. Then other forces must make it last.

You need to become friends. You need to become a team. You need to treat each other with respect. Gradually, over time, you need to learn about each other's points of vulnerability, and then take steps to help the other get strong where they were weak. Couples come apart when they use the intimate knowledge of each other's vulnerable points to hurt the other person.

This is why so many of us resist intimacy, and why my old teacher said love was a form of psychosis. You show another person where you can be hurt. You expose your most vulnerable parts, un-adorned. You do this literally in physical nakedness, but—even more risky—you do it figuratively in exposing your hidden feelings and your past hurts.

Not only that, but you struggle. You compete for time, for leisure, for choice of movies and TV shows, for control. You vie with the person you love.

Marie and Fred did all of this. They lived through a lot but still came back for more, stronger for what they had lived through.

This is the reward people find when they can make closeness last. Although the initial burst of energy subsides, a new kind of energy starts to rise up over time. If the first was a flame on a match, this second energy is like the warmth of day. It lasts longer, it doesn't burn, and it covers a wider terrain.

The love that Marie and Fred have now is much stronger than what they started with, and it is growing still, being tested still, I'm sure. Who knows if it will last forever—I believe it will, but sometimes people break apart for reasons no one could predict. Still, what they've created so far is made of the real stuff of intimacy: passion, conflict, pain, and finally, an old shoe called lasting love.

◦~~~◦

EIGHT

Friends

AT MY WEDDING I had eighteen ushers. People laughed, but it meant a lot to me to have as many friends as possible take part. I've followed my father's advice and always made sure I kept up close ties with my friends. It was the best advice he ever gave me.

No one needs to be persuaded that friendship matters; we all believe that. However, adults let go of their friends too easily. Letting go of friends is like dumping money into the river. Not only that, it can cut years off your life.

The usual excuse adults give is that friends take too much time or that friends are undependable. Sure, friends can hurt us and disappoint us, and it can be hard to make time for them. But they are crucial to a long and happy life. When my father used to tell me that I'd be lucky if I had one or two really good friends, I'd think to myself, Well, I certainly hope I have more than one or two! As time has passed, however, I have learned the wisdom of his words. It is hard to keep up friendships with many people when you are busy raising a family and working for a living. Many people do not, in fact, have two close friends.

It helps in holding on to good friends to get rid of your bad friends. These are the people who do not treat you right, even while claiming to be your friends. It is such an obvious statement; don't be friends with people who are not good to you. You would think no one would be friends with someone who is not nice to them, but this is not the case. In fact, most of us have stuck with friends who weren't good to us somewhere along the line. We might stay friends with such a person because we hope *someday* they will be nice to us; or we like the advantages they give us, such as prestige or money or influence; or we just can't think of a polite way to get out of the relationship, so we stick with it to avoid a confrontation. But staying in such relationships is bad for you. It makes you sick, and it corrupts your heart. As the saying goes, life is too short.

If you get rid of your bad friends—if you weed the garden, so to speak—you have more time and space for your good friends. This is a strong reason to get rid of your bad friends.

I'm not saying that good friends won't put you through bad times. They will. But good friends, even when they lean on you, don't make you feel as if it's a one-way street. You hang in there for them, and you know they'll do the same for you.

My friend Peter Metz and I met in 1979, when we were both starting our training in psychiatry at Mass. Mental. I'll never forget how I decided we had to become friends. It was such a guy thing, as they say. I saw Peter present a case. Now, Mass. Mental was a Harvard teaching hospital, and as such, it could be very competitive. When I saw Peter present his case, I was blown away by how good he was—articulate, smart, even self-effacing! He roused all my competitive feelings. I decided then and there that I had to either kill him or become his friend. Fortunately, I chose the latter.

We have been friends now for twenty years. He is the godfather of Lucy, our daughter, and I am the godfather of Sarah, his daughter. I love his wife, Phyllis, very much, as well as Sarah and David, his son.

We have stayed friends not only out of love for each other, although we do feel that, but also because we made it a priority to see each other regularly.

We do this by playing squash on Tuesday afternoons. Again, a guy thing. Every other Tuesday for the past twenty years, Peter and I have left work early and met at a health club where we play squash. We started playing as residents, and we haven't stopped since, except for vacations and travel. Both of us have turned down career opportunities in order to preserve our squash game on Tuesday afternoons. I remember a fellow resident of mine being shocked one day when he heard me say to a senior attending who had just offered me a job, "Will the position allow me to leave early on Tuesdays so I can play squash?"

"How could you have asked that?" my friend gasped later. "Don't you know how hard it is to get that job?"

But there's always a job. There isn't always a friend, however. And as it turned out, I was offered that job, with the proviso I could leave early Tuesday and make the hours up later in the week.

After we play squash, Peter and I go out, have a beer together, and talk about everything under the sun.

That Tuesday afternoon squash game and conversation has become one of the high points of my life. It is, in its own way, as important as church.

In addition to my Tuesday games with Peter, I have another regular game scheduled on Sunday morning at eight. I've been playing Sundays for seventeen years. It started with my friend Bart Herskovitz, then expanded to include two other guys, John Ratey and Jeff Sutton. Every Sunday, the four of us meet and play one another round-robin style. If someone is away and there are only three of us, one of us sits out and reads the paper or rides the exercise bike while the other two play, then we trade off, so everyone gets in some games. Afterward we take a shower and sit around and talk and drink coffee.

Then I come home, pick up Sue and the kids, and go off to church. It is a whole morning of connection.

The point I want to emphasize is that these regular games happen only because they are scheduled. If we left it to chance, we'd almost never play. But because we set aside the time, we show up. Then, over time, the magic happens. You get so much more than you ever thought you would. Deepening and sustaining a connection with a friend *requires* that time be spent. You need a structure, a routine, to prevent you from drifting apart.

Keeping up with a friend is something *everyone* can do. Before you say you don't have time, or you can't afford the time, or you don't have any friends you like that much, stop and give yourself a chance to imagine how you could do it, if only you decided to. Because if you do it, you'll *always* be glad you did!

In my practice, I see examples every day of how friendships save people from sadness, and how much they enrich life. But I also hear instances of the frustration they can engender. A patient of mine said to me recently, "I don't know if friends are worth it."

"Why?" I asked, expecting to hear him tell me of some betrayal. Instead he told me of a simple conversation in which he was not understood.

"The other guy, his name is Jack, just took what I said and told me a story from his own life. All he really wanted to do was tell me *his* story. Me being there was just an excuse for him to talk about himself. Is that all friendship is?"

"You know it is more than that," I said.

"Sometimes it feels impossible, though. Even for me, a modern, enlightened man!" This patient, Chris, who often laughed at his sensitivity to others, also took great pleasure in friendships.

I said, "That's just the downside of being who you are. You can get disappointed when you don't connect. Other people wouldn't even notice!"

"Maybe they are the lucky ones," Chris said.

"No, they go around wishing they could find something deeper in their lives. When they can't, they go fishing or write books."

"Is that why you write books?" Chris asked me.

"No," I replied, "I think I write books to tell people about the fish I've caught."

"Well," Chris went on, "what is the good of having a friend who is a stiff like Jack?"

"But you have told me at other times that Jack is a good guy. Maybe he was just having a bad day."

"I guess so."

This kind of dialogue between Chris and me was unlikely a few decades ago. Two men, even in psychotherapy, didn't talk openly about friendships and seemingly petty feelings. Women have taught us men a lot about the power of relationships to sustain us. Now men feel permission to have feelings, even petty ones, and to talk about them, even to explore them! This is a great advance for us all, men and women alike.

Once you get a friendship going, if you attend to it, it will attend to you even when you are not at your best. Let me give an example of four good friends who have hung in there for one another over twenty years now. They all talk to one another every week, and have for many years, even though they live in different parts of the country. These four women, Maeve, Sarah, Susan, and Jann, have deliberately kept up with one another, so that now they have made a kind of family of friends.

All Roman Catholic in background, one (Maeve) adopted, they found one another by chance, but a lot more than chance has held them together.

They met over a period of four years back in the seventies. The four women became roommates for differing lengths of time, depending on who was where doing what. A kind of energy field was jelling between them, a force that has only strengthened in the ensuing years, so that now not a week passes that all four are not in touch with one another, even though they now live in different parts of the country.

As Maeve told me about it, "We always had good times. We dated some of each other's friends and we even dated some of each other's old boyfriends. That always got dicey, discussing how we thought and felt about these different men. But all in all, it worked out."

"All in all" took in a lot of all. Part of the reason it worked is that this was a group of four friends, not just two. So, when the four got together, either in person or on the phone, they had the crisscross of the relationships of four people to support them, not just the line of two.

As time went on they all paired off, they all had children, they all developed careers. Interestingly enough, they all ended up in helping professions: Maeve became a psychologist, Sarah became a doctor specializing in psychoneuroimmunology, Jann became a massage therapist, and Susan became a music therapist. As Maeve said to me, "Now we all have kids, which adds to what we have to talk about. Finally we are all on the same page at the same time! We're in our forties now."

They have held together. "This is nineteen ninety-eight," Maeve said. "Every year we've gotten together, just the four of us, for a long weekend. We've been doing this for twelve years now. The first five or six years we got together in New Hampshire and went skiing in the winter. Just us four women. No children and no spouses. We began by giving Jann a shower for her wedding. We had so much fun we said, let's do this next year. We started by doing something physical, usually some kind of sport or hike, and then we began to talk more about our spiritual lives and our family lives, and then we created rituals when we got together on the long weekends. We also just hung out and read books."

"What are some of the rituals?" I asked.

"Simple things. We go to eat, then we all sit together in a room. Sometimes we light candles and have a ceremony if one of us is moving in or out of a career. We have some spiritual rituals, too. For example, if somebody is going through a hard time, we spend a while just letting them speak, unconditionally supporting them and talking. We've done some body therapy together, basically talking through problems as you're receiving a massage. Jann and I learned some of that, so we did it with one another. It usually brings up unfinished business from the past and from childhood. It's very intimate and very personal. Our relationships have gotten so much deeper in the process."

"It sounds wonderful," I said, thinking to myself how many of us could make great use of such weekend get-togethers, if we would take the time to set them up.

Maeve went on. "We try new things. Susan learned about something called energy therapy, and she practiced that on us at one time. Another time we just walked for hours. Sometimes we go to raunchy movies together and talk about those. Or sad movies, and we all cry. And of course we all talk about our husbands." She smiled. "I think our husbands, each one of them, have had moments of being really paranoid about our foursome. Like, oh, are they going to say bad things about us? But it has also dawned on them that it is actually good for them, too, that we get together. All of us getting together and talking about our lives has helped our families, including our husbands—because *we're* a kind of family. And I think that, as a family unit, we all have an investment in the other persons' marriages working well. If any one of us were to think of getting divorced now or were to have trouble in the marriage, there would be an enormous amount of support to try to heal it, as opposed to, 'Oh, you should get out of that, that's awful.' The effort would be in trying to keep it whole. That's the support none of us gets from our families of origin. We get it from each other instead. All of us have said at one point or another, you're more family than any family I've had."

"So you don't feel jealous of the husbands. Instead you feel you want to keep the marriages happy and intact?"

"Yes," Maeve said.

"When you first met, were you all poor?" I asked.

"Oh, church mouse poor," Maeve quickly replied. "We were all scrounging for everything. But I have to tell you, I don't think any of us ever had the rich-husband conversation. I don't think it ever occurred to any of us. I think all of us had a career idea instead. All of us had an idea of being self-sufficient. All of us wanted to get married, too. Well, Susan didn't want to be married, but all of us wanted to have kids. But none of us knew exactly how it was going to happen."

"And now you all have careers, marriages, and children. So it happened. How often do you talk?"

"I would say I talk to one or the other once a week or more. If two weeks go by, usually something is wrong. Now we also E-mail. We stay connected."

Even though one is in Tennessee, one is in Boston, and two are around Chicago, if they don't hear from one another, they know something is wrong. So far, they always hear.

Twenty years of close friendship. It has sustained them all. But how have they done it? How is it possible in today's world to make friendship such a priority? I wasn't surprised by Maeve's answer to that question.

"Sheer determination," she said without a moment's hesitation. "I *need* to keep up with these friends, because they're my lifeline. They have history with me. I trust them completely to have the intention of goodwill, of believing in a mutual spiritual meaning in life that is so powerful. I just think I would die if I let it go. There is no question it is every bit as important as my marriage for me. In fact, it's made it possible for me not to run away from my marriage, which would be my more natural thing to do. By now we've all met all of our parents and all of our siblings at one time or another. And we've all been to family parties of some kind. Like at weddings, you

meet everybody. All the old friends know who we are. I can imagine us sitting in rockers at the end of our lives. We're a powerful
group. It's like a soul connection."

Maeve went on. "When there's painful times, whether somebody
gets sick or somebody's having trouble with a husband, we say, 'You
married this person for a reason, what do you think it was? What is
this for, now? We know we meet each other for a reason, bigger than
we understand, so what was this for? Why is this on your path?' Or
let's say someone is having a fight with an administrator or a boss.
We'll ask, 'Why is this person in your life? What are you going to
learn from this? Where are you emotionally or spiritually? What
door do you need to open?' These are the kinds of things we say to
each other. It works so much better having one of us ask us, instead
of our asking ourselves."

I nodded in agreement.

"The other piece," she went on, "is just listening without judg-
ment. I think that's the spiritual piece. Instead of judging or saying, 'Well, this is what I think you ought to do,' we say, 'I don't
know why you're having this hard time and I don't know why this
pain has come to you, but I love you.' And there will be enough un-
derstandings so you can keep going and hang in there. We feel a
sense of being *for* each other, not just doing activities together. That
sense is there all the time. And when we call each other, we immediately connect with it. We often say to each other, 'I'm here all the
time.' We trust in the unseen things in the world—because we've
known each other, and gone through our lives together, and made
it possible for us to say, 'Well, I can trust in the unknown in my life,
in what I can't see, because I know you're doing that with me. I
share that with you and it allows me to do more.'

"This has worked for us," Maeve said. "Miraculous things seem
to happen. We keep seeing our lives interweaving with each other.
For example, now we all have therapeutic practices. One's in medicine, one's in psychology, one's in music therapy, and one's in massage therapy. You have the physical, emotional, intellectual, and
spiritual. This isn't something we planned. This is something that
evolved out of our lives; and making sense of them together, we
gave to each other. It's a gift. We were offered the gift of each other,
and we took it."

"Couldn't anyone have this?" I asked.

Maeve smiled, then said, "There are times when I think it's unique. But I have actually learned from having these relationships and watching us go through it that it's possible for me to have this kind of closeness with my husband if I want it. I have this with my children, and I see it growing, because I know how to do it. It feels like once you believe and you practice it, it becomes more and more part of your relationships. Soon you can't do without it. You think, this is so good, why would I give it up? In that sense, I feel like everybody can have it, but you have to experience it once, and then you have to take the gift and go. It is a spiritual source, like this lake. It feeds you and it's always there. You just have to jump in and take the risk. You just have to say, it's there, why didn't I see it?"

"It becomes like a gift each day," I said.

"Yes, and it creates a feeling of support and understanding. Kind of an intuition about the other person's life. This is the unexpected gift. You're standing there talking and all of a sudden you see the other person's life and you can say something that is useful. Not dogmatic, not pragmatic, but really emotionally useful. This requires a huge amount of trust. It is a gift. The four of us didn't know what we were getting when we all met. We had no idea. Once you feel it, you just can't do without it. It's very life-making."

Very life-making. I can't think of a better term for the power of connection.

NINE

~

Work, Part I

CREATING GOOD CHEMISTRY

IF I COULD make three wishes for my children, one of them would be that when they grow up they like their work. (The other two would be that they stay healthy and be happy in love.)

Most of us spend so much of our time at work that if we are not happy there, we suffer a great deal. On average, according to Juliet Schor's book *The Overworked American*, people in this country are spending 160 more hours at work than we did three decades ago. One hundred and sixty hours equals four forty-hour workweeks, or one month more of work per year than we worked in 1968. Hard work has always been at the core of American values, and we are certainly carrying that value out in our lives today.

But these numbers only underscore how important it is that we develop a positive feeling about our work. Working long hours in a job you hate is a surefire way to kill your spirit.

Some people have no choice but to do this. However, most people have more of a choice than they realize. Finding the right work and place of work is as important as finding the right mate for happiness in life. It is worth looking around and not settling for less than what you want.

More and more, people are seeking satisfaction from work beyond just a paycheck. For example, lawyers, traditionally content with their work just because of its intellectual challenges, are now demanding a positive atmosphere at work, instead of settling for intellectual challenge alone. A recent survey of lawyers "showed conclusively that dissatisfaction is a function of the work environment—the decrease in satisfaction is due to the fact that negative work factors have increased and other positive factors have decreased. The presence of intellectual challenge is no longer an overriding factor."

Doctors—another profession that traditionally reported very high levels of job satisfaction—are now deeply dissatisfied. A recent editorial in the *New England Journal of Medicine* reported widespread malaise, because doctors feel insurance companies are preventing them from practicing good medicine. These companies sabotage a doctor's connection to his or her patients.

Money is surprisingly missing from these complaints about work. People who are happy at work usually tell you they are happy because they feel a sense of mission, or they like their boss or coworkers, or they like the flexibility in the job that allows them to spend time at home with their children. All these are conditions of *connection*. They have nothing to do with money. Of course, you must be paid a fair wage, and more is always nice, but money is far less a factor in job satisfaction than most people assume.

People who are *un*happy at work usually wince and tell you horror stories of office politics, overbearing bosses, or the isolation they feel on the job—all conditions of disconnection.

To be sure, money matters, intellectual challenge matters, but often neglected in lists of factors that matter is the one that may matter most: connectedness in the workplace.

I am not a business executive, but I do *treat* business executives, entrepreneurs, high-level money managers, CEOs, physicians, lawyers, and architects, as well as employees at every level.

Time and again the mistakes I hear about have to do with careless disregard for people's feelings, or unintentional neglect of someone's point of view.

For example, one of my patients, a research physician at a world-famous Boston hospital, is doing excellent research, but he is unhappy, not because he is underpaid—all the doctors are underpaid at this hospital—but because the politics of the lab are so poisonous.

He tells me stories of data being hidden, of colleagues refusing to help out, of the principal investigator scapegoating innocent workers, and various other tales of perfidy and ill will. "The atmosphere in the lab is paranoid," he says. "It is very hard to work when you are constantly on guard."

I wonder out loud with him why it has to be that way.

"You tell me. You're the shrink," he replies with a laugh. But my answer is, *I don't know*. I don't know why one work group can get along so well, while another seems bent on mutual destruction.

My impulse is always to jump into the middle of the group and say, "C'mon guys, cut it out. Just get along. Everyone will be better off if you do." Sometimes this helps, but sometimes it backfires. You never know, when you are dealing with a group of people. Groups can behave in crazy ways.

Groups are unpredictable. It takes a very skilled leader to create an atmosphere of positive connection. Usually what makes the biggest difference is respect for the individual person. When people feel disrespected or devalued, their worst starts to come out.

So my advice to my physician/patient was to control what he could: be respectful to everyone, don't get involved in group plotting and scheming, do your work as best you can, and if it becomes intolerable, look for a different lab. In other words, try to connect as positively as possible, but keep in mind that leaving might be the best solution.

If an individual tries to create a connected atmosphere in a disconnected workplace, he must be prepared for the group to attack him. The members of a disconnected workplace often have hidden reasons for wanting the workplace to stay the way it is. This is why, early in my training, I was taught the adage "No good deed goes unpunished."

Jumping into the middle of the fray and saying, "Cut it out, let's be friends!" is risky, perhaps foolhardy, but it remains my first instinct. I still believe that positive energy begets positive energy, and as a consultant, I have seen it happen many times.

There is data that shows that in the long run, such a respectful, positive approach works best. Arie de Geus, an executive with Shell for thirty-eight years, studied what factors make companies live long and prosper. He was intrigued by the fact that most companies, even the big ones that get off to a great start, don't last. Many die young. For example, by 1983 *one-third* of the companies among the 1970 *Fortune* 500 had disappeared! Through merger or breakup or acquisition, these "great" corporations had vanished. De Geus wanted to find out what makes a company last.

He studied thirty companies that had done well—and done well over time, from one hundred to seven hundred years. He found that they all shared four qualities: tolerance of new ideas, conservatism in financing, sensitivity to the world around them, and *awareness of their identity*.

This last factor is connectedness. De Geus reported his findings in the *Harvard Business Review*: "No matter how broadly diversified the companies were, their employees all felt like parts of a whole. . . . The feeling of belonging to an organization and identifying with its achievements is often dismissed as soft. But case histories repeatedly show that *a sense of community is essential for long-term survival*."

We know it in our gut, and hard data like that provided by Arie de Geus prove it, and yet you still hear some managers talk as if connectedness didn't matter. "Chainsaw Al" Dunlap was brought in to take over Sunbeam because he promised to cut costs, cut jobs, cut people, cut anything—hence his nickname. Wall Street loved his approach and Sunbeam's stock went up—over the short term. But then the plan started to fail. Chainsaw Al himself got cut. He left, promising lawsuits.

You just can't overlook your people. Arie de Geus found that the most successful companies looked at their assets—their money—like oxygen: necessary for life, but not the reason for life. A company must generate profits to survive; but when assets come to matter more than people, de Geus found, the company starts to die.

Most of us have worked at both kinds of jobs: one dedicated solely to money, and one that respected its people. We all have done better in the second setting.

Modern medicine is a perfect example of how a job can be ruined by neglect of the human connection.

The practice of medicine in the United States is in a shambles. We spend more money on health care than any country on the face of the earth, and yet our health care statistics are way down in the middle of the pack. Furthermore, both the patients and the practitioners are suffering. Doctors do not get to practice medicine the way they should, and patients don't get to spend any time with their doctors. The only people who are happy are the insurance companies.

The big problem in medicine is disconnection. Doctors and patients are not being allowed to spend the time they want and need with each other. Insurance companies won't let them. I met with a physician who told me she was quitting her job, a job she'd held for twenty years, as a cancer specialist at a certain hospital because the HMO that had taken over made life so bad she'd rather leave medicine altogether than work for them. I asked her to give me an example.

"Well, the head of the department told me I should be able to see five patients an hour with a first-time diagnosis of metastatic cancer. That means he expected me to sit down with a patient and, in *twelve minutes*, both break the news to him that he has a possibly fatal illness, and then go over a treatment plan! That's disgusting, if you ask me. So I quit. Now I have no idea what I'm going to do, but at least I can look at myself in the mirror, because I'm not going to be doing that!"

Something is wrong. When a country is spending more than any other country in the world on health care and yet is getting mediocre results, something is wrong. When both the patient and the doctor are dissatisfied, then something is wrong. Somehow or other we have to reconnect the doctor and the patient in a positive way.

The field of medicine is just one example, although it is an egregious example, of how disconnection can plague the workplace. We live, after all, in the age of the cartoon character Dilbert. If you haven't read any of Scott Adams's strips about Dilbert, the fictional denizen of the corporate cubicle, they brilliantly depict the alienated, cynical world so many corporate employees inhabit.

Dilbert is all about disconnection.

The people who I treat for depression complain more about disconnected conditions at work than anything else.

"I wouldn't mind the extra hours they demand," Hank said to me, "if they gave me some respect." This is the number one complaint I hear, *by far.* Hank worked for the electric company. He had been there for almost twenty years. He had weathered changes in management before, as well as downsizing, abrupt changes in his job description, and an office witch-hunt around sexual harassment, all like a good sport. But when he got a supervisor who treated him with open contempt, that's when he started looking for another job. I knew him well. He was not a quitter. But this one supervisor almost drove him out. Luckily, the supervisor got fired before Hank quit.

"Why would he treat me like that? Why would he treat *anyone* like that? Isn't it obvious that people don't work well when you abuse them?" Hank asked in exasperation.

Creating a connected atmosphere in the workplace not only makes employees happier; it prevents them from leaving or burning out. We may scoff at the goal of happiness at work. Henry Ford's assembly line, after all, was not full of happy workers. But today's workplace, in our knowledge-based economy, demands far more of the intellect than the assembly line did. Productivity depends more on alertness and creativity than on rote performance. Therefore the mental management of each employee has become a top concern of the most enlightened managers around the country.

Let me give you another example. The Department of Chemistry at Harvard University, especially the graduate program, can be compared to a high-pressure environment. The three-hundred-plus graduate students and postdoctoral students are all striving to produce important research. The competition is stiff and the stakes are high. Everyone is extremely smart—there are five Nobel Prize winners in the department—and everyone works very hard.

Science is unforgiving. Either you get results or you don't. Everyone is competing for limited amounts of grant money, and the grants must be competed for year after year. But not only are the professors and students competing for money; they are pressing also for that most difficult of prizes to capture: new knowledge. Who will make the next big breakthrough? And who will get the credit?

In this intense atmosphere, bad things can happen. In the summer of 1998, a terrible thing happened. One of the graduate students committed suicide. He was one of the most talented students, one whose future seemed dazzling. He was doing well, so very well, but one day he took his life.

In the aftermath of that suicide, the chairman of the Department of Chemistry, Jim Anderson, consulted with me. He and one of his graduate students had read my book about worry and seen in it some ideas they thought might be helpful to the department.

In consulting with Jim Anderson, I found a man who wanted to change the way things always had been done. He was deeply concerned that the department wasn't doing enough to look after the emotional development of the graduate students and postdocs. "I want Jason's suicide to lead to something better," he said to me. "It is time to reassess how we do business."

Within weeks Jim, with the advice and consent of the other faculty, had made strategic changes in the structure of the chemistry department. He changed the advising system so that each student was given three advisors rather than one. This was intended to defuse the sometimes tense relationship that can develop between one advisor and a particular graduate student.

He also took a number of steps to increase communication, contact, and support between graduate students and faculty. He started having regular meetings with each class of graduate students and postdocs to find out their specific concerns. He arranged for anyone who wanted it to get psychotherapy paid for by the department. Although Harvard has a university health service, it is run like an HMO, so psychotherapy is limited. He asked me to give a lecture to all the graduate students and postdocs on practical ways of dealing with stress, and then he asked me to write it up as a short document that could be passed out to the entire department. (I append it at the end of this chapter.) He set up a series of lectures, to be given by recent graduates of the department, on various career options open to graduates of the Harvard program. He let it be known that his door was open for anyone to come to him with a problem, and indeed, I have never seen his door shut. He started making more of a big deal of departmental get-togethers; for example, he hired a string quartet to play at the Christmas party and had it catered by an excellent Cambridge caterer. And he instituted a tradition of regular buffet dinners, served in the department library, every couple of weeks for all who'd like to come. Many have.

I attended one of those dinners. Having gone to Harvard myself, I knew how stuffy department libraries could be. NO FOOD OR DRINK ALLOWED would be the usual sign. Not under Jim Anderson. He filled the library with food, and good food at that, and told the 250 students who showed up to dig in. Next thing you knew, groups of students were eating all over the library, sitting at tables, on the floor, at study carrels, everywhere. I could see connectedness spreading through the department as if it were a chemical reaction, catalyzed by Jim Anderson, driven by people's natural desire to bond. Despite the suicide, or perhaps because of it, by Christmas the atmosphere in the department, as best I could see, was more positive and connected. The students I spoke to all confirmed this observation. Life was not stress free—indeed it was high stress—but at least the students felt less alone.

The various steps Jim took all were geared toward adding emotional support to the graduate experience. "A lot of these students are pretty macho," he said to me. "It goes with the field of chemistry. They are not going to ask for support unless it becomes part of the culture to do so. Some of them will actively reject it, saying they prefer to do it the hard way. But I want to offer it, at least. It is time." It is time everywhere, I would add.

The early results are promising. Students appreciate what is being done. Time will tell exactly what impact Jim's new program will have, but after just a few months, faculty and students approve of the changes. Indeed, one graduate student said to me, "This should become a model for other universities."

Whether you are talking about the Harvard chemistry department, a big-city law firm, or some high-tech corporation, the management of minds under stress is becoming a top priority in workplaces all over the world.

How you deal with it varies from work site to work site, but positive connection at work will always reduce stress, help prevent burnout, and allow people to function at their best.

If you don't have it where you work, try to set it up. Connection at work will make you live longer and work better. The data prove it.

Below is the brief document on stress management I prepared for the Department of Chemistry at Harvard. It was intended to be simple, practical, and concrete. My effort was to provide steps that work, and steps that can be used by anyone.

QUESTIONS AND ANSWERS ON THE
CARE AND MAINTENANCE OF THE HUMAN BRAIN
FOR THE HARVARD CHEMISTRY DEPARTMENT

Q: Why should I care about this?

A: Attention to our emotional foundation leads to increased productivity, as well as enhanced feelings of well-being. Risks of ignoring emotional life are similar to risks of ignoring a whine in a car engine or a pain in the chest: car breaks down or heart fails. Normal people, just like cars, need care and maintenance.

Q: Even at Harvard?

A: Stress is common, indeed inevitable, among highly intelligent, creative people, such as grad students at Harvard. The more ambitious and aggressive the program you are in, the more likely you will encounter the friction of stress, just like a car that drives fast all the time. To acknowledge this is wise and strong, not whiny and weak. You would never tell someone who brought his or her car in for a tune-up to shut up and stop complaining.

Q: How common are stress-related problems at a place like Harvard?

A: Extremely common. Virtually every member of the Harvard community would do better if they broadened their emotional foundation.

Q: What are some of the signs of wear and tear on the emotional system?

A: Reduced productivity, underachievement, loss of interest in activities that used to be of interest, increased irritability, fatigue, insomnia, weight loss or gain, reduced motivation and confidence, increased pessimism and cynicism, decline in mental efficiency and powers of concentration, reduction in creativity, tendency to perceive criticism or rejection where none is intended, recurring gloomy (even suicidal) thoughts, increased use of alcohol or other psychoactive substances, increase in self-criticism, excessive worrying, tendency to pull away from others and reject help when it is offered, various physical complaints that yield no medical diagnosis.

Q: If I feel any of these symptoms, how can I tell if I have a problem—as opposed to just having a bad day or a bad week?
A: If any of these symptoms occurs with sufficient intensity and duration to hold you back, either personally or professionally, then it is worth taking corrective steps.

Q: What are some of the corrective steps I can take?
A: • *Never worry alone.* Talk to someone you trust. A friend. Your advisor. A relative. Any person with whom you feel comfortable. This is good preventative medicine, as well as good treatment for bad times when they hit.
  • Get the facts. Very often stress and worry emerge from the imagination, not from reality, particularly for creative people working alone. We (as a writer I experience this all the time) tend to imagine all kinds of negative outcomes or negative judgments that simply have no basis in outside reality. We take a little tidbit of reality and exaggerate it and amplify it in our imaginations until we have turned a chance remark into a prophecy of doom. Get the facts.
  • Get enough sleep.
  • Eat right. Don't skip breakfast. Try to include some protein with breakfast.
  • Get plenty of exercise. This is one of the best things you can do for your brain.
  • Pray or meditate. Learn how to put yourself into a quiet place mentally and turn off your critical voice.
  • Learn how to talk well to yourself.
  • Make a plan to attack your worry; don't be the passive victim and let worry attack you.
  • When stressed, do not withdraw. Tell others.
  • Don't be macho when it comes to your emotional life. That is as misguided as driving on a flat tire.
  • Maintain your support system. Make time for friends. You can still be a crazed, frantic, hyper grad student and have time to say hi to a friend or send an E-mail to your old mentor back home. It is good for you to feel connected.
  • Remember that to be productive over the long haul and not burn out, it is key that you learn how to manage your mind—not just keep flogging it to produce more and more.

- Keep a sense of humor. Laugh a lot. Life is funny.
- Don't use alcohol or other substances to medicate your stress and worry. It is fine to drink, just don't drink as a form of self-treatment.
- Make sure you get enough sunshine. People who work indoors long hours can develop depression simply on the basis of not getting enough sunlight. If you can't get out in the sun, there are lights you can buy that will provide the kind of light you need.
- Take quick exercise breaks when you are working long hours, e.g., run up and down stairs a few times, or go for a brisk walk around the block. This has the effect of pushing the reset button on your brain.
- Have music playing in the workplace, in your lab or office. Pick music you like. Experts on the effects of music on the brain recommend Mozart.
- Have a friend or colleague massage your shoulders from time to time. Stress tends to accumulate in the trapezius (back of shoulder) muscle.
- Do not hesitate to seek professional help. There are good remedies now for toxic worry, depression, excess anxiety. Both targeted (not endless) psychotherapy and the new generation of medications work well.
- Don't spend too much time on-line. A recent study out of Carnegie Mellon reported that even an hour a week on-line was associated with increased feelings of loneliness and depression. Beware of the tendency I see all the time among my very bright patients to become addicted to your personal computer and to the Internet.
- A corollary to the previous item: avoid excessive TV. This also blurs your brain. Especially important is not to consume too much news, via TV, print, or in any other way. The news is upsetting. It is meant to be upsetting to get you to pay attention to it. Resist this.
- Hire experts to help you. Don't be afraid to ask for help— whether it is in chemistry, or in money management, or in how to do laundry. Stress builds when you feel incompetent in any particular task.

- Complain. Complaining—to the right person—is good for the soul.
- Don't invoke the moral diagnosis. In other words, don't call yourself weak or a wimp if you feel sad, worried, or gloomy. Think of these emotions as noises in your car engine. Investigate them, don't rebuke them. Improvement comes from knowledge, not from self-blame.
- Sing, whistle, smile. Sounds ridiculous, but stress goes down if you sing. It is hard to worry and whistle simultaneously.
- *Never worry alone.* A repeat of the first item, because it is the most important item on this list.

Q: What if these measures are not enough?
A: Professional help can make a big difference. The University Health Services are always available. You can also call Dr. Hallowell and see him or ask for a referral. The department will pay for this service. His phone number is 781-643-0728. His E-mail address is EHallowell@aol.com.

TEN

Work, Part II

THE VALUE OF THE HUMAN MOMENT

THE CHIEF FINANCIAL officer of an international consulting firm holds his cell phone to his ear while waiting for the next shuttle from La Guardia to Boston. He listens to the messages that have piled up since he last phoned in, three hours earlier. After he flips the phone closed he sits down to wait for his plane, and he starts to brood. A detail in one of the messages caught his attention—a valued employee has asked for a transfer to another division. Questions begin to ricochet at hyper speed through his mind: What if the employee complains around the organization that he asked for the transfer because I am a lousy boss? What if the employee plans to take his team with him in the move? What if, what if . . . ? The CFO becomes lost in a frightening tangle of improbable—but possible—outcomes, a tangle that will snarl his mind the entire flight back to Boston. The minute he gets home he will dash off an E-mail, outlining his new concerns to the employee, and eagerly await a reply, which, when it comes the next day, will only upset him further due to its ambiguity. More brooding will ensue, making it difficult to focus on the present day's work as this new, imagined problem takes on major dimensions in the CFO's mind.

A slightly different version of this chapter originally appeared in the *Harvard Business Review,* Jan-Feb. 1999.

In another setting, a talented brand manager at an electronics company is growing increasingly alienated within a large and far-flung organization. The problem started when the division head didn't return his phone call for several days. She said she never got the message, but then the brand manager noticed he was not invited to an important meeting with a new advertising agency. He wonders: Is something wrong with my performance? The man wants to raise the question with the division manager, but the opportunity never seems to arise. All of their communication comes via memo, E-mail, or voice mail. These they exchange often. But they almost never meet. For one thing, their offices are fifty miles apart, and for another, both of them are frequently on the road. The rare moments they do see each other in person—on the fly in a corridor or in a parking lot—it is inappropriate or impossible to discuss complex concerns. And so the issues smolder.

In these scenarios, the anxiety consuming the CFO and the brand manager had a simple antidote: talk. The CFO and his departing employee, as well as the disenchanted brand manager and his moving-target boss, needed to reconnect—in person. They needed to shake each other's hands, settle into their chairs, look each other in the eye, catch up on each other's lives a little, even laugh together. They needed to experience *the human moment:* a face-to-face conversation. I have given the human moment a name because it has started to disappear from modern life.

What exactly is the human moment? The two prerequisites are (1) people's physical presence and (2) their attention. That's it. Two or more people together paying attention to one another create a human moment. Physical presence alone isn't enough; you can ride shoulder to shoulder with someone for ten hours in an airplane and not have a human moment the whole ride! And attention alone isn't enough; you can pay attention to someone over the telephone, but that is not a human moment.

Human moments are powerful and require energy. This is why they should be used judiciously—rare is the person who can perform effectively in a human moment for hours on end! (Indeed, some of my patients suffer not from a deficiency of the human moment but from an excess!) The human moment can be brisk, businesslike, and brief. It does not have to be emotional or touchy-feely at all. A five-minute conversation can make all the difference in the world, if the parties participate actively. To make it work, you have to set aside what you're doing, put down the memo you were reading, disengage from your laptop, abandon your daydream, and bring your attention to bear upon the person you're with. Usually, when you do this, the other person (or people) will feel the energy and respond in kind, naturally. If they don't, you will feel frustrated and disappointed. This is why human moments can be so draining, annoying, and counterproductive when they do not work well, and it is one reason many people avoid them. But if the other person (or people) does respond, then you are cooking. You quickly create a force field of exceptional power.

A human moment can promote creative activity long after the people involved have said good-bye and walked away. The human moment is like exercise in this fashion: its benefits last after it has ended. But they do not last forever. To continue to get the benefits that the human moment (or exercise) can provide, you must engage in it on a regular basis. But this isn't hard, because it is stimulating and usually enjoyable.

We all know the emotional impact of the human moment; unfortunately, we all may be about to discover the destructive power of its absence. I don't say this as an executive, but as a psychiatrist who has been treating patients with anxiety disorders for fifteen years. My research is not quantified, but I can tell you without a doubt that virtually everyone I see comes to me because of some deficiency of human contact. Indeed, I am increasingly sought out because people feel lonely, isolated, or confused at work. They feel cut off.

To be sure, people have felt lonely at work in the past. Henry Ford's early factories provided no touchy-feely encounter sessions. But from the 1950s onward, work did gain a central place in people's emotional lives. There became an expectation at work that people would talk with one another in the office, and that they would even play together after the day was done. And when it came time to connect with distant clients or suppliers and the like, people got on planes. Meetings happened in person. Yes, they were time-consuming and costly. But they also fostered trust and some level of comfort. Not incidentally, it was also more fun.

But in recent years—let's say the last ten—technological changes have made a lot of face-to-face interaction unnecessary. I'm talking about voice mail and E-mail, mainly—modes of communication that are one-way and electronic. Face-to-face interaction has also fallen victim to *virtuality*—people working at home or otherwise off-site. I will certainly not try to make a case that these changes are bad; only a Luddite would do so. And indeed, no one has planned it this way exactly; it is simply happening naturally, with the inevitability of water flowing downhill. We have the technology, so we are using it.

In fact, many of these changes are good. They are making our lives much better, for the most part. I myself enjoy every day the efficiency and freedom wrought by voice mail and E-mail. I communicate with people when and where I want. Since I travel the country giving lectures, I keep up with my messages from patients and my office through voice mail, and I log on from hotel rooms to collect my E-mail every day. Like most people, I don't know how I ever managed without these tools (which I have learned to use only in the past decade!).

But from where I sit, there's a problem with losing the human moment that cannot be ignored. Human beings need human contact to survive, and most certainly to thrive. They need it for their mental acuity as well as their emotional well-being. I make this assertion having listened to and counseled literally thousands of patients whose jobs have been sapped of the human moment. And I make it based on strong evidence from the field of brain science.

Let's talk about my patients first, the people I see each day. More specifically, let's talk about what they feel is missing. It should sound familiar to you, for it seems everyone knows how vital, invigorating, and often electric a meeting in person can be. You meet with a colleague to discuss a certain project, and you each come in with your agendas set in mind, but the next thing you know, some chance remark sparks an unplanned response. Suddenly you are discussing other concerns altogether, and you are feeding each other information that triggers fresh associations as you hop from talking about a certain problem to talking about your kids to talking about the latest educational technology; and then, in the midst of a sip of coffee, one of you wonders aloud, "Why don't we develop that software?" You interrupt and overlap your sentences, which quickly become half sentences or single words, and the energy builds as each of you reaches into his briefcase to bring out some other document or fragment of an idea that sparks further enthusiasm in the other, which leads both of you to ratchet your thinking up one more notch, until one of you rises up out of his chair and pounds his fist into his hand and says, "That's it! We can do it!" Such a scene happens because an extraordinary energy infuses the human moment, energy that is absent in all other kinds of communication—in particular, electronic ones.

In the absence of the human moment the mind becomes vulnerable. Let me give some examples of how things can go wrong when the human moment takes a backseat.

Harry, a senior partner at a Boston law firm and a patient of mine, was representing a bank in a complicated real estate deal with the developer of a commercial property. Many of the details of the agreement were being worked out in E-mail between Harry and the developer's counsel. At a key juncture, when a technical point came up, the developer's counsel E-mailed Harry, "Of course, your client won't grasp this, because he won't understand what we're talking about." When Harry's client read this message, mixed in with other documents, the client became furious and went to the brink of canceling the deal. Trying to patch things up, Harry met with the other lawyer, who was stunned to hear how his message had been misconstrued. "I was trying to be ironic!" the lawyer gasped in horror. "Your client is an expert in the field—saying he didn't know what we were talking about was just my way of being funny. I can't believe what a misunderstanding this is!"

Harry was second-guessing himself and asking me if he had some unconscious wish to fail in that he allowed the message to reach the eyes of his client. But the real problem was not in Harry's unconscious but in the mode of communication. The deal was saved—but it almost was lost because E-mail is so devilishly easy to misconstrue. It has none of the nonverbal cues, like body language, tone of voice, and facial expression, that are so key to proper understanding, especially among sophisticated people who are prone to subtlety, irony, and wit. This is the reason that as a psychiatrist I usually decline to do consultations over the telephone—let alone via E-mail!

On a deeper level, the neglect of the human moment can cause permanent damage. I recently treated a man—let's call him Zack—who came to see me because he was waking up in the middle of the night worried about the company he had just sold for $20 million.

"What's wrong?" I asked him.

"I had intended to stay on with the company for at least a couple of years, but I'm worried it's going to be impossible. I can't deal with the COO. He's in Texas, where the headquarters are, and I'm in Boston, and he keeps sending me E-mails with lists of things he wants me to do. This may sound petty, but the way he phrases them just makes me crazy. When I sold the company I knew my role would change, but this is totally degrading."

"Can you give me an example?" I asked.

"Sure. I turned on my computer Monday and got an E-mail that simply said, 'Last communication unacceptable. Redo.' I E-mailed back asking for specifics. He E-mailed me back, 'I don't have time to explain. Can't you figure it out?' Suddenly I'm feeling like a third-grader. But I tried to rise above it. The next day he E-mails me, 'Your people up there have to do longer weekend hours.' Then I started to lose sleep. That's when my wife told me to call you."

"Is this their way of getting rid of you?" I asked.

"It looks like it, doesn't it? But the fact is that they need me. They know that. But I can't deal with this."

"Can you talk to the COO?" I asked.

"He's evasive. When we have met, he's polite but insubstantial. He does all his damage in E-mail. All the objectionable stuff."

Although Zack had been determined to make the transition and stay with the new company, gradually his resolve broke down, as he felt increasingly at odds with headquarters, particularly the COO. Zack started to worry about work, instead of enjoying it. He started to brood about the direction and purpose of the company, issues he had felt confident about when he made the deal. "I've become a worrier, instead of a problem solver," Zack told me. "I never used to be this way."

When Zack submitted his letter of resignation he was deluged with evidence that the company did indeed want him to stay. But by then the damage had been done. His heart was not in it, he was getting interested in new ideas for other businesses, venture capitalists were approaching him from the minute he had leaked word of his dissatisfaction, so the company's attempts to keep him proved to be too little too late.

When we discussed his resignation, he told me how easy it would have been for the new company to have kept him, if only he had felt treated with even minimal respect by the COO. "My problems really came down to those E-mail interactions. The irony is that the COO did need me."

It sounded as if the COO couldn't handle his competitive feelings, so instead of dealing with Zack face-to-face, he took him on in E-mail. Indeed, I would hypothesize that the COO was somewhat passive-aggressive. He used E-mail as a weapon for his negative and angry emotions. In person, he would have had to submit, if you will, to social convention. His dark feelings would be forced into the light.

The human moment, then, is a regulator: when you take it away, people's primitive instincts can get the better of them. Just as in the anonymity of an automobile stable people can behave like crazed maniacs, so on a keyboard courteous people can become rude and abrupt, as did Zack's COO.

Less dramatic but more common are the instances when people come to see me because they simply feel worn out by all the non-human interactions that fill their days. "I feel like I'm going brain dead and losing the skill of listening and interacting with live people," said Alex, an executive in a health care system. He consulted with me because he actually thought he was losing his memory. "Thirty to 40 per cent of my work is done by leaving voice mail messages, playing phone tag, or by E-mail. I think my brain just isn't working right anymore."

A few simple tests conducted in my office revealed Alex's brain was in fine shape. However, his way of working was not allowing his brain to function at its best. He was not taking into account what his brain needed for smooth operation. It was as if he sprinted up ten flights of stairs and then thought something was wrong with his body because he needed a moment to catch his breath! Most people lose mental efficiency if they stay on-screen, on-line, or on the telephone for extended periods, just as most people run out of breath after a ten-flight sprint. Alex needed to do the mental equivalent of catching his breath. He needed to refresh his mind

with a bit of exercise (like walking around) or, even better, a moment or two of conversing with a live human being! Both exercise
and the human moment refuel the brain. The brain can be as
starved for a human moment as it might be for oxygen. (This is
why punishments like banishment or solitary confinement are so
painful.) All the coffee in the world can't make up for the brain-
dead state many people in jobs like Alex's feel about three o'clock
in the afternoon.

It may be that the disappearance of the human moment under-
lies the feelings of worry and stress more and more of my patients
report at work. Humans are remarkably resilient and able to deal
with almost anything, as long as they do not become too isolated.
But my patients, from many different kinds of businesses, tell me
that although they are electronically hyperconnected, they are losing direct personal contact all the time.

"I don't talk to live people anymore. All I do is receive memos
and directives," Ray, a senior systems manager in a large investment
company, told me. Ray had come to see me to inquire if he was suffering from burnout. "It's not that I don't like my work. I do. And
my company loves me. I'm a techie who can talk. That makes me
golden. But when I get isolated as much as I am now, I start to
think funny. My imagination can run wild. I start worrying about
my performance, even though I know it is excellent, and I start to
wonder if I am appreciated for what I do, even though I know I am,
and then I start to feel resentful inside. I become irritable and less
effective."

When I asked him if he could give an example of this, he told me
the following story. "A guy sent me an E-mail that said, 'We were
not able to access the following application, and we need to know
why,' and he cc'd his supervisor, solely to show the supervisor that
he was doing something about the problem. What bugged me was
that line '*and we need to know why.*' If he had spoken to me face-to-
face we could have solved the problem, but no, I get this E-mail
with its peremptory tone, and he cc's it. My immediate response is,
back at you. So I write an officious-sounding E-mail, with a cc to a
bunch of other people, including his supervisor, explaining that I
had submitted a change management ticket, and if he had gone to
the meeting where that was discussed he would have known about

it and wouldn't have even tried to access that application. I don't like what I did. I overreacted. I became that guy's adversary instead of solving the problem. But I felt goaded into it. I'm doing this kind of thing more and more. Do I have a problem?"

My answer is, no, Ray doesn't have a problem. The problem is in the neglect of the human moment. Ray didn't need a psychiatrist; he just needed confirmation of what his basic instincts were telling him. The problem was in the mode of communication: As the human moment gives way to the electronic, the mind tends toward a more vulnerable, unregulated state.

In that state, the mind becomes more vulnerable to toxic worry. I recently published a book about worry (*Worry: Controlling It and Using It Wisely,* Pantheon, 1997), and my research led me to distinguish between helpful, good worry and destructive, toxic worry. Good worry leads to constructive planning and corrective action, and is essential for success in any endeavor. But toxic worry immobilizes the sufferer and leads to indecision or destructive action. My research showed over and over again that the people who are most prone to toxic worry are those who are most cut off from live human contact.

For example, someone on the road who is living by E-mail and telephone messages and doesn't have the benefit of staff meetings or daily personal contact with colleagues is likely to feel cut off. In that isolation he might develop inaccurate ideas about what is going on back in the main office. Feeling cut off is like being in the dark. It is a fact of human nature that in the dark we all feel paranoid. Try the experiment. Go into a room at night and turn off the lights. Your whole body will respond. Even if you know the room well, you will probably feel the hairs on the back of your neck rise up a little as you wonder who might be lurking in the corner! The human moment is like light in a dark room; it illuminates dark corners and dispels suspicious fantasies. Without it, toxic worry grows.

But is there hard data showing that a lack of the human moment is bad for people? Yes, there is a huge amount of it, not just from psychology but from medicine, biology, anthropology, and epidemiology as well. Some of this was presented in the Introduction and Chapter 1. In our culture we are rightly proud of our self-reliance, but we ignore our need to affiliate at great peril. People need people—in person—and the scientific literature bulges with evidence of this fact.

Years ago Rene Spitz showed that infants who were not held, stroked, and cuddled, even if they had parents who fed and clothed them, suffered from retarded neurological development. Emil Durkheim's classic studies of suicide showed that social isolation, which he termed *anomie,* was a major risk factor for completed suicide. (Might there be a special kind of anomie endemic to the virtual workplace? And might the specific antidote be sufficient doses of the human moment?) Further evidence of the special nature of contact in person is that children of deaf parents cannot learn language from tapes or television, but must be placed with other children and adults in order to learn to use language properly. And researchers at McGill University have shown the extremely toxic effects of sensory deprivation; only hours in a sensory deprivation tank can lead to an altered sense of reality, even frank hallucinations.

The first study of the use of the Internet at home bears out my thesis about the importance of the human moment. Conducted by researchers at Carnegie Mellon University, this study followed individuals for two years and found that people who were on-line for just a few hours a week experienced higher levels of depression and loneliness than those who were on-line less. These people got worse as time went on; in other words, being on-line so much made them worse than when the study began.

The *New York Times,* reporting this study on its front page, wrote, "Based on these data, the researchers hypothesize that relationships maintained over long distances without face-to-face contact ultimately do not provide the kind of support and reciprocity that typically contribute to a sense of psychological security and happiness, like being able to baby-sit in a pinch for a friend, or to grab a cup of coffee."

It has also been shown that social support prolongs life after heart attacks, improves immune function, reduces the risk of the common cold, and even speeds up wound healing! The point is that, at a physiological level, *something* indispensable happens in the human moment.

What exactly is that something? We don't yet know the whole story, but we do know that the human moment can reduce the levels in the blood of the stress hormones epinephrine, norepinephrine, and cortisol. In addition to the stress hormones that regulate the body's response to danger, nature also equips us with hormones that promote trust and bonding (other than the sex hormones). Most abundant in nursing mothers, these hormones are always present to some degree in us all, but they rise when we feel for another person. They contribute to the natural feelings of empathy, caring, and bonding that flow through us all now and then. These hormones, oxytocin and vasopressin, are most potently stimulated in the human moment, face-to-face. Indeed, one of the reasons that it is easier to deal harshly with someone via E-mail than in person is that these bonding hormones are not usually stimulated off-site, in E-mail (although they can be by a moving scene in a novel). And one reason it is more difficult for most people to sustain a harsh attitude face-to-face is that eye contact tends to stimulate a sympathetic response, in part due to the production of oxytocin and/or vasopressin. This helps explain studies cited in Chapter 1, showing that sustained connections prolong life and promote a sense of well-being.

Of course, not all human moments reduce stress and promote trust. Indeed, some interactions increase stress and reduce trust, depending upon what happens in a given human moment!

But we fare better with it than without it. The scientific evidence presented in Chapter 1 shows the value of the human moment in bold relief. The MacArthur Foundation Study on Aging in America, for example, conducted over the past decade by a team of eminent scientists from around the country and just completed, showed that the top two predictors of well-being as people age are frequency of visits with friends and frequency of attending meetings of organizations. The import of the human moment is highlighted further by the finding that while those who have religious belief on average live longer than those who don't, those who actually attend religious services or ceremonies do better than those who simply believe, without going to a service in person.

If science has proven that human contact can prolong life, reduce stress, improve physical health—as reflected by a host of measurements—and enhance a sense of well-being as people age, doesn't it stand to reason that the lack of it can have a negative effect on people in the workplace?

Doctors—not just psychiatrists—see evidence of this in their offices every day. It is estimated that one-third of all visits to primary care physicians are prompted not by medical necessity but by emotional stress. More and more people consult with me because of problems that turn out to be at least in part related to a lack of direct human contact at work. On the one hand these people rejoice in the convenience that electronic communications afford, but they also increasingly complain of problems that relate directly to their being cut off from live interaction with other people. Problems like depression, feeling left out, toxic worry, mistrust, and mounting cynicism all can stem from a lack of human contact.

As one CEO told me, "High tech requires high touch." When I asked him what he meant, he explained to me that it is his company's policy to structure in new kinds of human interaction whenever he develops virtual office places. "Look what's happened to banks because of ATMs. You don't know Alice behind the counter anymore, or you don't know any of the agents behind those glass walls, so when you go in for a loan there's no familiarity, no trust. It makes everything much more difficult for both sides. Does that mean ATMs are a bad thing? Of course not. But it means the industry has had to think of new ways of creating the high touch that the high tech has taken away." Whether you call it high touch, as this CEO did, or the human moment, as I do, we're talking about the same issue.

But there is good news. In addition to problems related to the lack of the human moment, I have also found many examples from today's business world where the power of the human moment has been put to good use.

Jack W. is a major real estate developer in the Boston area with offices and interests that have in the last decade become worldwide. He runs his large operation from a suite of offices located on the ground floor of a Back Bay brownstone that he refers to as the "batcave." A former football player at Yale, Jack finds teamwork the key to his company's success. When I asked him how he dealt with the recent growth of his company, its increasing diversification, the expanding numbers of people working for him, and the global dimensions of what was once just a Boston development firm, he laughed and told me about his Thursday lunch.

"About ten years ago I realized I wasn't seeing people as often as before. It dawned on me that I was running around and so was everybody else. We were missing something important. I never got a chance to sit down and talk, and neither did anyone else. Since I rely on the conversations I have with people, this was a very bad thing. Being a simple man by nature, I decided to try a simple solution. I instituted a practice of ordering pizzas on Thursday. I know this is not an advanced management technique, but it did the job. We have a bunch of pizzas and Cokes—and bottled water, of course—delivered to the batcave, and whoever is there that day sits around the big table in my office and we talk. There is no agenda except the food. The group averages about fifteen people, and changes members every week, but there is a core five or six who provide continuity. They meet even when I'm not there. We all look forward to it, not as a business meeting per se but as a forum. People catch up with each other, they brainstorm, they bring up stuff that doesn't fit anywhere else, and it works like magic. That missing something is back. Visitors talk about what good morale we have, how well we communicate, and they ask me what system I use. 'Thursday pizza' is my reply."

While Jack W.'s pizza lunch was a simple idea, David P.'s performance groups were considerably more complex, and were created against much tougher odds.

David runs a large consulting firm catering specifically to the retail furniture business. About a decade ago he found that his clients were becoming increasingly cut off. As he put it, "We are in a very fragmented industry. The retail home furnishing industry is made up primarily of mom-and-pop stores still. It's the last of the mom-and-pop businesses, and it has gone through considerable consolidation. The problem is that the chains have now bought up so many of the stores that the sales reps go to the head office of that chain. So there are no longer five stores in town to see. Three or four of them are now part of a chain, and you get one major independent hang-on, if you will. Well, that guy is not getting any attention. And with telecataloguing he doesn't even need the sales rep at all. So he's not getting any of the grapevine information the sales rep used to supply. And he's not getting the social aspect of those visits that used to support him. You used to learn from the reps that stopped by your store what was going on in the marketplace. And a lot of those relationships were very close. Well, as the chains have proliferated, the major independents, the one-to-four-million-dollar stores, are getting more and more isolated."

Seeing the root of the problem as the isolation the dealers were facing, David wanted to start what he called *performance groups*, groups of independent retailers from different parts of the country who would get together three times a year to talk business and implicitly offer support. But when he presented his idea to his colleagues at his consulting firm they laughed at him. "You think these guys are going to open up and talk about their business problems in a group? You must be joking!" David's associates thought the idea was ridiculous, especially given the notoriously guarded, private nature of independent furniture retailers. While there may be a need for such contact and communication, David's colleagues believed it could never be made to happen.

But David persisted. In an end run, he went out and started a new company, a sister company to his consulting firm, and he found people to work for him who believed in his vision. He knew that the automotive industry had used what they call *twenty groups* (so named because the maximum number of members in each group was twenty) since the 1930s, when independent dealerships realized they could benefit from getting together and discussing their problems and concerns. "And so I went to my clients and said, 'Look, I'm going to start these performance groups where you will get together three times a year with other retailers from around the country. We'll facilitate the meetings to make sure you get through your agenda, to make sure no egos take over the meetings, and that the people who talk too much don't talk too much, and that the people who don't talk at all at least contribute. You will have to submit financial statements to us and be willing to share those statements to the rest of the group.' It's that full disclosure of their financials that is something ten years ago people would never have done. We've had people in our groups now who say that their father would roll over in his grave if he knew they were sharing the financials of their company with other retailers. But sharing those financials creates a trust and a bond. And they have a noncompetition agreement. They get together with other retailers from different parts of the country three times a year for two days, and they share their best ideas, they benchmark performance, and they give each other the support they need."

Not only did David face the resistance of his own company, which he dealt with simply by starting a new company; he had to sell his idea of the power of the human moment to a group of highly skeptical customers as well. Why did they buy it? As David put it, "The pain of change is something you agree to only when the pain of staying where you are gets worse than the pain of change. It may be a little difficult to reach out for help, but under threat of the kind of competition that exists today, more and more people are finding that they need this type of assistance. But they don't want to go outside of their business and they also don't want to sell their souls to people they don't trust. The performance group allows them to talk to people who know the business and know the traditions."

David then went on to tell me what a positive impact the groups have made. He now has six different groups going, representing over sixty stores nationwide, with a waiting list for future groups. Contrary to the hard-as-nails reputation the members have, they let themselves become vulnerable in the meetings. "The sessions can be very emotional," David said. "We have had guys break down in tears in these groups when the group looked at them and said, 'Fire your son.' Or said, '*You* have to step in.' These groups give them a forum of people who know the business to help work things out."

After three years, David asked the members of the first group he formed what was the single most important thing about being in the group. "The most interesting thing to me," David went on, "was that they all unanimously said, 'Being around people that care. I looked across the table at somebody who cares what happens to me and my business.' And I'll tell you, these are tough cookies. To have them say that the number one reason to be with a group of people was that they really cared about them, it's a pretty pansy thing for them to say, you might think. But again, that comes back to the value of leaving yourself vulnerable. It is a very difficult thing and it is only under the fear of extinction that they do it.

"I have another group that just started this year, which is the Strivers. Now the Strivers are all major guys, making fifty to sixty million. These are people who are already the number one leaders in their marketplace for the most part. They are constantly looking for ways to distance themselves from the competition. They have a different reason for being in the group. The other guys are looking to avoid extinction."

I asked David if it wouldn't be more efficient to have these meetings on-line, over the Internet. He said that the groups have in fact used E-mail and other electronic communications to great advantage in augmenting what they do in their three-times-a-year meetings in person. But he believed the meetings in person were indispensable. "I think caring develops when you're dealing with somebody face-to-face more often than over the Internet. Over the Internet you tend to be very precise with questions-answers, questions-answers, and you miss the emotion of what is going on. I don't believe people open up over the Internet like they do face-to-face. You're chatting with somebody and you see by their facial expression that you've hit on a very sensitive subject. It may be a signal to avoid that subject and it may be a signal to go further, depending on the situation. And it might be that you see the sense of the subject and you stick a bookmark in it and then over dinner that night you might say, 'I noticed this morning, when we were chatting about what your brother-in-law was doing in the business, that there seemed to be a little something more there.' Well, you would never see that over the Internet. But that does not mean that the Internet is not valuable as well. In fact the next stage with the performance groups is to give them each a chat room; each group will have a code and be able to go into the chat room and get questions and answers handled between meetings. But I don't believe we would give up the meetings for anything."

David's developing performance groups in the retail furniture business seems to me a brilliant example of using the human moment judiciously. As David led his initially skeptical colleagues and clients to realize, these moments may be needed in ways many managers have not thought necessary or even possible in today's world. Obviously, we don't want to turn back the clock and dispense with the tremendous efficiencies afforded by our electronic communications, but we do need to learn how to deal with the hidden problems they can create.

Technology has created a magnificent new world, fresh with opportunity; it has opened up a knowledge-based economy worldwide; and it has freed people from being chained to a desk. We are all in its debt—and we're never going back!

But one job of the shakedown cruise we're all sailing is to notice the snags and kinks on this new boat of technology. One snag appears to be the disappearance of the human moment. Without meaning to, we are letting go of one of our most powerful tools: face-to-face conversation. It is vanishing like pigment bleached out of a painting hung in the sun. We look at the painting day in and day out and it looks the same, hanging right where it always has. But then one cloudy day we notice it has lost its zest and color.

The human moment provides the zest and color of our daily lives. As long as we arrange our lives properly, it should be easy enough to preserve. All we have to do is take note and make it happen.

ELEVEN

~~~~~

Beauty

THE CONNECTION WE make, or could make, to beauty is easy to overlook. Often we take beauty for granted or we ignore it. One of the simplest ways to deepen your connectedness in everyday life is to start noticing beauty. You can't go through a day without finding it somewhere. You certainly do not need to go to a museum.

Nature offers us her museum each day. If you get up with the sun, look at it get up with you. Or if you chance by one of those spectacular moments nature can offer as you drive along, stop and take it in. Beauty, as much as friendship, prayer, or a pet, can comfort the soul.

I know a woman named Susan whose whole life embodies connection, not only to beauty but to friends, places, nature, the past, family, ideas, and mission. Susan came to art early on. I asked her how her connection with art began, and soon her whole connected tapestry emerged, starting in her childhood.

"I think it goes back to a very early experience with my father, going hand in hand up a path, up a hill behind our house in Burrville, identifying wildflowers together. We identified these flowers by the color, the shape, how many petals, the shape of leaf. Those early experiences of looking together, I think, laid the foundation for me for the later work of looking at paintings."

"So you learned to look closely, early on, with your dad?" I said, enjoying the image of Susan and her dad walking up the path of wildflowers.

"Yes. For example, I remember discovering what the hepatica was. Hepatica is a beautiful little wildflower that grows in spring. The bank between the waterfalls near our house was covered with hepatica. Ever since, I've sought them out. They're very rare, they're hard to find. I've actually transplanted a few to a stream near our house here."

"What color are hepatica?" I asked.

"They're a very pale pink, white, or blue, and they have a liver-shaped leaf, which is why they are called hepatica, which is from the Greek for 'liver,' I think. They're very delicate. There were also Jack-in-the-pulpits, and Dutchman's-breeches. There were all these beautiful rare wildflowers in upstate New York that I learned to look at and identify with my father. Now I associate it with my home and my earliest memories.

"Then as I grew up, I began to think about a direction, and I happened to take a course on Picasso, when I was a freshman in college. It was at McGill, actually. McGill summer school. And I was presented with all these bizarre shapes and colors and a vocabulary that was completely foreign to me. When you're looking at paintings, not wildflowers, there is a whole set of meanings imbedded in them, so that the shapes and colors are more than shapes and colors. A painting expresses ideas and emotion, and it's connected to history and tradition, and something far larger."

"There was one teacher at McGill," she went on, "who made a special impact on me. I was in a course a little over my head. I was the youngest. He reached out a hand, just as my father had, and taught me how to look. That was a very, very moving experience. As soon as I got back to New York and to Finch College, I took out a membership at the Museum of Modern Art. That became my home away from home. And that opened up a world to me. It was a place where I felt at home, and I began to look and feel that I was affiliated with an institution."

The gates of the visual arts gradually opened up to Susan. "Were you intimidated by MOMA at first?" I asked.

"No, not really," Susan said with the confidence of one whose connection is true. "I felt it was my place."

"What made you feel that way?" I asked, wanting to know how she established the connection so securely.

"I think it was my entry into modern art through that one course that gave me confidence. Also, the connection with a particular artist, Picasso, who became *my* artist. In addition, it was cultural. I was young, I could identify with all the rebellion that went with modern art. Plus, I was in New York. It was the nineteen sixties, and everything was happening there. There was Pop Art. Abstract Expressionism, Conceptual Art. Everything was happening all around me. The city was filled with art and artists and galleries. So again, I made a connection to a place through art. Once it became apparent to me that art can connect you deeply to a place and time, both your own time and the past, that was the psychological entry that I needed to devote a lifetime to studying art.

"It was such a thrilling time to be young, to be in New York, and see everything happening all around me."

For a while Susan drifted away from art, but she found her way back to it when she spent a few years in graduate school at Harvard. Again, it was a relationship with a teacher that reconnected her to art. "I found my way back, after a few years' interlude, through the work of a man whose books I had read, Rudolf Arnheim. His field was the psychology of perception. He taught me how meaning is expressed through visual form, and how that's different from writing. This interested me very, very much."

Now we see a turning point in Susan's life. We see her taking a chance to make what proved to be a pivotal connection, with a great teacher, who might have seemed unapproachable. But Susan approached anyway. How often in the lives of my patients do I hear of this moment, when they could strike and make a momentous advance, or hold back, thinking they are not good enough.

Susan struck. "Just from reading his work I felt bold enough to write to him. He was at Harvard at the time. I was no way qualified to be a student on that level. But I wrote to him anyway, and he responded. I had an interview with him, and he took me on as a special student.

"My ambition was to teach art on the high school level. And he was willing to accommodate a young person without a portfolio and without credentials to come and be a special student, to take in his courses and his seminars. Now I had a real mission. Learning to look and opening the visual experience to others. That's what took me back to graduate school, and that's what determined the shape of my further career."

I love the way Susan put it. She had a love, a mentor, and a mission. Three kinds of connection. A great recipe for success.

And succeed Susan did, way beyond her early expectations. She got a Ph.D. in art history, published a book on Picasso, and earned a job as a curator at one of New York's most treasured museums, the Frick Collection.

Her mission, which was not just one of personal ambition, continues to this day. Her mission is to open the doors of art to other people. She has created a program at the Frick that brings school-children into the museum "to learn to look," as she puts it. She is introducing these children, many of whom would otherwise have no exposure to art whatever, to the world of visual beauty. And the kids love it! That alone is testimony to how well she does it.

"I always loved the experience of being in the classroom," she said, "of working with young people to help them open their eyes." Susan's attitude hearkens back to her father, who was a doctor, in a helping profession. So, too, did Susan make her mission that of helping others; in her case, to understand visual form. Unfortunately, the connection to art is a connection many people never make. They need a guide, like Susan.

"Art can be very intimidating. People don't know how to look, and in addition they feel it's not for them. To open up a museum to children from all parts of the city, to bring them in the doors so they'll want to stay, that's not easy," Susan said.

"How do you overcome the intimidation they feel?" I asked.

"First of all, a staff member goes into the schools to present who we are to the faculty and then to the students, to prepare them in their own place. Then we organize a trip for them to come, and we take them through the museum ourselves, because often the teachers don't feel qualified to. We give a lot of individual care. We take them through in small groups. We stand in front of a Rembrandt and say, 'What do you think? What are your impressions? Tell me more. What do you think is contributing to your impressions?' For example, if a student says the painting looks lovely, we might reply, What is it in the painting that you can point to that gives you that impression? Is it its color? Its shapes?' And then we get them look-ing and talking to each other, and the connection deepens. They're not only connected to the work of art, they're connected to each other, and the experience of looking."

"You see this happen before your very eyes?" I asked, impressed by the simplicity of her method.

"Oh yes! It's thrilling, because their impressions are so vivid, honest, and uneducated, in the sense that they're not trained. We're just trying to give them a little vocabulary of how to look at art, how to begin to understand it in visual terms.

"Of course, going on a museum field trip is not a popular idea with your average kid," Susan went on. "I've been on these trips with my own daughter, so I know what the reaction is in the class-room. They don't want to go. But I've seen in the museum when things go right; it's just magic. You have kids who didn't want to be there start to get excited, responding to what they see. Every-thing they say is relevant, everything they say is right. There is no wrong. It's what they see and what they feel. It's a completely vali-dating experience. They see more as they look and discuss, and they connect with each other as a group. They've taught me a great deal in the way they express themselves."

Susan then gave me a memorable example of how the kids have taught her. "We had looked at an Ingres portrait, a very finished work of art. Right next to it was a Monet. I asked a little girl, 'What was the difference between the two?' The girl replied, pointing at the Monet, 'He painted out the shadows.' Well, that is what Im-pressionism is all about. No one has ever said it better than that girl. It was a creative way of looking."

Susan's methods could be used anywhere to develop in people of all ages a connection, as she says, "to the pleasure of looking. That's our major goal. Even if they don't come back for another twenty years, we want them to have those early experiences, to remember that they came when they were very young. Then they'll have that as the base of their later experience."

She summed up our conversation with a story about Matisse and Picasso. "I think back to a remark," Susan said, "that has to do with the fact that all art builds on earlier art. That's particularly true of Picasso. He and Matisse were the two great artists of the twentieth century and were the most immersed in the past, and intent on carrying it forward through their own work. One of the things that concerned them both was who would continue to carry the past into the present. They saw themselves as the end of a tradition. Picasso asked Matisse toward the end of his life, 'Who will carry us in their hearts, as we carried the artists of the past?' "

❦

TWELVE

The Past

> *You must know that there is nothing higher and stronger and more wholesome and useful for life in after-years than some good memory, especially a memory connected with childhood. People talk to you a great deal about your education, but some fine, sacred memory, preserved from childhood, is perhaps the best education. If a man carries many such memories into life, he is safe to the end of his days, and if we have only one good memory left in our hearts, even that may sometimes be the means of saving us.*
>
> Alyosha, speaking in the epilogue to
> Fyodor Dostoyevsky's The Brothers Karamazov

WHEN I WAS eleven, my mother asked me if I wanted to go to boarding school. I said sure, since it was clear my stepfather and I were not headed toward peace anytime soon. Plus, I figured that by going away, not only would I escape Uncle Noble and his drunken tirades, I'd also get out of doing homework. I reasoned that at boarding school, since you didn't go home, they couldn't give you homework! So I was sent away to a school my mother picked, called Fessenden, a boys' boarding school in West Newton, Massachusetts. I started there in the fifth grade and graduated four years later. By the time I discovered the homework fallacy, it was too late.

A few years ago I was invited to give the graduation address at Fessenden. It was 1995, thirty-one years after I had graduated. The theme of my talk was that life can be good. When I was sent away to Fessenden, it was because life was bad. But thirty-five years after my first day and night spent as a Fessenden student, I returned to the school with the message that life is good.

Many of us have painful memories from our childhood. Many of us are haunted by them even as adults, while others do their best to forget them. I think it is best to hold on to them if you can; just change how they make you feel. Bad memories have something to teach.

If you can walk back into the memories, if you can preserve the connection to your past instead of breaking it, you might find that there is some goodness or usefulness left back there, even if it is only in giving you a sense of continuity.

One of my patients, let me name her Sarah, related a dream to me that illustrates this point in the surreal way of dreams. In her dream Sarah was lying in a narrow hospital room on an examining table, naked, with just a sheet covering her. There was a single window at the end of the room behind her head, but it was painted black, so little natural light could get through. Overhead, bright fluorescent lights filled the room with a sharp glare and made a low humming noise. Beyond her feet was a door. Through the door came a series of four men. The first man started making love to Sarah, then left. The second man entered the room and picked up the process of sexual intercourse at the exact point where the first man had left off. The third man did likewise, and then the fourth and final man came in. At the moment of penetration, his job was complete, and he died. His body disappeared, leaving Sarah alone in the room.

When she woke up, she started to sob at the horror of the dream. "What was so horrible was how disconnected I felt," she said. "I had no past, no future, no friends, no family, nothing but the present moment in that cold room. That was all there was to my life, just me in that moment. What horrified me was not so much what the men did, it was how cut off from everything else I felt. When I woke up from the dream I felt overcome by feelings of gratitude that the dream was only a dream. For the first time, I felt grateful that I had a past. My childhood was horrible, I was abused and battered and often abandoned, but the fact that I *had a past at all* suddenly gave me a huge sense of relief. In the dream I had experienced what it was like to have no awareness of the past, and I realized that that was worse than having a painful past. In a way, having a history gave me a reason to live, a motivation to go on. At that moment I became grateful for my awareness of who I was, and where I had been, painful as it might be. I feel that sense of gratitude to this moment."

We don't usually think of the past as providing a motivation to go on, as Sarah said it did for her. We usually think of motivation in terms of the desire to achieve future goals. But Sarah calls attention to a basic function of the past, one that we typically take for granted, namely, to lift us on. The past is like a wave that we ride. Without it, there is nothing. I think this is partly what Sarah meant by the past providing motivation. It gives a context, a foundation, a wave.

A painful past, like Sarah's, can spur one on to make things better now. I know one of my chief motivations to provide for my children is my desire to give them the happy childhood I wish I'd had. By giving it to them, I somehow create for myself, as well as for them, what I did not have. I know that Sarah takes great satisfaction in making a good life for herself now in part because she didn't have it years ago.

By preserving our connection to the past, even if the past was awful, we add something important to the present. The past gives depth to the present, gives it its contrasts, ironies, and feelings of triumph.

The past, like time itself, transcends good or bad. It just is. Memories are like stones that are part of a fence; if you start throwing aside the stones that don't please you, pretty soon the whole fence falls down.

If you go back in search of a stone you really loved, a happy memory of a person you've lost, who knows what magic you might do? A sixty-five-year-old woman told me what happened to her in this regard: "My first boyfriend, in high school, was a Holocaust orphan. He poured his heart out to me, and this made for a terrifically close bond, as powerful as a blood relationship. While I was in college we lost touch, but I never stopped caring, worrying, wondering about him. I'm still happily married to my husband, whom I married in nineteen fifty-four, and I've raised five children, but I regularly prayed for this boy's parents, and bought a piece of a Torah in their names, lest they be forgotten. In the summer of nineteen ninety-seven, after forty-seven years, I decided that I had to find him, to know whether he was dead or alive, well, happy, or what. I decided to get that book on how to find people, went out grocery shopping, and came back to a message from my college alumni office: *he* wanted to find *me*, and he left his phone number. I called, and it was overwhelming for both of us. To me, it felt like finding a long-lost twin. He was in deep despair, having lost his wife to cancer after a multiply tragic life. We got together, my whole family included. He says this changed his life and his luck. Since then he found a widow who is a perfect match for him. They have married. We stay in touch, and have promised that we will never lose each other again. He says he is happier than he has ever been, and his happiness enhances mine."

It is never too late to go find someone who meant a lot to you. Most of us can think of such a person. Finding him or her might be disappointing, but probably would be just the opposite.

I suppose the ultimate search like this is an adopted person's search for a biological parent. A thirty-year-old woman described her search in a note to me:

About two years ago, I looked for and found my biological mother. This was something I knew I would do at some point in my life. As I was preparing to get married, it seemed time—time to close a chapter in my life as a single woman and open the chapter of being a married person and hopefully a mother myself. My reason was just this, as well as medical reasons (I got no information growing up). My reason was *not* to replace anyone. I had and still have a very close and special family that I never knew was so important to me until this period.

When I first phoned my biological mother I was wondering (and worrying), What will she say? How will she react? As she answered the phone and I heard her voice, my very first thought was, I've heard this voice before. I was adopted at four months old, so obviously this connection was twenty-eight years old. When I did find my biological mother she was hesitant at first, but warm, welcoming, and loving. What was significant was, when I knew she was out there and alive, that meant there was someone out there who was connected to me.

Yet as positive as this experience turned out to be, I felt threatened in some way. My family that I knew, loved, and relied on all these years felt threatened. This foundation felt shaken, just by the mere fact that I was reunited. My family (adopted family) gathered around to help me with my fears—three-year-old fears in a twenty-eight-year-old body. I could not imagine doing this at a younger age, because as a high-functioning and relatively stable person, I really needed to pull on every cognitive insight and family reassurance to balance these "little girl" fears.

Looking into the past, as this woman points out, can be dicey. You never know what you'll find or how it will make you feel. But as she went on to say, "This to me was and is a profound demonstration of the intensity and importance of connection, but it also shows its tenuous nature, how it needs rather consistent maintenance to keep secure. At different phases in life, certain connections may be rattled, shaken, and reevaluated, and reinforced." Often, it is a person from the past or a memory that prompts these reevaluations.

If you are lucky enough to have had a happy childhood, then as Alyosha says in *The Brothers Karamazov,* you are safe to the end of your days. Preserve those memories and keep them alive. Tell them to others and talk about them. They are not dusty old postcards, but food for the living soul.

Developing a connection to the past—your past—is very important. Much of the spiritual teaching written these days emphasizes the importance of living in the moment. "Be here now" is the standard command, urging people to stop living in the past or in the future so that the present won't pass them by.

But I don't believe these writers mean that it is good to jettison the past. It is good to connect to the past, vividly and in detail, as Alyosha described. This does not mean that you live in the past, but that you *bring the past into the present*. You keep it alive. As you do this, it helps keep you aware of who you are, by reminding you who you were and where you've been.

Our historical connectedness can be suddenly enlarged and jolted by coincidences or chance experiences. For example, at a lecture I recently gave, a woman about my age came up to me and asked, "Did your father play hockey at Harvard?" I said that, yes, he did. "And he graduated when?" she asked. I told her 1936. At that, a tear came to her eyes. It turns out her husband's father was named Dunny Holmes. Holmes, along with a man named Hovenanian and my dad, comprised one of the most famous lines in Harvard hockey history, the "H-line," of Holmes, Hovenanian, and Hallowell. We talked for a few minutes, instantly being taken back to the scrapbooks we both had seen from the Boston papers detailing the exploits of that line. I gave her a hug. The past came to life in a burst of shared memory; our historical connectedness deepened.

The next week I got a note from her:

My husband's father, Dunbar (Dunny), died two days before Christmas. He was a wonderful man. My own father died about nine years ago and wasn't in the best of health for a few years prior to his death, so Dunny filled the role of father and father-in-law for me. Dunny was a very active man, a lawyer and a public servant, helping to found the Big Brother Association in the 1950s as well as serving on many boards in Wayland. He loved and supported his schools, Belmont Hill and Harvard, and he enthusiastically kept up with tennis and hockey, playing tournament tennis up until six months before he died.

So when I spoke to you at the conference, asking by chance if your father had played hockey at Harvard in the 1930s—and we then made the discovery that your father and my father-in-law, Dunbar Holmes, were indeed line mates on the famous H-line—I could barely contain myself. Thanks for the spontaneous hug. I needed and appreciated it. I oh-so-wanted to be able to call Dunny and tell him whom I had just met. It was difficult to hold back the tears—as it is to do now as I'm writing this. Is your father still alive? I hope so.

Of course, I had to give her the news that Dad had died twenty years before. It made me sad that Dad hadn't kept up with Dunny—although maybe Dunny was the man I remember at the funeral.

This chance connection to the past was like a gift through time. If I couldn't bring Dad back, I could meet the children of one of his best friends, a friend that had shared life with Dad in his glory days.

The effort to develop historical connection can pay unexpected dividends. One woman told me, "I'm currently working on my family tree. Although I'm only at the beginning stages, so far I've had more thorough and meaningful contacts with various relatives (father, mother, uncle, aunt) than I've had before, and I have found that my research is creating a more connected feeling all around. As I share the information that I've gathered, other relatives are joining in with their own information and research. Communication has opened up where there was little in the past."

Of course, you don't want to pursue the past as your reason for being. An awareness of the past should not replace human warmth in the present. I know some Mayflower descendants who can tell you every last detail of their lineage but can't crack a smile or give anyone a pat on the back.

Nonetheless, a connection to the past makes life richer. Many children are growing up with almost no sense of their family's history, let alone that of their country or region. If researching a family tree seems too ambitious, try just collecting stories of your family as they come up. Older people can teach the past just by telling some of the many stories they have lived. A tedious conversation with an aging grandparent or great-aunt can come alive if you just ask a few questions.

Family traditions can connect us to the previous generation even after they have died. "After my grandmother's funeral service," a woman told me, "we were all gathered at the home of a cousin. We—me and four cousins, all sisters now in their forties—were seated around the table talking about Grandma and reminiscing about our childhoods, growing up with her. Even though we live in other parts of the Northeast—many states apart—we had similar memories of Grandma, and we were all talking about our connection to her and to each other. We realized we shared many of Grandma's customs and traditions as adults in our own homes. One cousin brought out a cake and left it there on the table, saying, 'Grandma always would say just place the cake there even if no one wants it—someone will eventually eat it.' And we all found ourselves munching on the cake after a while. We felt such a strong connection to Grandma at that time as well as to each other because of her presence and influence in our lives."

Even if, as was my own case, your parents die before your children are born, you can bring your parents to life for your children by talking about them, their habits and customs, their appearance, how they did Thanksgiving, any details that come to mind. Instead of holding back the memory or wiping away a tear, put it into words.

"My mother died when I was thirty-three," one woman wrote to me,

before my children were born. After a few years my son, then my daughter were born. These long-waited-for children were, and are, such a joy. My only sadness was that my mother was not alive to know her grandchildren, to be part of their lives and to enjoy them. They are wonderful kids.

It was important to me for my children to feel connected to my mother. In the course of daily life, family celebrations, and holidays, I tell my kids stories about her and add a comment about what she might have said. For example, I might say to my daughter, "Amy, your grandmother would have said you were a real trooper." Or I might say, "Let's bake some of your grandmother's sugar cookies. I still have the recipe card she wrote for me." Or, "Daniel, I'm giving you this book today because I got it from grandmother when I turned fourteen." By weaving these tidbits into the fabric of our days, my children have some sense of their grandmother, her personality, her interests, her quirks, her humor. Together we have built a relationship between my children and their grandmother. The benefit for me personally is that I can remember specific situations and qualities about my mother that help me remain connected to her. I have conversations with her to help me figure out a problem, to share some happiness, to tell her something she would have enjoyed. I also tell my kids I do this and use this as a strategy to cope. I've told them they can tell her their stories, too. Consequently, we all feel a connection to a wonderful woman who we still learn from and feel loved by.

There are countless other ways you can develop your children's sense of where they came from. For example, something as simple as your child's name can tell a huge story. My daughter, Lucy, for example, is really named Lucretia Mott Hallowell. Lucy is her nickname. At first she thought Lucretia was a dumb name to have, and she wished we hadn't given it to her. But now she is proud of it.

She has learned that the original Lucretia Mott was a courageous Quaker lady from the Civil War years who fought to free slaves and later fought for women's rights. She made a deep impression on Elizabeth Cady Stanton and is remembered as one of the shapers of the Seneca Falls women's rights convention.

She is my great-great-great-great-grandmother, and is Lucy's (plus one "great") as well.

As Lucy becomes a mature woman, carrying the name of Lucretia Mott will mean a lot to her, not only connecting her to the past, but contributing to her sense of who she is.

From memories to family trees to names—you can find your history in many places. In teaching your children about it, you enlarge their sense of who they are. You get closer to touching, at least metaphorically, the ghosts and spirits who brought you here.

~~~~~

THIRTEEN

Nature and Special Places

PLACES HAVE A spirit. The ancients called this the *genius loci,* or the character of a place.

You walk into your old school, let's say. A detail grabs you—the odor of the sweeping compound used to clean the floors, for example, and the odor takes you back in a flash. The spirit of the place has captured you and put you under its spell.

Places speak to us. Our old playground. The tree we used to climb. The dentist's office we remember too well.

Nature, in general, is one "place" we all connect with, in a myriad of different ways. For some, the connection with nature is almost their religion, providing them with the peace and meaning others may take from God. For some, nature *is* God. And for almost all of us, nature is a kind of mother, hence "Mother Nature," who holds us all our lives, sometimes terrifying us, sometimes inspiring us, sometimes hurting us, but always surrounding us with her powerful presence. It is a connection no one can avoid and most people celebrate.

As with the connection to pets, only one member of this connection speaks words. But like pets, nature speaks back in her own way. "I will lift up mine eyes unto the hills, from whence cometh my help," spoke the psalmist.

Nature, like the best of mothers, is always there, offering sustenance if we will but take it. You can feel the presence of nature wherever you are. The more you talk to the trees and the hills and the woods and the sea, the more they will talk back to you. The more you talk to your garden, the better it will grow. The more you embrace nature, the more it will embrace you.

I lived on Cape Cod as a little boy, before the days of Uncle Noble. I remember playing tag with the waves many times on the Outside Beach beyond Pleasant Bay, racing up the sharp slope of shore as the breaking waves chased up behind me. When I reached a certain distance I would turn around and let the foaming water churn around my ankles. It would slosh there for a moment, then begin a tug on my legs as it swept sand and periwinkles back past me down to the ocean. Standing my ground against the undertow, I loved the feeling of the sand and shells and water tickling my toes.

Now that I am fifty, I can see that little boy back there playing tag with the waves, confident and unthinking about anything other than the next wave, the next grilled hot dog, the next trip to the Outside Beach. I can feel the undertow as I write about it now, as if I were there today; only today I know that one of those waves, one of these days, is going to take me with it.

Most people have some place in nature they call holy, some place that carries special meaning, that opens their hearts and minds as no other place can.

For me it's the beach, especially the beaches on Cape Cod. I was in Wellfleet on business one wintry day, and on my way out of town I pulled into an empty parking lot by a beach. Thronged with people in summer, these beaches lie empty in winter. Seagulls and terns provide the only company.

I walked the sandy stretch, my coat pulled up around my ears, and felt the salt air flick around my face. The distinct colors of the beach in winter worked on me. It was usually this way when I visited the beach alone. A kind of cut-to-the-bone honesty and loneliness would come over me. I could never stay long, alone, or I'd get too blue.

The slate gray ocean, whitecapped; the off-white sand, speckled with blue-green clumps of dried seaweed; the stalks of yellow-green beach grass bending in the wind; the sky (this day gray, as so often it could be, but a gray of many shades) all sparked their own associations. There was the hint, or at least the hope, of sun this day, as opposed to the dense gray of other days. I could intuit a golden glow.

No other place but the beach stirs in me the same feelings. The beach on the Cape—the colors, the smell, the wind, the feel of the sand underfoot—takes me instantly to a feeling I know but never feel anywhere else. I *intimate* it elsewhere, but never feel it.

It is a melancholy feeling, composed of fear, loss, and sadness. It's odd that I like it, but I do. I think I like it because it takes me back to where I began. It was just my bad luck that those years were tough. But I hold on to them no matter if it hurts.

I go back to the beach to make sense of life. It is only fitting that there should be pain in the place where I try to make sense of life. It is a work in progress, this work of making sense. The beach is where I feel the power of the past most acutely, and so it is a place that draws me to it, as well as causes me fear.

Other places can hold a special sway over us. Some people's special place may be an old bookstore, or a road they walk down every day, or the corner news store where they buy coffee and the paper and have friendly conversation each morning.

You may find yourself wanting to go to a place, rather than a person, when you feel sad. You may find in that place a kind of comfort that another person just can't provide. I have a patient who grew up in Vermont and now lives near Boston. She says at certain times she simply *has* to go for a walk in the woods. She loves her family and friends, but she finds at times she has to go into the woods to feel right about life. Fortunately, the surrounding areas of Boston are full of woods, so my patient has a lot to choose from. The woods take her in like a welcoming friend.

I have another patient who says she *has* to go to New York City now and then or she'll "go flat." She gets a dose of energy from New York that she can't get anywhere else. New York affects a lot of people that way. All you have to do is drive into the city to feel a surge of intensity.

Churches and other places of worship, of course, become special places for many people, due to the meanings associated with the places as well as the beauty they usually possess.

But the homeliest of places can become special, even holy. The tree house you had as a child was probably not very elegant, but I'm sure it was special. The pool hall you frequented in high school maybe has memories like nowhere else, or the tavern you frequented in college. Dives of all kinds, although unattractive and downright dangerous, can become treasured memories.

The more you associate strong feelings with a place, the more hallowed it is likely to become to you. This is why mundane places like movie houses, ballparks, and bus stops can strike such deep chords within our hearts.

Just as many places speak to us depending upon what happened to us there, nature also speaks in many different ways. I have described the potent feelings the beach brings out in me. For some people it is the prairie, or a canyon, or the mountains that work on their soul. Sometimes they feel these places in a positive way, but more often than not there is some fear, or at least awe, mixed in.

I remember a friend in college who came from Montana. He was an atheist, but he told me he did believe in the mountains. I asked what he meant by that; after all, the mountains were not a belief system. He said the mountains gave to him what organized belief systems, like religions, gave to other people.

I have a patient, a confirmed skeptic and believer in nothing but nothingness, who has started to "go spiritual," as he ironically puts it. He feels the tug of "something" when he walks his dog. "Maybe it is just old age," he told me. "Now that I'm fifty, maybe I'm just looking for magic. But I have been reading some Native American writings about the spirit of the plains, and you know, I'm starting to swallow it. Tell me I'm crazy, OK?"

"If you're crazy, you're in good company," I said to him.

Nature can inspire just about anybody, but if you develop and nurture your connection to it, it can lead you to states deeper than simple wonder.

Seasons can change our moods. Autumn seems to be especially therapeutic. The colors of fall tend to improve mood, studies have shown. Bernard Vittone, director of the National Center for Treatment of Phobias, Anxiety, and Depression, in Washington, D.C., believes that walking in the woods in fall is good for emotional well-being. "We encourage our patients to take advantage of fall color. A drive in the country makes people feel better and takes their minds off their troubles."

There are so many different ways to connect with nature that you can choose what you like. One of the more unusual ways is bird-watching. I am not a bird-watcher, but I know bird-watchers. They are devoted. They will get up at 3 A.M. to drive a hundred miles for the chance to see a particular bird at daybreak. And they find the experience riveting. Listen to the drama in one person's description:

> While in Arizona in May, I had a close encounter with a Great Roadrunner. As the trip began I had wished for a good look at a road-runner. I define "good look" as one where the bird stands still for at least a few minutes and I get to study it. We had already seen a couple of roadrunners dashing across the road in front of us, and I figured that was all I was going to get. Then, while walking through Catalina State Park in the early evening, I noticed that the mesquite trees were in bloom and had moths and smallish birds in them. I stopped to try to identify the birds, and the rest of my group moved on. I could not identify the birds even when I was standing right next to them! I was about to give up when I heard a rustling of leaves. A roadrunner ran up, stopped not twenty feet away from me, and pulled itself erect, as if it was tuning into the world. I tried to stand still (it was difficult). The roadrunner stood perfectly still (seemingly without any diffi-culty), and we remained like that for a few moments. I could see the blue and red color around its eye, and I was perfectly happy. Then I moved, and the roadrunner was off. Later I thought, we sometimes are granted our wishes, often when we least expect it. And often when we are trying to do something else.

As in this case, the connection with nature often prompts reflections about life. How many times do we think long, long thoughts as we stand and stare at the sea, or at a sunset, or at a Great Roadrunner?

Nature is always there for us, waiting to be joined.

FOURTEEN

Pets and Other Animals

YEARS AGO, WHEN I was director of an inpatient psychiatric ward at a state mental hospital, I decided to get a cat to have as a pet on the unit. I'll never forget the hoopla the bureaucrats put up. You would have thought I had advocated cocaine as a form of therapy. "You can't do that!" the man in charge barked at me. "What about patients who are allergic? What about diseases like cat scratch fever? What if a patient gets too attached to the cat and then wants to take it with him when he gets discharged? What if a patient's family sues us because of something the cat does?"

"Like what?" I asked, trying to imagine what on earth this man might be thinking of.

"I don't know. Something unforeseen. People will sue about anything. Why take the chance?"

"Because the cat will give these patients a relationship that matters," I replied. "Many of them don't have that."

"But they won't own the cat. They won't be able to keep the cat," the man protested.

"That's an important lesson for them to learn, too," I replied. "After all, we're always talking to them about how there are limits on all relationships. Well, why not let them practice with the cat?"

The bureaucrat in charge let me do it, I think, just to get me out of his hair. The hospital offered no support, but it did allow the cat to live on the ward. Once, the cat jumped out the window, which was three stories up. He broke his hip. The vet told us we could either put him to sleep or have hip surgery, which would cost $300. We opted for the surgery, funded by me, of course, as the hospital took the attitude of "I told you so."

But it was worth every penny of it. That cat did a huge amount of good over the years. Patients would talk to the cat when they would not talk to anyone else. Patients played with the cat, fed the cat, cleaned up after the cat; and when the patients didn't, the residents (psychiatrists in training), nurses, and other staff pitched in.

We had a contest to name the cat. My favorite name was suggested by the chief resident: Oedipus, or Eddy-puss. But the patients didn't like that one. They voted for "Mr. Fenwood," a name derived from the street the hospital stood on, Fenwood Road.

Mr. Fenwood lasted longer on that unit than I did. I left after three years to do something different. I remember in my final year the hospital had a big shindig to celebrate its seventy-fifth anniversary. The *Boston Globe* came to do a story because of the anniversary. As the reporter toured the hospital, he heard about Mr. Fenwood and wanted a picture. I'll never forget the chief bureaucrat saying to me, "What did they want a picture of? Your damn cat!"

Pets can inspire loyalty and warmth as Mr. Fenwood did. Patients who could not make contact with humans could love Mr. Fenwood.

Pets are good for you. Everyone who can should have a pet. They bring out good feelings. Studies show that people who have pets live longer.

People who have a hard time with other people can find something special in a pet. For example, one fifty-two-year-old man told me, "I do not have a strong sense of connection to anyone, including my wife, or any institution, including my job. But I do feel a strong bond with our dog. She is a seven-year-old shar-pei who loves me unconditionally, and I reciprocate that love. I talk to her as if she could understand me, and she makes her little shar-pei noises to carry on her part of the conversation."

We sometimes dismiss as trivial the relationships people make with animals, but that is a big mistake, as millions of cat owners, dog owners, horse owners, and other animal owners can attest. For example, a twenty-seven-year-old woman told me about her close relationship with her horse.

"Although I feel connected with my family and friends," she wrote,

I feel an especially deep connection with my horse, Webster. I've had Web for twelve years. My father bought him for me my junior year in high school. Web and I went to horse shows regularly in the South. Because we traveled alone, we developed a special sense of friendship.

When I graduated from high school, I made arrangements to attend college without Web. By Christmas I had found a barn for Web to live in near my college town. I felt that my first semester was somewhat lonely because Web was not there to share it with me. I missed being able to see him daily and visit with him. My parents brought Web down after Christmas break. We had a few months together. In March I went home for spring break but left Web at school.

Soon the barn where Web lived called to say Web had a case of colic. I went back to school early to be with him. These "colic" episodes continued to occur every time I would leave him for more than a few days. I began to realize that Web missed me and our daily visits so much that he would develop this stomachache. So I began to take him home with me during the long breaks so that he wouldn't become ill.

Horse owners would think I'm crazy, but I'm convinced Web's illness was a result of his missing me. During my junior year of college, at spring exams I was too busy to go to the barn every day and visit Web. Sure enough, the barn called and Web was sick. Usually when I went to see him things got better for Web. This time was different, though. Web had worked himself into a genuine illness, which eventually required surgery later that evening. I was upset, because I felt I had let my friend down. He was always there for me, but I had been too busy for him. I spent several nights with Web at the hospital. The doctor told me he would be fine after a lengthy recovery. Web had a miraculous recovery!

He graduated with me the next year, and we moved home to our farm in Tennessee, where Web lives in the backyard, within viewing distance of my bedroom window. Web and I lived at home for a few months until I got my first job, in South Carolina. Web went with me, and we lived in South Carolina for two and a half years. Unfortunately, the drive was too far for Web to come home with me for visits, and he got sick a few times.

Today, Web and I are back in Tennessee on the farm. I go see him daily and spend time grooming, riding, or just loving Web. He is a wonderful animal that I feel very connected to and loved by.

Pets are one of the most available connections. Shut-ins, people in nursing homes, patients in mental hospitals should all be given access to animals if at all possible. Their power to heal is extraordinary, and they are not in short supply!

FIFTEEN

Ideas and Information

I HAVE A patient whose father used to take her fishing. On these trips they would enjoy special one-on-one time, each person revelling in being with the other. Not surprisingly, my patient developed a love of the outdoors. "I wanted to learn more," she said to me. She wrote a paper on ecology in high school that won a prize; she majored in environmental studies in college; and she now runs an environmental consulting firm. "It all began on those trips with Dad," she said. "I just naturally wanted to learn more."

"Naturally" we all want to learn more. Before formal learning turned natural learning into drudgery, as it does for too many, learning was a happy, creative experience for us all, even when it got us into trouble! Trial and error—that's what childhood, and learning, are all about! The desire to *understand* defines us as humans. The presence of her father may have been the emotional impetus leading my patient to become interested in the outdoors, but then her natural curiosity took over. Once that happened, she was unstoppable!

We all are born curious. We all are born avid for new ideas. We all are born ready to connect to ideas and information.

If you nurture your connection to the world of ideas and information, that world will nurture you as you grow older. It will give you pleasure year after year as you look forward to reading a certain journal, or can't wait for the publication of the next book by a certain author, or eagerly await the results of the next experiment in a certain field. You will start to follow oceanography or politics or car mechanics or whatever realm captured your imagination years ago.

Making this positive connection early on is *the* chief goal of a good education. Many parents and educators make the error of believing that demonstrating knowledge is the chief goal of a good education, and so they stress test scores as a measure. However, many children who score well can't wait to stop learning, and many children who score poorly end up making great contributions. For example, the writer John Irving took five years to complete his four years of high school, and he needed remedial help in, of all courses, English! After he nearly flunked out of high school, he went on to become one of the world's most acclaimed novelists!

What he did develop was a positive connection to the world of stories and of words. Even though school did its best to discourage him and convince him he was stupid, he found a wrestling coach who brought out the best in him and kept his spirits up. That wrestling coach helped him preserve a positive connection to himself and to life, which in turn allowed him to keep trying.

Too often people dismiss the connection to information and ideas as only for intellectuals, but this is not true, not true at all. A car mechanic may develop a deep connection to the world of information and ideas about cars. A lover of sailing may become expert on all the complex science involved in sailing, from navigation to boat design to weather forecasting. A gardener may not get a Ph.D. in botany, indeed he may have no formal education at all, but he can become expert in how to make things grow. The connection to information and ideas can expand constantly over a lifetime, giving pleasure every day.

We take an innate pleasure in mastering a new body of knowledge or grasping the meaning of a complex idea. Remember when you first learned some simple laws of probability, that every time you flip a coin the chances of a head are fifty-fifty, even if you've flipped ten heads in a row? And if you went on and learned more about statistics and probability, you probably felt the pleasure of better understanding truth, if you had a good teacher.

Or at a younger age, can you remember starting algebra? I recall asking my teacher in an exasperated way, "Well, what *does* x equal, anyway?" Then, gradually the meaning of a variable dawned on me, like a ship emerging from the fog. It is a concept that is old hat to me now, but it once was pretty cool.

Connections to ideas provide some of life's most lasting pleasures. Furthermore, now more than ever, getting a good job depends upon how comfortable you are with information and ideas and how confident you are in the midst of uncertainty and change. Such confidence directly relates to how well connected you feel to the world of information and ideas. It does not relate to how many ideas and how much information you have memorized. It does relate to how comfortable you feel in playing with what you know, and finding what you need to know. It doesn't matter how *much* you know nearly as much as it matters how easily you can identify what you need to know and then find it—in other words, how easily you can connect with information and ideas.

There is one major reason people do not develop a full and confident connection to information and ideas. It is not that they lack intelligence. It is not that they lack motivation. It is not that they didn't attend the right school or have enough computers at home or in their classrooms. It is not that they watch too much TV, or don't eat right, or any of the myriad explanations we often hear for why so many people can't easily get around in the worlds of science, math, and language.

What gets in the way of people of all ages from developing a confident connection with ideas and information more than anything else is one single thing. It is fear.

Fear is the most pernicious learning disability. It is also by far the most common. It affects nearly everyone once in a while.

Some people never learn to operate a computer, not because they lack the intelligence to do so, but because they are afraid.

Some people never learn to ride a horse, not because they lack the athletic skills, but because they are afraid.

Some people never get good at math, not because they can't, but because they are afraid.

I have specialized in treating learning disabilities in children and adults for years. Conditions like dyslexia, attention deficit disorder, foreign language disability, and nonverbal learning disability are my specialty.

However, none of these holds a person back nearly as much as fear can. I have seen brilliant people never make use of their brilliance because they could not overcome their fear.

Sometimes people fear other people, or they fear going outside to work, or they fear responsibility, or they simply fear being anything less than perfect. These are concerns I took up in my book *Worry: Controlling It and Using It Wisely.*

But there is a fear that is even more common than the states of worry I discussed in my previous book.

This is the simple, stark fear of learning something new.

It can hold a child back in school, but more commonly it holds an adult back. This is because in school we have teachers to lead children into the new fields they may fear. We have teachers to help them overcome their fears of learning something new. But adults usually do not have teachers, or if they do, adults are often afraid to ask questions, for fear of looking stupid.

We all need to develop a comfortable connection to the world of information and ideas. You can do this in any number of ways. Let me tell you how I did.

When I was in the first grade, in the public school system in Chatham, on Cape Cod, I had a teacher named Mrs. Eldredge. (Back then in Chatham, most of the town was either Eldredge or Nickerson. I had Eldredge.) She was a sturdy woman, in her fifties, I imagine, and was an old hand at teaching first grade. This was 1955, and when it came to learning, the diagnostic categories as far as most people were concerned were "smart" and "stupid." All Mrs. Eldredge had to help her was her experience. But she also knew that not all kids who were slow to read had a case of stupidity.

I was a lousy reader. Mrs. Eldredge told my parents that I wasn't stupid but that I had dyslexia. My father told me this meant I was a mirror reader. I thought that meant I had a mirror in my brain. I can remember looking for the mirror by peering into my left ear in the bathroom mirror.

In retrospect I am impressed that Mrs. Eldredge diagnosed my dyslexia. She could have just called me slow or stupid and left it at that. But I am even more impressed at how she treated my dyslexia.

What did she do? What was my treatment plan, my IEP, or individualized educational plan, as it is called in today's bureaucratized system? Mrs. Eldredge never heard of an IEP, but she had an idea of how to treat children who couldn't read.

What she did was make the classroom safe for me. She made it safe for me to fail. She was a big woman, built sort of like a washer and dryer stacked vertically, and wherever she sat she carried the weight of authority. During reading period she would sit next to me. Back in the fifties in Chatham, we learned to read by reading out loud. Each child would read a paragraph. "See Spot run. Run, run, run," and so forth.

When it was my turn to read, I couldn't do it. I would jumble up the letters. I would stammer and stutter. Some words I'd nail, but others would come out wrong. In most classrooms I would have been embarrassed, but not in Mrs. Eldredge's. When I read, she put one of her big arms around me and squeezed me just enough to make me feel secure. She wore white dresses, as I recall, with red apples on them. I can see the red apples out of the corner of my eye even now. When I read, none of the other kids laughed at me, because I had the mafia at my side. I stammered and stuttered, and Mrs. Eldredge squeezed, and reading class went on without missing a beat. No shame, no embarrassment, no fear.

I fell in love with words, thanks to Mrs. Eldredge and thanks to my great-aunt Nell, who would read aloud to me every day. Even though I was a slow reader— and am *still* a slow reader—I went on to major in English at Harvard and graduate magna cum laude. That degree belongs as much to Mrs. Eldredge and Aunt Nell as to me.

Mrs. Eldredge couldn't cure my dyslexia. But what she could do was make the classroom safe for me. She could make it safe for me to be a slow reader. Because I felt no shame, I was not scared off from reading.

Because of Mrs. Eldredge, and Aunt Nell, and a host of other teachers, I developed a comfortable connection to the world of ideas and information. I was a setup to do just the opposite—to develop a hatred of school and of reading. But it didn't happen that way.

Mrs. Eldredge's arm has stayed around me since first grade. It is around me now, giving me the courage to learn new things, to write books, to explore new areas. I was an English major who went to medical school. Fear has not slowed me down academically, because I always had that arm around me.

Anyone can find that arm, but the younger you do it, the better. Children should be challenged in school, but they also should be reassured. As she leads them into new areas, the teacher should allay the children's fears, always letting them know they can succeed. This combination of challenge plus reassurance creates a strong connection to the world of information and ideas.

Along these lines, there is an innovative group in Boston called Boston Partners in Education, which has organized a program in the public schools called Power Lunch. Once a week, business executives, lawyers, and other professionals go to a Boston Public School and meet with one particular child for forty-five minutes. They eat lunch together, then the adult reads aloud to the child. The adult can stay with the same child for up to three years; the program stops at the end of third grade.

This is such a perfect model of connection! I asked Olivia Matthews, one of the staff of Boston Partners in Education, how the kids liked it. "The overwhelming majority love it," she told me. "That was the big question when the program started. Would these kids want to give up their lunch hour and their recess to sit with a grown-up and read? It turns out they really do. They get so excited. One of my favorite moments is seeing their faces when their volunteers walk in. They come up to me when I'm there and they say, 'Is my partner coming today? Is my partner coming today?' And as you can imagine, the businesspeople love it, too."

The companies that participate also provide the funding for the program. It is a great example of the business community supporting the schools and the children in a grassroots fashion. Over three hundred executives and professionals participate, from over twenty-five different organizations. The large law firm Ropes and Gray sends thirty-four adults alone. I love the image of thirty-four lawyers at Ropes and Gray leaving for lunch once a week to go read to a child in the public school system of Boston!

In terms of earning power, the connection to information and ideas is one of the most important connections anyone can develop. In terms of self-esteem in adulthood, it is also key.

But most of all, a comfortable connection to the world of information and ideas is crucial because it allows for the full development of your mind. It allows for a kind of mastery, like hitting a home run or making a slam dunk, that is one of life's most hard-won pleasures.

SIXTEEN

Institutions and Organizations

A CONNECTED MAN IN A CONNECTED PLACE

ONE GRAY AFTERNOON in a suburb of Boston, Bob Tobin, age forty-one, crawled into bed and started to cry. He felt depleted, ashamed, and out of luck. He was making no money, and had to rely entirely on his wife, Maurine, to support their family of five children on the small salary she made as a teacher. An Episcopal priest, Bob was pursuing graduate studies at Harvard, but he felt worthless because he was not contributing to the financial support of his family. To make matters worse, he was cross and grumpy all the time, barking at his children and his wife every day. This man who had played college football in Texas and ridden bareback broncos for fun was now breaking down.

But as he lay in bed crying that afternoon, something wonderful happened. His children and his wife all came and crawled into bed with him. They must have made quite a picture, five kids, age six to sixteen, one mom, and one dad weeping all in one sagging bed.

But their spirits did anything but sag. When Bob said, "I feel so ashamed, I can't even give you kids money to go to the movies," the kids rallied. They immediately volunteered, "Dad, we'll go out and get jobs." The very next day two of them had jobs as ushers at the Cleveland Circle Cinema. Everybody pitched in. Life began to improve.

Not long after that bleak afternoon, Bob found work. But he has never forgotten that day. He came up from the depths, with the help of his family and his God, but he still talks openly about the experience, with characteristic humility. He continues to look back at it, and share it with others, knowing it is the kind of crisis that can befall us all. These are the moments when we need our connections the most.

Now sixty-three, Bob Tobin has built his life on connections of many kinds. Christ Church in Cambridge, where Bob has been rector for eleven years, is as connected a place as Bob is a connected man. I know, as my family has been attending that church for ten of those years.

Bob grew up poor. His dad had a decent job in the printing business, but he was a drinker, so he gave most of what he made to barkeepers. Due to his father's alcoholism, Bob and his sister, Bess, often had to fend for themselves, relying on the help of neighbors or strangers.

He started going to church, which became a kind of refuge. One of his first vivid moments of outside connection was when a woman in the church stopped him and asked, "Bobby, how *are* you?" She must have known he was hurting. Bobby, the boy, said he was fine, but Bob, the man, still draws strength from the kindness of that gesture.

Looking outside his home for support, he got attention playing football in high school. High school football in Texas is high school football at its most intense. If you are good, you are somebody. Bob was good. He went on to the next level, playing college football, but his life was to take a big turn in college.

At the University of Texas, he found a calling. Merrill Hutchins, who was working with the chaplaincy program, took him aside and said, simply, *"I know you."* Bob immediately knew what Merrill meant. They had never met, but Merrill sensed something in Bob, this rugged football player, that spoke of spiritual depth. Bob had always known it was there, but he hadn't pursued it until Merrill Hutchins made the connection.

Seminary followed college. Socially, the times were changing, but not very fast. So Bob began to play a different, in some ways tougher brand of Texas football, the fight for social justice.

Before Bob could be ordained he had to be interviewed by a psychiatrist in Austin. The day of the interview Bob was marching in a picket line protesting segregation at a lunch counter. He had to leave the line to go for his interview. When he walked into the psychiatrist's office, he found the doctor standing at his window, looking down at the protest Bob had just been a part of. The psychiatrist was cursing the "niggers and all the people who support them," Bob recalls. Bob passed his sanity test by saying nothing to the psychiatrist that would lead the psychiatrist to disqualify him. After the interview he returned to the picket line, having had one of his first lessons in the practical aspects of idealism.

To this day Bob has been committed to ending racial discrimination, as well as all other kinds of prejudice. One of his first jobs as a priest was in Borger, Texas, then a John Birch Society town. On the day President Kennedy was assassinated, one of the local bankers went on the radio and said Kennedy's death was the best thing that could have happened to the country.

Bob tangled with people like that. When he challenged the local Rotary Club by pointing out it was against the bylaws of the organization to have a biased political speaker without having a speaker from the opposing side, a member of the club, one J.C. Phillips, threw a stack of books at Bob, along with a handful of laminated cards that read on one side, "I am a card-carrying American," and on the other carried the pledge of allegiance.

Bob sprang at J.C. like the old halfback he was. He got in J.C.'s face, something that J.C. was not accustomed to. Bob, still not long out of riding broncos bareback, took this overweight, middle-aged Rotarian by his lapels and warned him *never* to do that again. "Pretty macho, huh?" Bob says now with a chuckle, as he tells the story. "But that was the language those people spoke."

Bob continued to speak the language of connection through his various jobs.

Christ Church, the place that has employed him for the past eleven years, also has been speaking the language of connection— all the way back to the eighteenth century. Christ Church sits about a hundred feet off Garden Street, right at the edge of what is now the hubbub of Harvard Square. It is a simple wooden building, painted gray, built before the Revolutionary War, in 1759. George Washington worshipped there, and Martin Luther King gave an important speech there announcing his opposition to the Vietnam War.

Bob Tobin is rector now, a job few people have held. One fact that attests to the strength of this church is that Bob Tobin is only the fifth rector since 1900.

It is hard to tell how many people consider themselves regular parishioners of Christ Church, since many more people attend from time to time than are on the official rolls. As is probably the case in many other parts of the country, religious faith in Cambridge, Massachusetts, is a sometime thing. People catch it and lose it, flirt with it and reject it, embrace it and give up on it on a regular basis, so the attendance at any given service varies from week to week. There is no promise of damnation if you don't show up, and there is no absolute proof of salvation if you do, so attendance fluctuates.

Nonetheless, there is a core group that always comes, and they preserve a strong sense of connection within the church. About three hundred people show up every Sunday, around 250 at the ten o'clock service and another fifty or sixty at the eight o'clock service. The congregation is made up of Harvard Square street people and Harvard University faculty, Cambridge working people and Cambridge leisure class, old people who have been members of the church for fifty years and brand-new members who are just sniffing it out.

Sue and I joined in 1988, just after we were married. I'll never forget the first time we went to Christ Church. We were struck by how simple it was. None of the stained glass I remembered from Saint Michael's church in Charleston. Just clear glass windows, a simple cross, hardwood pews with red cushions, and a congregation that looked as diverse as Harvard Square, much more diverse than your average Episcopal congregation. Some people wore suits or fancy dresses, while others wore jeans or cut off shorts. Most were neatly groomed, while one or two were in dire need of a bath. Most were white, but there were more than a few people of color. The service was Rite II from the Book of Common Prayer. I hadn't prayed those words since I left Charleston, and when I started to pray them again I could tell they'd been changed a little bit, but not that much. Gone was the line from the General Confession "and there is no health in us." I was glad to see that line go. But many words were the same, enough to keep the connection coming.

Sue and I, a little shy, didn't stick around after that first service; we just filled out a pew card asking for more information and went home.

The next day we got a call from Louise Conant, the associate rector. "Hello," she said. "We picked up your pew card. Would you like me to come visit you and tell you about Christ Church?" I had been accustomed to people calling to ask if they could come tell us about a life insurance policy or vinyl siding. But no, this caller was offering us God.

I'll never forget Louise's visiting our condo on Linnaean Street in Cambridge, sitting down with us in our small living room, and gently opening up the arms of the church. She seemed to me then, and still does now, one of the gentlest, strongest women I've ever met.

Sue and I had both been away from church for years. We were looking for a way back, but not for a lecture or a set of rules. Louise gave us the reassurances we needed, sipped her coffee, ate her cookie, answered our questions, and left, I imagine, to another person's home or bedside. She made no pitch, told us none of the benefits of believing in God or attending Christ Church, just smiled her gentle smile and answered our questions. We've been members of the church ever since, and our three children were baptized there.

Christ Church is a very inviting old place, situated next to a graveyard. The Episcopal congregation feels connected—to God, to one another, to *something* they do not find in everyday life.

I don't know everyone in the church; far from it. But each year I get to know a few more. Whenever I go there I feel better on the way out than I did on the way in.

It is interesting how deeply the place and the man—Christ Church and Bob Tobin—both embody the power of connection. In fact, Bob arrived at Christ Church for the first time not as rector, but as a parishioner. He came during that difficult period in his life, when he ended up in bed, crying and depressed. That winter, he and Maurine were looking around for a church.

"I was totally disconnected and feeling very lost," he recalls. At the time Bob was a vice-president in the administration of an educational institution and he had become distraught because of the politics of the place. "It was the epitome of disconnectedness," he said. "There was ongoing terrible manipulation and dishonesty there. I was feeling completely fragmented. Then one day I resigned. I left bitter and angry.

"Then I started coming to Christ Church. It was my first encounter with this kind of place. Having been a priest since nineteen sixty, I had been involved in parishes and had had good friends who were, but when we came here we found something special about the atmosphere, something Maurine and I had never felt anywhere before.

"I remember we came for the first time on a Christmas Eve. We went out that afternoon not even knowing whether we were going to go to church or not. We had been sledding with the kids, and we were still in our sledding clothes when we looked in the paper and saw there was a five o'clock service at Christ Church, so we decided to run over here. We got here a little late and came in. Here was Murray Kenney, my predecessor, telling stories and wearing a grinch hat. Not your stereotypical, stuffy Episcopal church. The people felt so alive. They obviously enjoyed being in this environment. We decided right on the spot that we really wanted to come back here. And so we did. We started coming here until we went back to Texas in nineteen eighty-one. Then I was called back as rector in nineteen eighty-seven."

Bob told me what a contrast the warmth of Christ Church struck against the environment of fear he had lived with when he was in educational administration. "The place ran on fear and intimidation. I should have realized it sooner than I did. No one dared even laugh when they were at administrative meetings unless the boss laughed. I remember I told a joke at the third executive committee meeting that I attended, thinking that it would loosen things up a bit. I said something to the effect of, 'Well, I haven't been here very long but I'm finding out why it's so hard to get our jobs done.' And the boss looked at me and he asked, 'Oh, why's that?' And I replied, 'Well it's hard to do your work when you have to go around with both hands covering your ass.' Well, you could have heard a pin drop. *Not a soul laughed.* That was my first clue about the environment into which I'd stepped. That's why Christ Church became so important to us. It was the total opposite."

Many institutions, unfortunately, are run on fear. Fear creates disconnection, which creates factions, backbiting, conniving, opportunism, and most of the discontents of unhappy organizations.

There is no reason for it to be this way. While all organizations require authority and order, fear as a management tool is the refuge of bullies. Almost everyone has worked for a ruthless boss or had a cruel teacher. From corporate America to professional sports to classrooms, these kinds of leaders may produce good results in the short term, but in the long term they kill organizations and drive away the best people. Bob was driven away, but he came back to a different part of greater Boston, this time to a connected center.

When he was chosen as rector, Bob was overjoyed, because he got the chance to come back to the place where he had felt so welcome. "I never would have thought that would be possible. It was a real gift to me. It's been an opportunity for me to give something back to Christ Church and its people."

Bob's experience in coming to Christ Church seems representative to me of the experience of many people who come there. They come from a place of suffering to a place of connection. Bob puts it well: "I guess why this place is so important to me is that there is a pattern of people taking care of each other, just being there without a lot of public display. A friend of mine came up with the definition of community that I've always liked. He said, 'Community is a place where when there is a crisis or difficulty, the people involved know what to do without having to be asked.' Frequently I see that happen here. There is an awareness of others in all corners of this place. I still find out things that are going on that I didn't know about. People will meet spontaneously, or take care of someone else in the congregation without anyone knowing about it. That just seems to be part of the fabric here."

Bob's being only the fifth rector of Christ Church in this century is highly untypical of Episcopal churches around the country. As he told me, "I have worked as a consultant with other congregations where people attack the leadership, wanting to strike it down. There's a lot of scapegoating. That doesn't happen here."

"Do you know why?" I asked.

"I think it's the tone that has been set through the decades. *It's just not acceptable to do it that way here.* We operate on the belief that we are a community, and that it's not acceptable to divide ourselves. It's just not part of the way things are to be done."

Instead, people help one another out, often, as the saying goes, in mysterious ways. "A few years ago," Bob told me, "there was a young woman who came to help make Advent wreaths. She was at Harvard, and she was graduating. She had just finished her thesis and it was due on Monday. This was Sunday, and she just wanted to do something to help out around church. So she helped the kids make Advent wreaths. She put her backpack outside the door, but when she came back out it was gone. Her thesis was in it, and she had made no copies.

"Before I tell you what happened, I have to give you some background. The first week I was here I wanted to get some rocks out of the rectory garden. I saw this guy hanging around and I told him I would be glad to pay him to do some work in the garden for me. He said, 'I'll do it.' He came back that afternoon, but he was high as a kite. He picked around and said, 'There are rocks in here, that's too hard,' and after a while he was sitting on the porch, not doing anything. I said, 'Paul, that's fine, here's some money, I'll see you later.' He said, 'Well, I haven't finished.' And I said 'That's all right, don't worry about it.' Well, the next morning, Maurine and I were eating breakfast and we saw a head sort of going back and forth outside the kitchen window, and it was Paul. He finished the job beautifully, didn't say a word, and went off.

"Subsequently he did some other things for me. One time he said, 'I would never ask you for any money, I've always worked for it, but now I'm going to ask you for some,' and I asked, 'Why?' He said, 'I'm in charge of the laundry for all the people in Tent City, and I need fifteen dollars in quarters,' so I gave it to him. That was our relationship. We see each other on the street. Sometimes he's sober, and sometimes he's not.

"Well, after this student lost her backpack with her thesis in it, I went down to the square and saw Paul with a friend of his, and I said, 'Paul, I have a problem. There was a backpack that was taken at the church. A young woman had her thesis in there, and it's very important to get it back, so could you just ask around and see if you can help me? We don't care about the backpack, but we do care about the papers in it.' He said, 'I don't know anything about it.' His friend was sort of looking at me funny, and I said, 'I'm just asking for some help.' He was over at Au Bon Pain in the middle of the square. I had just walked over and happened upon him. I asked another guy I knew to help look around too. He went around the neighborhood and actually found *two* backpacks, but neither one of them was the right one. Well, within about three hours the student's actual backpack was returned, and she got her thesis back. I didn't see Paul for a couple of weeks. When he saw me on the street, he said, 'We took care of that one, didn't we?' "

Quite a few Pauls populate Christ Church, people whose usefulness to the community may not be apparent until someone loses a backpack.

Street people find a place in the web of Christ Church, right along with the well-heeled professionals, "and that's a real joy to me," Bob says, "but it scares the hell out of some people. We have two or three every day. They come in and get coffee, and we always keep the coffee pot on for them. Then there's what we call our latrine ministry. Especially this time of year, a lot of young kids that are hanging out in the square come in to use the bathroom and usually clean themselves up a little bit in there. That's not quite what we intend, but that's what happens. I'll come in and see they've used all the paper towels." The latrine ministry started back in the sixties when the protesters could not find bathrooms because Harvard Square shut down.

"We have another guy who comes to church every Sunday and he always comes to Bible study and never says a word, doesn't talk to anybody, but he's always here. Then there's John Lee, who's schizophrenic. John paces, and he tells my son Robert that I don't understand, people are after me, but he's here to protect me. Right now his haunt is over there in front of the fence. Sometimes he comes inside and just sits. Sometimes he's dressed very well, and sometimes he deteriorates, but he sees his role as protecting us. When we renovated this building he was furious with me because we had to shut the building down. This meant he couldn't come in for a while. I would see him on the street and he would say, 'You son of a bitch, you son of a bitch.' He didn't come back for about a year, but then he did come back, after he decided that everything was all right again."

Most everything is all right at Christ Church, as it tries to make life better in a world where so much isn't all right. The church could use more money—it runs on a budget of about $400,000. How it gets as much done as it does on so little amazes me. If some billionaire somewhere would donate the interest he or she earns in one day, or even in one hour, Christ Church would get more mileage out of that money than any institution I can imagine. But until then the church makes miracles out of the bits and pieces it collects from parishioners.

Christ Church has many programs—from feeding the homeless on Thursday nights, to participating in a drive called the Greater Boston Interfaith Organization (GBIO), which aims to marshal the strength of all the faith-based denominations in the Boston area for social good, to supporting Bible study, to the Thursday lunch group of elderly people, and on and on.

These efforts lead somewhere. People get fed. People in despair make contact. Children learn about faith. Harvard Square has a safe haven. Sick people get visited and prayed for. Politicians hear from parishioners about affordable housing. Souls come in for a landing. Goodness gets a plug. And, every day, the doors are open to everyone.

I mentioned GBIO. This is an organization Bob Tobin particularly supports. It is based on the practices and principles of the Industrial Areas Foundation (IAF), which, in the words of Derek Bok, former president of Harvard, offers "the greatest hope we have, by far, for achieving social justice in this country." The IAF and the GBIO operate by bringing people together first, *then* by deciding on which programs to advocate. The key to it all is called the "one-on-one." People meet one on one, just to talk. They find out from each other what their major concerns might be. Then, gradually, they built a network of concerned people, all coming out of one-on-ones. This is truly a bottom up, rather than top down, organization.

In San Antonio, IAF led to the construction of infrastructure— paving of roads, setting up of flood control—where there had been none, at the cost of over a billion dollars. This happened only after the people had been meeting in one-on-ones for an extended period of time. IAF builds connections first.

The method relies on the power of grass-roots connections. For this reason it is no wonder Bob Tobin is so active in the IAF-based GBIO. He has found skeptics in his congregation, however. Around Harvard, after all, people often prefer to discuss policy rather than meet other people. Many prefer the structure of an intellectual debate to the open-ended emotionality of a one-on-one. But GBIO is gaining great strength, and Christ Church has voted to donate 1 percent of its budget to the support of GBIO.

On November 22, 1998, I attended the opening rally in Boston for GBIO. After two years of one-on-ones, the organization was ready at least officially to declare itself alive in greater Boston. The leader of the Catholic Church, Cardinal Law, was there, as were Bishop Shaw, the Episcopal bishop, Jewish leaders, Muslim leaders, and leaders of scores of local churches, parishes and other faith-based organizations around the city. There were people of every color. There were infants and schoolchildren and young adults. There was a steel band, some gospel singers, and a whole lot of energy. Four thousand people packed the Boston College High School auditorium, while an overflow crowd watched next door over closed-circuit TV.

The leaders gave speeches. The members of the audience, like me, sang songs, listened, and did one-on-ones with the people next to us.

What happened at B.C. High that night was best summed up by Bishop Shaw, who said, "I have seen many visions of hell in my life-time. Walking in here tonight, seeing all these different groups coming together, I got a glimpse of the kingdom of God."

Bob Tobin's work at Christ Church and Christ Church's work within its community through GBIO and the many other programs it supports embody the power of connection, not just through faith—indeed, many people who attend Christ Church bring as much doubt to church as they bring faith—but through goodwill and a basic desire to give and receive love.

Most people harbor stores of untapped goodwill. However, this positive energy can go to waste unless they can find a practical way to channel it. Such people—indeed, all of us—need a place, like Christ Church, and a leader, like Bob Tobin, to help us plug it in.

SEVENTEEN

Creating a Connected School

SHADY HILL

DIANE T. SAT sobbing in my office. "Are children just naturally evil?" she asked me through her tears. "Why would they do something like this?" She had come to see me because her son was being teased mercilessly in the fifth grade. In the most recent incident, a group of kids had taken off the boy's pants and underpants and run them up the school flagpole, leaving the boy curled up crying in a corner of the locker room while the kids outside hooted in laughter.

I have heard many similar stories. Kids can, indeed, be horribly cruel. Usually for no good reason. The only reason this little boy was being teased was that he was different. He hadn't done anything wrong, like tell on someone or provoke one of the leaders in the class. His only sin was that he existed.

Some schools and parents respond to this kind of behavior with a sort of law-of-the-jungle shrug. "What can we do?" they protest. "Children can be cruel."

But other parents and other schools take a stand. They say, "No. We will not tolerate such behavior. It is our job, as adults, to create a culture that constantly opposes cruelty."

But then these parents and schools must wonder *how*. How can they instill the values of cooperation, respect for all people, mutual empathy, and concern for community if their children are growing up in such a competitive, aggressive society? Sometimes they wonder if they *should* instill such values, fearing the child might turn out too weak. Parents and schools often feel torn between a desire to give their children a competitive edge and a desire to make sure their children grow up to be decent people.

This is a false dilemma. Parents and schools should unite against cruelty in any form. One of the great myths that should be erased from the annals of parenting is that you have to be mean to succeed. The study I did at Exeter showed that nice guys win, as have many other studies. Just look around at successful people in all walks of life. Not many stand out as being cruel.

In fact, one of the best ways to insure happiness and success in life is to teach your child to respect the rights of others, and emphasize the practices and values of connection—like empathy, sharing, and tolerance.

The practical question then becomes *how to do it.* How can we create a connected childhood for our kids, how can we promote the values of connection in a disconnected world? One of the best ways to do this (if you can choose your school) is to choose your school wisely. Next to families, schools offer the most powerful training grounds for children that we have.

Far from creating namby-pambies, the values and practices of connection create strong citizens who will stand up for what is right, instead of just what works best for them. These values create children who say, no, we will not humiliate that kid by running his pants and underpants up the flagpole.

Some schools are good at creating such a culture, some are not. I will describe one school that excels at it. It is a school I know well, the Shady Hill School in Cambridge, Massachusetts, which my children attend.

Shady Hill has created a connected community. As a specialist in learning, I visit many schools around the country, so I have wide grounds of comparison. Even before my children started attending Shady Hill, I admired the school. Now that my children go there, I love the school. Lucy is in fourth grade and Jack is in a combined first-and-second grade (what Shady Hill calls *mixed group*). Lucy started in prekindergarten (what Shady Hill calls *beginners*). What I have learned up close about the school in the six years my children have attended has only confirmed the best of what I had imagined I would find.

Let me try to describe what the school does.

There is an explicit belief at Shady Hill in the power of connection. From the head of the school—he is called the director—down to the man who delivers the milk and snacks to the lower school, everyone on the staff goes out of their way to do the little things that count. They smile and say hello. They make time for everyone. They answer questions directly. They are polite. They practice what they preach.

And what they preach can be summed up in one word. This one word was the only rule in Lucy's kindergarten class, and it was written in big red block letters on a poster in the classroom. The one word is RESPECT. Everything at Shady Hill comes back to respect. "Is that a respectful way to treat your classmate?" a teacher will ask, or, "Is that a respectful way to treat the environment?" Whenever a disrespectful act is done, it gets noticed and talked about. The children quickly pick up what's expected.

At circle time in kindergarten, the kids have discussions on what being respectful means. For example, they talk about respectful ways to solve problems, the right and the wrong way to resolve differences.

Lucy was in kindergarten when I learned about respect firsthand one morning. I was rushing to get out of the house to go to the airport when Sue asked me if I could help Lucy get dressed before I left. Lucy was then, and still can be, a first-class dawdler when it comes to getting dressed in the morning. "Lucy," I said emphatically, "please get dressed."

"I don't want to get dressed," she said.

"Lucy, I really need for you to get dressed right now. I don't have time to play games," I said sternly.

"I don't want to get dressed," she repeated.

"Lucy, you must get dressed right now," I insisted.

"I don't want to get dressed," she reiterated.

"Lucy," I said in desperation, "if you get dressed right now, I'll bring you a big present when I come home from this trip."

"Daddy," she said, looking me squarely in the eye, "that is not the right way to solve this problem!"

Respect. The right way to solve a problem. This is what she was learning at circle time. And she was starting to teach me!

By the way, she did get dressed. We both started laughing so hard when she told me my method was improper that the laughter seemed to break her stubbornness. She got dressed, and I caught my plane.

The school takes this ethic of respect seriously and applies it to all aspects of school life.

For example, Lucy has a learning difference. She inherited from me both my dyslexia and my attention deficit disorder. When it became apparent she was not learning to read as quickly as the other kids, the school handled the issue beautifully, talking to Sue and me about it, allaying our fears, and setting Lucy up with a tutor in a way that minimized Lucy's feeling of embarrassment. Lucy is now reading at grade level and doing well. For many kids in other settings, the problem is handled quite differently, which leaves the child feeling stupid, hating school.

Although the school is private, it has an extensive scholarship program. The pickup line each afternoon has its share of Land Rovers, Volvos, and Mercedeses, but there are inexpensive cars, too. Racial and economic diversity continue to grow at Shady Hill, as the school puts a priority on creating a student body from many different backgrounds.

This is not done out of a holier-than-thou, politically correct attitude. Shady Hill's diversity is built on an honest conviction that children do better the more varied their peers are. It works. The kids at Shady Hill are growing up without the prejudices that many of their parents still harbor today.

I asked Bruce Shaw, the current director of Shady Hill, to talk to me about connection, how he sees the issue in the world today, and how the school manages to create such a caring, connected world for children. Bruce, a young-looking, extremely affable man, has been teaching for thirty-one years. He has been director of Shady Hill for five.

Bruce smiled as (I knew) he warmed to the task. "For me at Shady Hill, connectedness is really a deliberate thing. It's something that our whole faculty pays tremendous attention to and sees as an extremely high priority. That word doesn't get used often, connectedness, but the idea lies behind everything we do."

"What are the words you use?" I asked.

"Relationship, a respectful community, a community that values multiple perspectives and diversity. All of those concepts kind of get lumped in my mind with connectedness. It is always in our minds."

One practical way the school does this is the grade head system. Each grade has a grade head, one teacher who understands both the academic profile of each child and his or her social issues and concerns. Each grade has an assistant and/or an intern as well, and they also know the kids in depth. As usual, the feeling of connection begins in the human moment, and these teachers spend most of their time in human moments with the kids. Small groups learning together.

Having a grade head is like having a parent at school. The grade head does much more than teach. She watches over her brood, looking out for signs of trouble, as well as noticing signs of strength. Shady Hill is a school where competence is developed more through encouragement than through correction.

When you meet with the grade head, which parents do at least twice a year in formal conferences, and can do as often as they like, you are talking to an expert on your child, but also someone who likes your child.

As problems come up, the grade head anticipates the next development. For example, in the fourth grade there was a problem of certain girls excluding certain other girls. This goes contrary to Shady Hill's ethic of including everyone, excluding no one.

The grade head began by alerting the parents who were not aware of what was going on, and reassuring the other parents who were upset by what was going on. He suggested both parents and he try to speak to the girls individually, seeing if they could be encouraged to empathize with the girls whose feelings were getting hurt.

This helped a little, but it didn't turn the tide completely. So the grade head made some structural changes in the composition of special classes, like art and music, and the school set up a series of group meetings, called "girls' talk." These groups of four girls each were led by the school psychologist. Their purpose was to talk about social issues, what it was like to be someone's friend, how you could manage having several friends at once, and other topics relevant to fourth-grade girls.

Gradually, the trend of excluding began to subside. While Shady Hill cannot change human nature, it recognizes that adults do have much more control than they think, if they will just use it.

Implementing this philosophy depends upon having a grade head who has a close relationship with the children in the class.

In addition to the grade head system, the school is set up physically to foster a sense of connection and belonging. Each grade has its own little building, or half of a building. These buildings are simple. They are all painted gray, and they sort of look like army barracks. There is nothing fancy about the architecture or landscaping at Shady Hill. But there is great warmth.

Each child starts the day going to his or her own building. There they store their books, store their clothes, and have most of their classes. Recess operates from there, and it is from there that they leave at the end of the day.

The end of the day involves another simple but important practice at Shady Hill. Each child shakes hands with the grade head before leaving for home. Not only the little kids, but even the eighth-graders do this. Bruce Shaw said to me, "We think the eighth-graders need that as much as eight-year-olds do in third grade. We think that doing anything less would be to drift away from what kids, including young adolescents, absolutely need in order to grow tall and straight and true. We also see that kids learn the three Rs better in communities than when they're not in communities."

Children do indeed learn the three Rs at Shady Hill. They do not learn just compassion and connection. They learn to think. The math program at Shady Hill is one of the most advanced and innovative in the country. Academic rigor thrives at this school; what is exceptional is that it is induced by pleasure, not by pain.

Central subject is one of Shady Hill's best-known innovations. I asked Bruce to comment on it. "Starting in third grade," he explained, "our students begin a long-term study of one subject each year. For example, fourth grade, where your daughter is going next year, is all about ancient Greece. Lucy will be in the fifth century B.C. The kids spend the entire year absorbed in the history and mythology and the art and the poetry of that era. They will know it inside and out when they are finished. And it will relate to them. We found that that particular subject works really well with nine- and ten-year-olds because they're thinking about their identity.

They're thinking about their social life or they're thinking about who their heroes are, and what being an adult means, and what are the gods.

"Plus, when they leave, they've developed an expertise. They really know something about ancient Greece. Lucy will know more about ancient Greece than you do, and more than most adults do. When she's thirty-five, because of the in-depth study, she'll still have a lot of that in her grasp, as opposed to me, who can't remember my fourth-grade teacher or what I studied. It's gone, obliterated from my memory at this point. But I've never met any Shady Hill alum who doesn't remember extensive details about what they studied as a fourth-grader here."

"So the whole message is to go in depth?" I asked.

"In depth, and *slow*," he emphasized.

"Sounds like the opposite of modern life," I said.

"I guess it is," Bruce replied. "The school also has a belief in material simplicity. That's a really hard one. Even these new buildings are going to be simple."

"All the buildings here are humble buildings," I said.

"Material simplicity is important," Bruce added. "The school doesn't have uniforms, which cuts both ways. Some people think that uniforms are a great equalizer, and others think that they don't in fact do that. But we really don't have much of a dress code beyond neat and clean. It doesn't look like going into a suburban school, where you see a little bit of dress one-upsmanship going on."

"How do you discourage that sort of thing?" I asked. "Some of the kids here come from very wealthy families, while some have very little money. What about bragging about vacations and things like that?"

"We discourage it in a number of active ways," Bruce replied. "For example, our faculty is trained not to come in on the day that school restarts in September, January, or April, and say, 'Where did you all go?' We don't discourage that conversation, but we don't encourage it as part of the group. The school has a comprehensive tuition so that paper, pencils, books, erasers, and colored pencils that every child gets is part of the tuition. They all get the same things. The interior of the buildings is furnished with everybody's cast-off couches and rugs, and that's just fine, because what it really says is, what counts is comfort, as opposed to having to make my classroom look better than your classroom.

"Last year we had a couple of sessions for parents on economic diversity. The school is going to follow that up. We are actively trying to look at what it means, knowing that we have very, very wealthy people here as well as people who are very poor. We know it means something. It's stupid to pretend that economics don't play a huge part in who a child is. But on the other hand, what doesn't it mean? How do you not label people in that way?"

"Do you find the kids of the poorer parents in any way feeling stigmatized?" I asked.

"Some do. I have talked to some parents who feel that way. People bring different things into the school. People have objected to the number of evening meetings here at the school. Because there is no child care, it's really impossible for them to attend. They just can't afford to go out night after night and come to a meeting here. Those are very real issues, and I think they deserve the school's attention."

I was getting ready to say good-bye to Bruce, but I asked one more question: "If my thesis is right and we're living in a more disconnected world, do you feel a very connected school like this is being asked to fill a bottomless pit? Do you feel parents are looking for the school to do more than it can?"

"Absolutely," Bruce replied. "The result of that is that the hurried parent who drops off the hurried child is now dropping him or her off into the hurried school."

"How do you solve the problem?" I asked.

"I think it's really very difficult. It's very hard to combat. Central subject is an academic way of combating it. The grade head system is kind of a social-emotional way of combating it. The ethic of material simplicity is a way of combating it. But it is so pervasive in society—we're all hurried, we're all a little tense and on edge. It's quite complicated."

"As you look at Shady Hill down the years, do you feel optimistic?" I asked. "Do you feel that the connection theme is something that can be preserved?"

"I think that it has to. I think the school has a role to play in feeding the child's soul as well as feeding their head. And I'm not quite sure how to take that on in school. Particularly in a secular school."

"But you take it on just by raising the question," I said. "Just by saying you think it matters and you're not quite sure what to do, that begins to solve the problem, don't you think?"

"Perhaps. I hope so. But you never know."

Bruce and I said good-bye.

Shady Hill has taught me a lot about the practical application of the principles of connection I believe in so deeply. While I can prove their benefit from scientific studies, as well as my own direct observation, sometimes I have wondered, along with Diane T., the mom whose son's clothes had been run up the flagpole, *Are some people just evil? Can they be taught to be kind?*

I have seen at Shady Hill—and at other schools—that children and adults alike will respond to the culture they live in. If you create a school culture that insists upon respect, people will gradually start to treat one another with respect. Similarly, if you create a family culture that insists upon respect, the same will happen at home.

People—both children and grown-ups—will be bad now and then. But in a connected culture, we are all much less prone to being bad.

The methods Shady Hill uses do work. The kids usually do practice what the school preaches. I think the methods and ideals of Shady Hill could be implemented at any school, as long as the average class size is small. If towns and cities commit to reducing class size by hiring more teachers and creating more space, they can give their children a connected education, and all the benefits that go with it. As long as you have small classes, you can have connection. And as long as you have connection, the chances are good you will have moral and spiritual growth, as well as the best education possible.

EIGHTEEN

Mission amid the Rubble

ONE CONNECTED INSTITUTION

DR. KEN DUCKWORTH is a man with a mission working in a place with a need. Fired up by his sense of purpose, he has helped maintain an invisible web of connection within one of the most understaffed and underfunded of institutions in any state: a state mental hospital.

Ken is six feet five inches tall. He is movie-star handsome. He could have any number of high-paying consultant jobs. But he chooses to follow his heart, and to fuel the connections within the hospital where he was trained, the Massachusetts Mental Health Center.

Ken is now on a campaign not only to improve the treatment patients receive at state institutions but also to teach young doctors how to care for the chronically mentally ill. He is also working on a national basis to dispel the stigma against mental illness that prevents many millions of people from receiving the treatment they need.

While I could have selected other institutions to demonstrate the power of connection, I chose Mass. Mental and Ken Duckworth because the odds against both have been so great. Mass. Mental, founded in 1912, has grown up without money, and Ken Duckworth, born in 1959, has overcome testicular cancer.

But both Mass. Mental and Ken Duckworth have thrived on the

power of connection. Ironically enough, there are few places where you can see more vividly the positive effect of human connections than on a good psychiatric inpatient unit. Most people are familiar with mental hospitals only in terms of lurid stories of "snake pits," or horrifying accounts of so-called back wards written up in journalistic exposés, or tales from Bedlam, the infamous English insane asylum, or images of the nasty Nurse Ratchett from the movie *One Flew over the Cuckoo's Nest*. While the horror did exist, and does go on today in some poorly run hospitals, in other hospitals you can find some of the most dedicated professionals and effective treatments in modern medicine.

We do not customarily think of a human relationship as a form of medical treatment. Medical treatment normally refers to medications, operations, changes in diet, radiation, or some other sort of physical or mechanical manipulation of the body. Even treatment of the mind, so long dominated by psychoanalytic thinking and the "talking cure," now has yielded to more physically oriented kinds of interventions, especially medications.

However, a human relationship can heal a sick mind. It happens every day.

I have spent a long time on psychiatric inpatient units, treating both adults and children, mostly in the public sector, where the craziest patients sooner or later end up. Rumor has it that the worst abuses occur in state hospitals—bad treatment by bad staff. However, I have seen over and over again that these state hospitals attract devoted professionals, angels in disguise, who give their whole heart to the treatment of their patients.

The Massachusetts Mental Health Center, in Boston—a state hospital treating the sickest of the indigent population, long regarded as one of the premier teaching hospitals for psychiatry in the country, affiliated with both the state of Massachusetts and the Harvard Medical School—introduced me as a professional to the world of mental illness. It used to be called the Boston Psychopathic Hospital, or just the Psycho, for short. It was where I treated Mr. S, whom I described in Chapter 3.

It was also where I met Ken Duckworth. He was my student when he was a first-year resident. We both loved professional baseball. I liked him right away when he informed me in one of our first meetings that Mass. Mental and Fenway Park, home of the Red Sox, were both built in the same year, 1912.

The Psycho, or what is now called Mass. Mental, was a laboratory of connection for both Ken and me. "The patient is the best textbook," one of the great teachers at Mass. Mental, Dr. Elvin Semrad, used to say. I remember Semrad's various aphorisms to this day: "Psychosis is the mind's last defense against unbearable feelings." "Trust your heart and rely on it." "Idealize no one; everyone's bad in part." "The therapist's job is to help the patient acknowledge, bear, and put into perspective painful feelings." "Everyone is either mad, sad, or afraid." The heart of Semrad's message was just that: the heart. "Love brings them to us," he said of patients seeking help, "and love sends them away." Stay with the patient, he taught, and above all stay with the feelings. Look for emotion, because it is emotion that makes us who we are.

When Ken entered the broken-down corridors of Mass. Mental and found that his only command was to "sit with the patient," he felt as if he had at last found his way out of a maze. He and I would sit and discuss his various patients in our teaching sessions, called supervision. Ken and I connected instantly because of a similarity in style.

I remember warning Ken: however much he started to love this dirty place and the great work being done here, he should know that bad things would happen. I told him about Justin. "He was a patient I knew only when I was on call at night, because he was on a different ward from the one I worked on. However, when I was on call I had to make rounds throughout the whole hospital, which would bring me into contact with Justin. Justin was a wise guy with a brilliant mind. He would insult me whenever he saw me, but he always did it in a way that made me want to stay and talk.

" 'Hey, Doctuh Hellwell,' he'd say in his New York accent, 'saved any minds today? You making rounds, or are you rookies still making squares?'

" 'Nice to see you, Justin,' I would reply.

" 'No, it's not. You think I'm a pain in the ass,' he'd snap back. 'It's OK to tell me I'm a pain in the ass. I'll like you better if you do. At least I'll know you're honest. I know I'm a pain in the ass. It's my shtick.'

" 'But Justin,' I'd object, 'I like you, and I don't like a pain in the ass.'

" 'Oh, Doc,' he'd protest, 'you like me—don't tell me that. Now you're gonna put me into homosexual panic.'

" 'Sorry, Justin,' I'd say.

" 'It's OK, Doc,' he'd reply. 'You're still learning. We have time.'

"Or I'd come by late at night and he'd be sitting up on a windowsill, leaning against the cage-covered glass. 'Hey, Doc, you're late tonight. Whatcha been doin', watchin' TV? Don't you know you got crazy people to look aftuh? Don't we rate?' Pause. 'You're supposed to tell me to get down out of this windowsill, you know.'

" 'You took the words out of my mouth,' I'd say.

" 'No, Doc,' he'd quickly reply, 'don't do what I tell you to do. You're supposed to make me think *you're* in control. If I think *I* control *you*, that makes me more crazy. Read my chart. It's all in there.'

"Justin and I sparred with each other like this every time I was on call. I looked forward to making rounds so I could kid around with him. I knew he was crazy most of the time, but whenever I saw him I learned something. He was so smart, and he was only thirty-eight. I hoped he'd leave the hospital and get a job, but he had tried to do that and failed many times before. He always ended up coming back. He was trying to learn to get it right, but life was very hard for him to do. 'When I get out there, I take a shellacking from the voices,' he once told me. The voices were his auditory hallucinations, of course.

"One night on rounds I found Justin on the floor in his room. He was dead. We did CPR and packed him off to the Brigham, where they did CPR some more and injected him with lots of medicines, but he stayed dead. An autopsy was inconclusive; the best guess was that he died because of a fatal arrhythmia.

"I felt awful about Justin," I said to Ken. "I still do. He was only a crazy pauper, why should I care? Most of the world certainly didn't care. But, of course, I had grown attached to Justin, as everyone else who spent any time with him also did. He was just a nut with a wise-guy shtick, a man who contributed nothing to society, and in fact cost it money. So why is it, twenty years later, that I remember him so well and respect him so much?"

Ken smiled, as if he already knew. But I explained, anyway.

"Because, to me, Justin was like a prophet out of the Old Testament. He was always calling me down, telling me to watch out, to cut the B.S. He was telling me to shape up, to learn my job, to study him well. Basically, he offered me himself—exposed, naked, a mess—and asked nothing in return but that I learn from him. If he couldn't make it in the outside world, he wanted me to learn about him while he was inside so I could help the next guy like him that came along."

I learned to "sit with" patients like Justin as the first line of therapy, and I tried to pass this skill on to Ken and others, as the tradition continued.

It was strange that so many of us, like Ken and me, should find such a deep connection in such a dump. After four years of medical school and a year of a medical internship, we came to this broken-down old hospital with no physical supports at all. The building was a shambles. There was not enough of anything, from food to toilet paper. Windows were grimy; the one in the on-call room had a bullet hole in it. Some lights had no shades, some shades had no lights. It was not like a hospital: no one wore white coats or carried stethoscopes, and there was no smell of antiseptic, or patients being wheeled around on gurneys. It was more like an old flea-bag hotel from 1912 that had never been maintained or upgraded.

And yet, and yet . . . It is hard to describe how inspired we were by the place, the people who worked there, the faculty, the patients, the history. In its glory days, the Psycho became the premier psychiatric teaching hospital in the country, one of the crown jewels in the Harvard crown of teaching hospitals. But some years prior to my arriving there, the hospital had fallen on hard times due to the state's withdrawing much of its financial support. Still, it remained a superb place to learn psychiatry.

I remember on my first day there the head nurse, Linda Nanni-celli, asked me to go meet a patient in the library. I asked her where the library was, eager to find a room full of books amid all this squalor. She pointed me down the corridor. What the library turned out to be was a little room that had one shelf of tattered paperbacks, donated by some ex-patient who didn't want to take his books with him when he was discharged. *"This is the library?"* I exclaimed to Linda, who had followed me down the corridor.

"Welcome to Mass. Mental," she said with a laugh. Finding out what the library really was made me sad and embarrassed for the place, but it also inspired me. How marvelous it was, I thought to myself, to have no library—but still have one. Sort of a make-believe library, a minimalist library, a delusional library. They don't have a library on this ward at Mass. Mental, so a patient bequeaths one by leaving a few ratty old paperbacks. The next thing you know, a grubby little room and those old paperbacks combine to form Mass. Mental's version of the Library of Congress. Creative. Make the best of what you've got. I was beginning to learn.

That inspiration only grew throughout my days at Mass. Mental and through my days on the teaching faculty there, right up until I left, in the early 1990s. The whole place is a library without books, a sham, a monument to the impossible, a tribute to hope and prayer, where patients in pain meet a dedicated staff and turn an empty room with a few paperbacks into a library.

Mass. Mental is built on connection. There is every reason this hospital should fail. The patients are as sick as you can get, the frontline doctors are just out of medical school and have no experience, the place is ridiculously underfunded and undersupplied, and there is little public support. The place works *only* because of the connection to the patient, and to an ideal.

When I met Ken, I knew I had just a few more years left there. I knew I would soon move on. There were other things I wanted to do. And there were so many prettier places to work! I was getting tired of the new kind of institutional psychiatry, with its emphasis on paperwork, staving off lawsuits, and rapid diagnosis and medication. Working with Ken made my leaving easier, as he took the ideas I had received and developed and ran with them. He developed them better than I ever had. He is now the clinical director of the hospital.

The Psycho—Mass. Mental—is still where it always was, at 74 Fenwood Road in Boston, a few blocks away from Brigham and Women's Hospital and Harvard Medical School. However, times in medicine have changed drastically from when I was a resident. While I could treat a patient for a year as an inpatient, or while a patient like Justin or Mr. S could stay at Mass. Mental for a long time, now patients are forced out quickly.

But it is still a laboratory of connection for those who want to learn. I have been away from the hospital for five years now, but Ken tells me the hospital still runs on connection.

"There's something very beautiful about the mission of it all," he said to me, "the whole idea of it, the whole thing. I think that's why I've stayed there eleven years now. When I got to Mass. Mental, I realized this was it. This is where I can be who I am and grow as a doctor. Now, I keep looking for jobs because I need a school system for my children and Boston doesn't have the greatest school system. But when I'm recruited for jobs, I keep turning them down. The reason is that I love Mass. Mental, I love the patients, I love the whole idea of working with really sick people in an environment where curiosity is welcomed. And I haven't found a place like it yet.

"The thing is, you have to keep a long-term view with the folks we treat at Mass. Mental," Ken went on. "Managed care has failed to appreciate that people who are paranoid take time to trust people. So you might spend a year talking about the weather. You might spend a year talking about baseball. You might spend a year talking about the CIA. Well, you just have to say to yourself, Let's hear what this guy says about the CIA. These people don't come in and say, 'I'm suffering, help me. I want to talk about my pain about being alone and isolated. Help me find a few people to count on. Help me to learn to get along with people.' This isn't how it goes. Most people start to talk only when they feel safe. They talk about their difficulties maintaining a relationship. Their sorrow about not having children. Or if they've had children, the heartbreaking fact that they lost their children because of their illness.

"We treat a very severe group of patients. They usually aren't able to keep their own children. The pain is staggering. It's interesting, though; we've also seen a few weddings of patients from Mass. Mental. Beautiful weddings. A woman who has gotten sober and is on clozapine meets a man who is trying to get sober and is on clozapine. People meet each other and love each other and stick together. Remember, these people have serious mental illnesses, like schizophrenia. We had a woman die not too long ago of cancer after she had married one of the other patients. Her memorial service was absolutely beautiful. The number of lives she had touched, all in the last three or four years of her life. She wasn't on clozapine. She improved just through talking out issues with her therapist. She figured out how to be with other people. It was a very sad day when she died, but it was a beautiful memorial service. The number of people who turned out was amazing. I found myself wondering, Is this really an illness of disconnection? Probably not, if you have the right medications, or the right therapist, or a place to stay. With somebody to love, even the most severely afflicted can make it. And we see that time and again. Very interesting."

Ken Duckworth still entertains offers to leave Mass. Mental. One day, no doubt, he will depart. But what he's left behind will never leave.

Mass. Mental teaches one main lesson: Only connect. Be with your patient. Be with your friend. Whatever state your patient (or friend) is in, go there. That is the simple lesson they still teach at Mass. Mental, the old Psycho.

~~~~

NINETEEN

Finding Your God

CONNECTING TO WHAT IS BEYOND

WE ALL HAVE our own connection with what is beyond knowledge, whether it be to a being we call God, or to nature, or to the cosmos, or to a higher Power. It is a connection—or disconnection—that we feel in our own private ways.

I offer my experience now as an example of one kind of connection to whatever is beyond.

I don't mean to suggest that my way is *the* way. That kind of my-way-is-the-only-way thinking has ruined religion for many people. The sins that have been committed in the name of God throughout human history have caused many people to give up on organized religion altogether and to consider it an evil institution.

My plea is that you keep your hearts and minds open. My hope is that you still allow yourself to yearn for, seek, and find a connection to what is beyond. It doesn't matter if you use the word "God." It doesn't matter what belief system you subscribe to, or even if you have a belief system at all. What matters is that you try, on a regular basis, to reach out to what is beyond.

You can do this by taking a walk in the woods with your dog. You can do this by sitting outside and looking up at the stars. You can do this by looking into a fire.

You can say a simple prayer: "Please, God, come into my life." Or you can pray for someone you love: "Please, God, help my daughter." Even if you do not know what you are praying to, you can still pray.

Doing this is good for you. Praying, meditating, reflecting—call it what you will—helps your body and mind. Studies show that people who attend religious services regularly live longer. Studies also show that in the prayerful or meditative state human physiology actually changes. These changes, induced regularly, lead to improved health, enhanced well-being, and longer life.

You do not have to join a religion to make a connection to what is beyond. You can ponder a question like "What happens after we die?" or "Why is there evil?" like a child looking at a Rembrandt for the first time. What do you see? Nothing? Well, that is a starting point. You must trust your own responses and not fake a response. All that matters is that you keep looking and keep responding. That is how a connection grows. It happens as naturally as the day breaking, as long as you keep looking.

We each develop our relationship to what is beyond in our own way. It is important that your way be yours, honest and heartfelt. You may use a guide, as many people do—a priest, or the Bible, or the Koran. But you may also do it alone. God, or the higher power, would never ask you to be intellectually dishonest. All I am urging is that you not ignore this connection, the connection to what is beyond knowledge, out of a feeling that you don't know how to find it or what to do with it.

If you open yourself up to the beyond on a regular basis, a connection *will grow.* It is like going to the exercise club. You need to exercise your spiritual life for growth to occur. Pray every day, or meditate, or simply take time to reflect. It is at least as important as physical exercise or a proper diet. You need to feed your soul.

You should find your own way of doing this. Mine is very much an emotional relationship with what is beyond, rather than a cerebral one. I *feel*—and have felt since I was a child, listening to my mother tell me that God was everywhere—that a spirit surrounds us. I feel there *must* be a God. "Jesus loves me, this I know," the song says, and I do feel that love, but only when I let myself feel it. I have to pause and reflect for the feeling to find me. Stuck in traffic, I do not feel the love of God unless I remind myself of God. Stuck in sadness, I do not feel the love of God unless I remind myself of God. My awareness of God's love does not beat within me as automatically as my heart does, nor does it come as naturally as my breathing. I have to open up and let it in. *Then,* I feel it. But if I don't pray or reflect, I could go for days, years, probably the rest of my life without feeling the love of God. In my personal experience, God's messengers do not break down my door. I have to open the doors myself.

However, if I do open up, I feel a response. Call me crazy, as some of my friends do when I tell them how I feel about God, but I feel that the spirit, which I call God, is always near us, trying to connect.

I sense that God is just on the other side of what we can see. God is on the other side of time, the other side of the edge of infinity. I use a visual model to explain this to myself. I imagine that the cosmos is a big bubble, and God lives outside it, signaling us the best God can.

I think God is *hoping* we'll get the message. The message has been sent to us in many different forms. The message I have received is the one sent in the Bible.

It is a message of love. People have complicated it, but at heart it is simple: *"Thou shalt love the Lord thy God with all thy heart, and with all thy soul, and with all thy mind. This is the first and great commandment. And the second is like unto it, Thou shalt love thy neighbor as thyself. On these two commandments hang all the law and the prophets."* That's it. Love God and love your neighbor. And always keep in mind that God loves you. This is what I read in the Bible.

Then there are the promises we Christians believe in, or try to. When I feel insecure, worried, or sad, I try to remember God's promise: *"Trust in the Lord with all thine heart; and lean not unto thine own understanding. In all thy ways acknowledge him, and he shall direct thy paths."* God promises us not only guidance, but eternal life. That is the big one. All sadness in life, it seems to me, comes from connections being broken in one way or another. The promise that we will never become completely disconnected—we'll never die—is the best news possible. If *that's* true . . .

If that's true, then it means I will never totally lose touch with my daughter, Lucy, or my sons, Jack and Tucker, or my wife, Sue. I will see my mother and father again, and my grandparents and uncles and aunts, and one day my children will meet them, too. I will always keep contact with my cousins, Lyn and Tom and Jamie, and my nephews, Tim and Jake and Ned, and my nieces, Anna and Molly, and my brothers, Ben and John, and my in-laws, Bill and Pat and Terry and Louann and Christopher, and my friends Jon and Susan and Peter and Phyllis and John and Michael and Ken and Mary and Alex and Jeff and Jennifer and Bart and Terry and Theresa and Paul and Susan and Sharon and all their children. Name the names.

Even as I write those words, I feel the part of me that is trained to doubt recoil, as if it were all just wishful thinking. "The idea of God is stupid," I remember a smart man saying to me. "I can't believe it when I see people filing into church. It is comical, like a big group delusion. Don't they know they're just inventing God out of desperation? It is pathetic if you ask me."

But then I feel something telling me that it's true, it's all true, and I believe that this is the voice of God, outside the bubble, urging me not to turn away. *It's true,* the voice says, *it's really true. I'm here for you all the time.*

Pathetic delusion, opiate of the masses—or truth?

I feel that the more I pray and the more I listen to that silent voice, the truer the voice becomes. How do I know it is not just my wish, or a self-fulfilling prophecy? How do I know I'm not kidding myself? I don't. There is no proof. I have treated many schizophrenic patients who told me God was talking to them, and I categorized their reports as *auditory hallucinations.* How do I know mine are any different? I don't. I just feel a force telling me they're not. To not believe, I would have to resist that force. To believe, I have to resist doubt. I feel the stronger pull toward belief.

I imagine God is outside the bubble rooting us on, the way we might root a character on in a movie who was facing a big decision, and we knew which decision would be the best one. I imagine God urging, as we in the audience might urge the movie character, *Don't give up now, you're almost there.* I imagine God beaming us hope. *Go with it, I'm here. Reach out to me, I will respond.*

Or as Yogi Berra said, "When you come to a fork in the road, take it."

My evidence for taking the fork toward faith is, as I said, emotional evidence. I *feel* God must be there, otherwise life makes no sense. It is a mean joke. George Wald, my old biology teacher at

Harvard and a Nobel Prize winner, gave a famous lecture every year in his introductory biology course. The title of the lecture was "The Meaning of Life." Professor Wald told us that as far as nature is concerned, we are here to pass along our germ cell before our soma, or body, gets destroyed. In other words, the meaning of life is the perpetuation of life. Nature's purpose in putting us here is to have us propagate. That's it. Nothing more.

I have listened to many others whom I respect as much as I respected George Wald tell me that religious faith is simply a balm, a drug for the soul. The cold, hard facts, these people tell me, support nothing more than blackness after death. Life *is*, and death *is*, and that's *it*.

But the voice I hear when I pray tells me otherwise. I hear God saying, *You don't have all the facts yet. Don't turn away from me just because you can't argue your way back to me.*

I heed that voice because it rings true. It rings truer than the cold, hard view. Love wins out. Who knows? Maybe I'm just a sucker for happy endings.

I have had a lot of sadness in my life, and I'm sure there's more to come. Death, illness, defeat. I need God. I need to believe that God is out there, loving us, waiting for us, for all this sadness and suffering to make sense.

But I don't think my needing God means there is no God, as some people suggest. I need food and oxygen, too, and we all agree they exist. Of course, we can see and measure them. We can neither see nor measure God.

And yet, I feel the vibes from the other side of the bubble. They feel real.

But then you hit the question of evil. How can you feel connected to God in a world bursting with pain? Why does God allow so many bad things to happen? My answer is, *I don't know.*

Ever since I was a little boy praying at the makeshift altar I set up in my third-floor bedroom in Charleston, I have been hoping against hope that God was out there, listening, watching, loving, protecting. Ever since I was a little boy I have looked to God. In high school and college I went through a period of agnosticism, spurred by my discovery of rational debate and science. Then I started to come back to belief, not out of any reasoned argument but because I felt in my heart that God, outside the bubble, was calling to me.

I can hear that call now. How do I know it is not just in my imagination? I don't. But I *feel* the warmth of God, as strongly as I feel the sun even when my back is turned to it.

There is an old joke about a man whose town gets flooded. The man goes up on his roof and waits for God to save him. A rowboat comes by and offers to take the man, but the man says no, he is waiting for God. A second rowboat comes by and offers to take him, but again the man says no, he is waiting for God to save him. With the water sloshing around his neck, the man declines yet a third offer of help from a third rowboat. A few minutes later, the man drowns. When he gets to heaven he asks God why God didn't save him. God replies, "What more could I do? I sent three rowboats."

I see rowboats everywhere. All the different connections we make are like God's rowboats. All we have to do is get in.

~~~

TWENTY

A Good Place for You to Grow

YOUR CONNECTION TO YOURSELF,

PART I

A GOOD WAY TO assess your connection to yourself is to ask yourself, *Do I provide a good place for me to grow?* Like a gardener, do you make sure the soil is fertile and the sunshine bright where you've planted yourself? Do you put burlap bags over yourself in times of frost, and do you find extra water in times of drought? Do you prune and cut back when you should, and do you try to keep pests from nibbling at your leaves?

Two of the greatest writers of all time, William Shakespeare and Joseph Conrad, gave succinct advice on how best to tend to this connection. Shakespeare's advice is the more famous: "To thine own self, be true," Polonius said in Hamlet. Conrad's advice, less well known, is equally apt: "To thine own self," he wrote, "be *enough*."

In America today—and perhaps anywhere, anytime—it is hard not to get tempted into making bargains with the devil. It is hard not to betray yourself, and it is hard to be enough to yourself. We all feel the pressure to *get* more instead of learning how to *be* enough.

The verb of the connection to yourself is the verb "to be," not a verb like "to get." *Be* true to yourself, *be* enough to yourself. This is the way to a good connection to yourself. Such a connection, however, requires daily maintenance, or, like a garden, daily tending. You have to tend to how you are, lest you become someone you do not want to be. How easy in a moment of temptation is it for us to betray our deepest values, or in a moment of greed to feel we must have more?

One of the best uses people make of me as a psychotherapist, I believe, is when they bring in dilemmas of self-disconnection. This is when they come into my office upset at the prospect of a decision they *sense* might lead them astray, astray from being who they really want to be.

For example, I'll never forget a scion in real estate saying to me, "I need your help because I know that whatever project I do next will consume me for ten years. I know I will succeed at it, but I want to make sure when I am done I know in my heart that this was the project I should have taken on." He wanted me to help him reflect on his decision in advance, to make sure that his work would be in keeping with what he believed in, with his image of who he should be.

I did this by allowing him to slow down enough to review his own thinking out loud. He had done the real work just by coming to see me. When he sensed that he might be going too fast, that he was at risk of making a big decision too quickly, one that he would have to live with for a long time, he put on the brakes. All I did was hold him still long enough for him to decide what he wanted to do. It is easy to say to yourself, *Stop and think!* But it is much easier actually to *do* that with another person. This is because another person can help diffuse the impatience and anxiety that waiting naturally creates in many people who are action oriented, as this man certainly was.

The worst decisions we make are not the ones that lead to failure but the ones that leave us disappointed in ourselves. These are the decisions that disconnect us from ourselves.

Some people are so talented that they will succeed at practically anything they try. Their Achilles' heel turns out to be not lack of talent or perseverance, but lack of self-knowledge. They work and toil for decades, only to "discover" toward the end of their work that they had never been doing what they wanted to do. I put the word "discover" in quotes because they really knew it all along. Their discovery was really more a belated acknowledgment. If you honestly connect with yourself, you acknowledge what you know now, not at the end of your life.

"I have made more money than my father made, more money than any of my friends have made, more money than anyone else in my family ever has made, but I am not happy," one of my patients said to me.

"Why?" I asked.

"Because it was all grunt work. I never took the chance to do what I wanted to do."

"What did you want to do?" I asked.

"I don't know. That's the worst of it. I never even took the time to ask myself what I really wanted. But I can tell you, it wasn't investment banking, which is where I have spent the last thirty-five very lucrative, stupid years."

Most of us would gladly have taken the lucrative part of those thirty-five years, and it may be hard for us to understand how bad it could be, if it was so lucrative. After all, money can make up for a lot of dissatisfaction.

But this patient, and several others like him whom I have treated over the years, would tell you, from hard-won experience, that as the end draws near the connection you feel to yourself becomes more and more important. Was this patient true to himself? He would say, absolutely not. Was he enough to himself? Again, he would say no.

It is not just money that can become fool's gold, the goal you pursue at the expense of your true self. Fame, glamour, power, influence—these are some other favorites.

We all have to make a living. But how much of a living? We all want to get noticed. But how much notice? These are the questions that can help you stay true to yourself and be enough to yourself.

Another one of my patients, a Harvard student who came to see me because he was depressed, used to berate me when I would question him along these lines. "I don't care how I get there," he barked at me. "I just want to be on top!"

"On top of what?" I would ask.

"On top of the heap! On top of wherever I am! Obviously! And don't you try to talk me out of it!"

"I'm not trying to talk you out of it," I replied. "I'm just trying to help you decide where you are going to spend your time."

"I don't care. Just as long as I am the one who finishes first."

"But first at what?" I persisted.

"It doesn't matter!" he yelled at me.

"But it does matter," I replied. "If you become the best at something you don't believe in, it won't make you happy."

"Doctor Hallowell, I think you are naïve," he answered. "Do you think the man who invented Tupperware *believes* in Tupperware? Do you think the president of Cambridge Savings believes in what he is doing? Do you think the average senior partner at Hale and Dorr believes in his job? Of course not! They all believe in the money they make and the power they have, that's all. They believe in how many people they can order around! I mean, I hate to tell you this because you are basically in a loser's profession, but what *really* matters is sitting in the front row."

I'll never forget how I squirmed in my chair when he told me I was in a loser's profession. Suddenly he was challenging me. *Was he right?* I wondered in a millisecond. Did the winners in medicine all go into heart surgery or brain surgery, and did the losers go into low-paying, low-glamour fields like psychiatry? In a flash I had to remind myself that I loved my work, that regardless of the opinion of the world, I was doing what I believed in, and that was the most important reward. Fast thoughts. I bit my tongue. I did not say, *So what's a winner like you doing seeing a loser like me?* Instead, I held to the therapist's role and empathized with him. "It must be hard to want to be on top so badly, and yet not have any guarantees."

"Yes, it is hard. But the solution is not to try to sell me on the cheap seats in life, which is what I think you are trying to do. I want the front row."

"Honestly, Jason," I replied, "I am not trying to sell you on the cheap seats. It's just that I know from experience that there are a lot of unhappy people in the front row, and a lot of happy people in the cheap seats."

"Like you?" Jason asked. "Are you happy in the cheap seats? Well, I'd rather be miserable in the front row than happy in the cheap seats. That's who I am."

"But you don't have to be that way," I continued. "After all, the reason you are coming to see me is that you are not happy in life doing things the way you have been doing them."

"Touché," Jason replied, with a slight grin.

T. S. Eliot put the dilemma well when he wrote, "The last temptation is the greatest treason, to do the right deed for the wrong reason." Outward success is never very satisfying unless it is accompanied by inner satisfaction as well. In other words, unless the connection to yourself is honored and tended to, success will not succeed.

Tending yourself is a skill you can learn, like gardening. Unfortunately, the skill many people learn is the opposite. Instead of a green thumb, they develop the equivalent of a black thumb when it comes to taking care of themselves.

Many decent, good people fit in this category. Many kind, generous people take care of everyone else but they neglect themselves completely. Their garden of connections makes a stunning display of the most beautiful plants and flowers, all lovingly tended to, except for the section of the garden devoted to their connection to themselves. This section is shabby, overrun with weeds, and so dry it's parched and cracking.

It is a paradox that the people who are the best at taking care of others are often the worst at taking care of themselves. I know many great physicians, for example, who can't tell you when their last physical exam was or what their cholesterol level is. However, they can easily recite these facts on all of their patients!

I have treated people who could make other people feel good—people turned to them for advice and solace all the time—but they could not soothe themselves. Indeed, they did just the opposite to themselves. They tormented themselves with endless criticism and self-doubt. These very people, who so skillfully advised others on how to be good to themselves, could never follow their own advice!

Even though they had the insight to see what they were doing, they had trouble stopping it. Even though they knew they were hurting themselves, they had trouble putting that inner voice to rest. And so it did its destructive work, like a boll weevil in a cotton field, worming its way into the boll of self-regard.

I think of a psychotherapist I once treated, Dr. P, a woman of all-encompassing empathy, a woman who comprehended the human condition so broadly that she really did live up to that axiom "To understand all is to forgive all." Forgive all, that is, except herself.

Here she was, so wise and understanding that I would gladly have put myself or any of my relatives or friends in her hands were we in distress, but she could not stop berating herself for all kinds of imagined transgressions.

I often wonder at these people. I marvel at how persistent they are, doing battle within themselves every day.

I believe they were never encouraged to treat themselves well.

Dr. P found help in making a connection with me. As usual, I didn't do anything magical. I simply did what Dr. P herself would have done. I listened, I responded, I cared. I speculated with her as to the reasons for her self-doubting: Was it her withholding mother that was the cause? Was it her distant father? Was it her repressive Protestantism? Was it the high standards set by the high school teacher she so admired? Was the problem simply in her genes? We didn't answer the questions, but tackling them together brought about positive change.

The relief really came in our connection, in the relationship we made, in our teaming up to look at her life. She spent her whole day doing this for other people, so it is not surprising that she found it helpful to find one place where someone else would do it for her. She didn't change radically, but each visit to me restored some peace of mind.

It was true her parents hadn't shown her much about how to care for her emotions. Conscientious parents often teach their children everything *except* how to take care of themselves emotionally. They teach their children to achieve, they teach them how to be polite, they teach them to please others. They teach them how to take care of their bodies—brush their teeth, cut their nails, get enough sleep and exercise—but they don't teach them how to take care of their feelings. They act as if this happens automatically.

Unfortunately, it doesn't.

When you grow up without any instruction, or even permission, to make yourself feel good, you don't suddenly learn how to do it when the need arises. Instead, you do the next best thing. You make everyone else feel good. That, in itself, is a form of pleasure, one that some people have perfected to an art.

I have seen such people in action. I am pretty good at it myself, but I am nothing compared to the experts. They can walk into a room of fifty or sixty people and within seconds identify who is unhappy. Like bloodhounds picking up on a scent, they instantly detect where unhappy feelings are, and then they begin to do their magic.

This is the second part of the art. Part one is identification, part two is fixing. The miracle here is not only that they can do it—the true artists can do it without your even knowing what's happening, so you don't have to feel grateful. Indeed, if you are the unhappy person, not only will you feel happy after you speak with one of these magicians, but you will feel that you helped them, instead of vice versa. So, not only do you get the gift of happiness, not only do you not have to take on the burden of gratitude, you can feel proud of yourself! The artists in this field would never allow you to feel grateful, unless, of course, you wanted to!

Impossible, you might say. And as I describe it, it sounds like magic.

But in fact it is very simple. Let's say you are the expert at helping. Once you find the unhappy person you just walk up to him and ask him a few questions about himself. Nothing deep, just enough to put him at ease. You are sniffing around for an area of interest to him. Once you find one, you tell him a problem you have (make it up if you have to) that relates to his area of interest. Then you listen as he tells you how to solve your problem. You thank him profusely, tell him what a great help he's been, and purr inside as you watch his unhappiness lift. Then you move on in the party to find the next unhappy person on whom you will work your magic.

That is just one approach. There are many others.

The point is that some people can spend a lifetime learning how to tend to others, but learn nothing about how to tend to themselves.

Not only do they not learn it; often they are cautioned against it.

One of the common misreadings of religious teaching is that a person should be utterly selfless in order to be virtuous. People can be brought up in the belief that any concern they might feel for themselves is immoral. They then strive to extinguish those concerns as desperately as they strive to extinguish any other "impure" thought. Self-concern gets tinged with the same brush of shame as sexual feelings, envious feelings, hateful feelings, or any of the other feelings that as humans we are bound to have yet have been cautioned against.

In making a healthy connection to yourself, accept that you have a self to begin with! Accept that you are human. This means that you have sexual feelings, angry feelings, petty jealous feelings, the whole bushel basket of feelings that make us human. The goal is not to eradicate these feelings, it is to regulate them and direct their growth.

A lot of people put a boll weevil in the field in the hope it will *kill* their "bad" feelings. That boll weevil eats in their minds for their entire life, but kills nothing but pleasure.

If you were never taught how to tend to yourself—if, indeed, you were taught to ignore your needs and feelings as if they were selfish and impure—it is still possible to learn how to make a healthy connection to yourself. It is still possible to kill that boll weevil.

Dr. P never killed it, but together we certainly stopped its spread. We laughed at it whenever it stuck its little head out, we ridiculed it as much as it had ridiculed Dr. P, so that when I would ask her how she was if she immediately replied, "Fine, and how are you?" we would both start to laugh. Then she'd catch herself and say, "No, that's not the truth. I feel perfectly awful, and right now I don't care to know how you are." "Bravo!" I'd say, and then we'd laugh, not because it was funny that she felt bad or didn't care about me just then, but because it felt good just to tell the truth and be real.

You can help yourself to grow. But some people, like Dr. P, have trouble letting it happen. They are so harsh on themselves they won't let self-growth occur. Any attempt is met, internally, with ridicule and criticism. These people need to practice. Even if they are gifted at helping others, they need to practice helping themselves.

I have found it helpful to suggest to my patients they ask themselves, *Is this helping me grow?* When Dr. P picked at herself over one imagined failing or another, I encouraged her to ask herself, *Is this helping me grow?* Then she could recognize in an instant that it was not—indeed, it was preventing her from moving ahead. This gave her a rationale for stopping it.

We *can* change the way we treat ourselves.

One of my greatest frustrations as a psychiatrist is watching people cling to the idea that they will never change—as if that cast-iron idea were a life raft—instead of letting go of that idea and trying actually to change. Change is the real life raft, not staying the way you are. One of the most worn-out bits of conventional wisdom is that people never change. *But they do.*

There is an old lightbulb joke about psychiatrists. *Question:* How many psychiatrists does it take to change a lightbulb? *Answer:* One, but the lightbulb has to want to change.

If you want to change, you can. The best way to change is through changing your connections, deepening them, expanding them, maybe eliminating a few, pruning others, and fertilizing still others. You may develop a new friendship, or deepen your connection to beauty, or develop your connection to God, or make peace with a member of your family. There are many different ways to change through changing your connections.

As these outside connections change, you find that your connection to yourself begins to change, as well. You start to become a better place for you to grow.

The person who has a strong connection inside is not prey to the whims and inconsistencies of others. He does not *have* to please in order to feel OK. He may choose to please —but the opinion of others is not his guiding compass.

There are times when we must look to the connection to ourselves, rather than anywhere else, for guidance. Franco Bernabe, appointed CEO in 1992 of the Italian industrial giant Eni, took that company from a corrupt, debt-ridden, government-owned, politically controlled mishmash to its standing today as a thriving publicly traded corporation. As externally connected as a CEO must be, Bernabe said his most important connection in accomplishing what he did was to himself.

"A person who has to make important decisions has to make them alone," he said in an interview published in the *Harvard Business Review* in 1998.

You can rely on no one. In Italian, we call this condition *solitudine.* If you are in a difficult situation, as I was for a very long time, then it can be dangerous to listen too much to others or to depend on them.

You have to watch every bit of the picture. And then you need an inner compass to indicate the way. In my case, that compass was my conscience. . . . The right thing to do was to pull the company out of the swamp of politics it was mired in. My compass told me where to go and what I needed to do to get there.

Connecting, therefore, does not mean merging with others, being enmeshed or entangled. The connected individual preserves his own privacy and inner sanctum. He is still an individual, able to step back and refer to his inner compass when he needs to.

~⌒~

TWENTY-ONE

Tapping Your Creative Side

YOUR CONNECTION TO YOURSELF,

PART II

BY FAR, OUR most untapped natural resource is our creativity. More good ideas go unused than mines undug or fish uncaught. Indeed, if we really put our collective creativity to use, we probably wouldn't need to mine any more mines or fish any more fish!

But most people lose faith in their creative side somewhere before age ten. We all are born creative. I have never met an uncreative two-year-old. But life scares most people away from sticking with their creativity.

It is not as if we grow out of creativity naturally, the way we grow out of, say, baby fat. Nature does not make us shed our creativity. And we don't need to grow out of it for social reasons, the way we need to grow out of, say, diapers. We lose creativity for many reasons, but none of them are good.

Often, adults give up on developing their creative side simply because they are afraid to look stupid or silly. But being creative depends upon your being willing to look stupid, to fail, and to fail again. Fear is the number one killer of creativity.

Whoever invented the wheel must have encountered a peer who sneered, "You *always* have to do it *your way,* don't you? The square has been around for centuries, but is it good enough for you? No-o-o-o-o! When will you learn?"

The creative person—and that person could be you, if you let it be—must first of all be bold, or at least so caught up in enthusiasm for his idea that he forgets all the reasons that make it seem stupid to pursue it! Children naturally forget they might get punished or ridiculed for whatever new escapade they pursue; they get into it, they forget themselves, and their creative side takes over.

Of course, not every one of these escapades advances mankind. When my daughter, Lucy, put peanut butter into her mother's hair dryer in an attempt to make peanut butter spray, this did not advance mankind. Lucy's mom rightly told her not to do that again, and she took a little money out of her allowance to help pay for a new hair dryer. But at the same time, her mom told Lucy that she admired the imagination that went into the act. The story goes that the young Steven Spielberg tried to paint his kitchen yellow when he was a child, using egg yolks for paint. That effort did not advance mankind, either, but still, we are glad he was not punished so severely for what he did that he never dared try anything new again.

Perhaps the reason we regularly stamp out creativity is that it is potentially so dangerous. As helpful as it can be, it can also be destructive. For every successful new idea, for every wheel, bobby pin, transistor, or microchip, there are thousands of peanut butter hair dryers and egg yolk paints. The safe course is to exclude creativity altogether. That is why Plato expelled poets from his utopian republic. They were dangerous.

But they are indispensable for progress. Our goal should be to nourish creativity and responsibility at the same time.

If you are a parent or a manager or a friend, and you want your child or employee or friend to develop creativity, start by trying to eliminate fear. Never ridicule. Praise people for making an honest mistake; don't scorn them. An honest mistake is good because it can be learned from. Never shame a person's honest efforts, unless you want to shut them down.

If you yourself want to become creative, you can begin by taking chances. You can begin by declaring your independence from the *laws of conformity,* declare yourself free of the *fear of what other people think,* and begin to *play.* Play is where creation begins. Look at children, the born masters of creativity. They play. Out of play come messes, fights, injuries, screams, bruises, wasted time, lost time, missed appointments, and a host of other miscues. But also, out of play comes one of the most important connections anyone can make: a confident connection to your imagination. Out of play comes art. Out of play come new ideas. Out of play comes just about every new thing in life.

If you can nurture in your child or employee, or in yourself, the capacity for play, you will be opening the doors to a creative life. The more you make play seem foolish, the more likely you will close those doors. The trick here is not to exclude play from the life of a child or an employee or from yourself, but to combine it with a sense of responsibility.

I see in my office every day adults who are desperately seeking to draw upon their creative side, but just as desperately they are afraid to try it. Long ago they were taught that being creative was too messy, or it was not efficient, or it was disruptive, or it was just a waste of time. Long ago they heard the commands *"Get serious!"* and *"Be sensible!"* and they heeded them.

They stopped trying to do it their way, and followed the directions instead. They stopped trying to fall in love, and married a sensible spouse instead. They stopped speaking up in meetings, and let someone else speak up instead. They stopped coming up with new ideas for where to go for dinner, and went with the flow instead. They stopped making funny remarks, and behaved "appropriately" instead. They stopped dreaming of opening their own business, and took up golf instead. They gave up on becoming a musician, and went to law school instead. They gave up on poetry, and wrote novels that would sell instead. In short, they gave up on what they loved, and did what made sense instead.

As parents, teachers, or managers, how many times, without knowing it, do we counsel exactly that? And as managers of ourselves, how many times do we advise ourselves to give up on what we love, let go of what seems to be leading nowhere, and instead get serious and make sense?

Without intending to, we kill creativity all the time, every day, and usually with the best of intentions—for the good of the other person, the business, or ourselves.

The solution is not to let chaos reign. The solution is not for us all to regress to toddler age and prance about "being creative."

The solution is, rather, to recapture the uninhibited, unafraid part of ourselves that we lost sometime in childhood. The successful creative person combines the discipline and responsibility of an adult with the freedom and spontaneity of a child.

To reconnect to the creative part of yourself, you have to move quickly, like a master fisherman catching a fish with his bare hands, because the creative part of you has been trained to dart away when it sees you coming!

You have to put aside "Yes, but" and replace it with "Yes, yes." You have to learn to get enthusiastic about the tiny good part of the very big bad idea. You have to embrace the stinking, unbathed wild child and get dirty in order to find the treasures embedded in the dirt under his nails. You have to be willing to say, "Let's try it again," when every fiber of your self wants to say, "No more." This is because creativity feeds on failure, not on success. It feeds on garbage, not prepared food. It takes garbage and failure and turns them into something fine. But the process is ugly. So, to be creative, you have to be willing to get ugly.

Most adults just aren't willing.

Let me describe to you a man who was willing. He is my dear friend Jonathan Galassi, editor in chief of Farrar, Straus & Giroux. To the world he looks like the model of control—a successful businessman, a conventional family man, a man of no bad habits, a solid citizen.

But I know him better than that. Jon grew up wanting to be a writer, specifically a poet. He was an excellent student in school, and he could have lived off his academic skills in any number of ways, but he wanted to develop his creativity as fully as he could. He wanted to take a chance.

I have known him since high school, and I have participated in his life as a close friend, so I have seen his story unfold up close.

At Harvard he got started in poetry with Robert Lowell and Elizabeth Bishop. Early on, he made the connection to a writer's life by taking courses with these eminent poets, not only learning their craft but observing their habits. Lowell was brilliant, but erratic. Bishop was also brilliant, but normal, on the surface at least. She particularly influenced Jon because, as he said to me, "She showed me you don't have to be a kook to be a good writer." Jon liked what James Merrill said about her, "She carried a lifelong impersonation of an ordinary woman."

Jon has done the same thing. He has impersonated an ordinary man. In some ways, any person who wishes to remain actively creative and hold a normal job must do the same thing. This is how *"Get serious"* and *"Be sensible"* can embrace, rather than destroy, the powers of the imagination. Neither force has to kill the other. Responsibility does not have to kill creativity, and creativity does not have to ignore responsibility, in order for either to thrive. The creative person simply has to learn how to dress up his creativity to take it out in public, and he has to be able to let it go unfed, crying in the night, now and then.

Jon's normal job became editing. After Harvard and a fellowship at Cambridge University, in England, he continued the commitment to creativity he made in high school by taking a chance in choosing a career. Instead of taking what would have been, for him, the safe route, going to law school or becoming an English professor, he went into the world of literary commerce. Few worlds are less secure, especially nowadays, than the world of book publishing. But as Jon said to me, "I didn't want to submit to the regimen of being a graduate student. More education just seemed too confining, so I decided to try being a publisher, and I got a job at Houghton Mifflin in Boston." There he started working with authors like Louis Auchincloss and Pat Conroy, helping them make their work better. But all the while he wrote his own poetry, too.

He flourished as an editor and soon took the big step of moving to New York, the big time of publishing, and a job at Random House. He was hedging his bets, as you must do to survive, between the *"Be sensible!"* side of himself and the artist side, in developing a solid career as an editor. He had learned from Elizabeth Bishop, in particular, that you didn't have to give up a normal life to be a good writer, and he wanted the pleasures of a normal life. He succeeded in securing them, getting married to a woman he loved, having two children he adores, and keeping up with friends he likes and hobbies, like gardening, that engross him.

The creative fire kept burning within him, indeed burning brighter as he got older. As he did all the "normal" things, he did not shut off his self-expression. He did not *"get serious"* in the sense of amputating his playful side. He simply learned how to regulate it well.

Life was not all smooth sailing. Jon remained loyal to his literary values and standards, which led to his getting fired from his job at Random House. But Jon had the pleasure of the last laugh. In his next job, at Farrar, Straus & Giroux, the first author he signed on was Scott Turow, with a book entitled *Presumed Innocent*. It became one of the biggest best-sellers of the decade. Since then Jon has shown a knack of finding quality books that sell well—an extraordinary skill that few people possess.

I see Jon for extended periods every summer. Every morning he disappears into a room somewhere to write for several hours. He works on his own poetry, a book of which was published just before he turned forty, while another one is almost ready as he now nears fifty, and he writes translations. His translations of the poetry of the Italian Nobel Prize winner Eugenio Montale were published to great critical acclaim in 1998.

Meanwhile, his editing skills grow apace, with Scott Turow and Tom Wolfe being his best-known authors, but many other notables thriving under his guidance. He was poetry editor of the *Paris Review*. He became president of the Academy of American Poets, and has served on various prize committees. He has risen to the top of the literary world.

But he did not become insensitive, as so many do in the process of gaining commercial success. He did not become invulnerable. He did not become aloof.

Amazingly enough, he doesn't even feel all that successful. "I don't know," Jon said, a little awkwardly. "I mean, I'm only now sort of backing into being a writer. I finally published a book of my poetry when I was almost forty. It was a goal for me to get it done before I turned forty. I'd done these Montale translations as sort of another way of backing into writing. Being an editor, being a magazine editor, being a translator were fine, but being a writer is something I didn't give myself full permission to do until recently."

If it was hard for Jonathan Galassi, with his many qualifications, to give himself permission to give time to his creativity, no wonder it is so hard for so many people who have fewer credentials. I asked him why it was hard for him, given all his experience and training, to let himself do what he loved.

"I think it was too awesome, or my own sense of self wasn't big enough to encompass it in some way," he replied.

Again, how often do our own fears, or feelings of being too small,

too inadequate, stand in the way of our most important ambitions!
"Some people are more intimidated by that than others," I said to
Jon. "Does it depend on how much talent they have?"

"Oh, no, I think it has more to do with their own formation, how
they've been brought up, and how much leeway they're allowed. I
think being an artist requires having an unfettered ego. As my
friend Christopher Hewat, a sculptor says, when you're doing art
you can't be nice, you can't be polite, you have to give in to the most
primal, primitive, uneducated facets of your personality. Some people are better at that than others. Some people have more access to
those parts. Some people are more repressive of those things than
others. I think that I don't always have that access. I think I've gotten it more as I've gotten older. As I've had more freedom or more
success in other ways, I'm able to give myself more permission. But
the desire has always been there since my teenage years."

So here is Jonathan Galassi, a man at the top of his field, still
struggling within himself to grow, to develop his art. He works to
give himself permission to do it, to be who he dreams of being. He
wants to do it not for the money or the glory, but for the sake of
doing it, for the joy of the connection. He continues to work at it,
to practice, trying to get it right, trying to give himself full permission, also trying to perfect his craft. "Being a writer," Jon said,
"being an artist, it's all about practice. It's a long way from stream
of consciousness to actually writing something that you want to
show to the world. But the main thing about art in my opinion is
not about sales. It's about self-expression. If it's good enough, then
it becomes something of value to other people, but there's a lot of
value in just doing it for yourself."

In other words, there is a lot of value in making the connection
to your creative self just for yourself, not to sell a product or earn
money.

"Take Emily Dickinson," Jon offered as an example. "She might
have published four or five poems in her whole lifetime, and yet she
is one of the two greatest American poets. Her communications
with the world were all delayed communications. She was writing
for herself. She was writing to understand her experience, to make
something out of what she lived. While she was doing that, she
didn't have any outward confirmation of its value to anyone else. It
was all her own communications with her own soul. Her own spirit.

That's the ultimate lesson of writing. You don't do it for the re-wards or other people's responses. In many cases that happens, but the ultimate level of reward is something personal and deep."

"What is that, exactly? Can you put it into words?" I asked.

"Well, I think the ultimate reward is making something. You feel you actually captured some idea or some image. You're plumb-ing your own plumbing. You're grappling with reality."

"Do you think a person can get to it in other ways than through art or beauty?" I asked.

"I think you can get to it in gardening," Jon, an avid gardener, replied. "You can get to it in teaching. Sometimes I feel I get to it in my work editing a writer. It's a question of feeling that you have gone as far as you can, in whatever it is. You can be a really great road paver and you will have gotten to the depth of something. I believe that. I think that there's no real difference as long as it's a true expression of your energy. As long as you're fully engaged by it, you're fully used up in it. Take gardening. Gardening is an art. If you see a beautiful garden it's an expression of aesthetic under-standing. And it's an expression of the personality of the person who did it. So it's very poetic, I think."

Jon has developed himself as a poet while making a career as an editor. He has kept the creative connection to himself alive, as he has nourished it in others.

This is possible for us all.

III

HOPES

and

FEARS:

CONNECTION

and

DISCONNECTION

$\backsim$

If Connection Is So Good, Why Is It in Such Short Supply?

WHY IS CONNECTION in such short supply? Because it's difficult. In the short term, it is *much* easier not to connect than to connect.

Most people feel a twinge of fear as they enter a room full of new people. We learn to hide it well, but we are afraid of other people initially. People who don't know me often say to me, "You seem so calm and confident. I can't imagine you ever have an insecure moment." And yet my friends can tell you, nothing could be further from the truth! I am a perfect example of the guy who worries about going to a party out of his own insecurity, then when he gets there has a great time. Indeed, my wife often has to pull me out the door as if I were a mule being dragged out of its stall just to get me into the car to go to the party—which, once I join in, I almost always revel in. I love parties; it's going to them that I hate!

Fear is the biggest obstacle to connection, but there are many others.

One is time. It is hard to make the time. And even if you make the time, it is hard to put up with the aggravation. It is easier to hold back. Every time you enter into a relationship of any kind you risk getting hurt, rejected, misunderstood, or simply feeling that it wasn't worth your time.

And yet by holding back over and over again, we create gaping holes in our lives.

The problem of disconnection has grown so large and so obvious that we almost take it for granted. Maybe it is just too obvious. But we should tend to the obvious before we start looking for more subtle answers to our problems. There is an old joke that makes this point quite well. Three psychiatrists drove to a lecture together. When the lecture was over, they returned to their car. The one who owned the car couldn't find his keys. They peered through the window, and there were the keys, sitting in the ignition.

"What do we do now?" one asked.

"Let's crawl under the car and see if there is a way in that way," one psychiatrist suggested.

"No, let's break the window and just take the keys," another suggested.

"Easy for you to say," said the third, the driver, "but I own the car. Why don't we just call my son—I know he's at home—and ask him to bring down the spare set of keys? We can go have a drink while we wait."

"Well, I don't know what we're going to do," one of the others interjected, "but whatever we do we better decide pretty soon, because I see storm clouds coming and the roof of the car is down!"

Connection is like the keys in the ignition. The keys are there, waiting to be taken. We only have to reach in.

But often we don't, because it is hard. Bearing with the tension of an angry conversation with a friend, putting up with your own nervousness and self-consciousness in some new social group, negotiating a curfew with an argumentative adolescent, putting up with a cranky relative, sitting still while a customer harangues you—all these moments of potentially valuable connection can strain you to the breaking point. It's easier to avoid these moments than to deal with them constructively.

So, connection is disappearing from modern life because a part of us *wants* it to. We want to get rid of the discomfort of the human moment. We want speed, efficiency, and control. Then we want rest and relaxation. The best way to achieve these goals is to deal with people *as little as possible.* They just get in the way!

A part of us all would rather be left alone than put up with the frustrations involved in human interaction. People are just so difficult! Ask anyone who deals with the general public on a regular basis, like a flight attendant or a shopkeeper or even a part-time

Santa Claus, and they can all regale you with stories of how *impossible* some people can be.

The reason we like to insulate ourselves from one another is that we find one another to be, well, a pain. Easier to watch TV or log on to the Web than to converse face-to-face.

However, avoiding one another gets us into trouble over the long haul. We need the human moment—time spent with one another in person—to thrive in life. The more we avoid one another, the more likely we'll get sick and die young, not to mention get depressed and lonely.

Yet people lose touch with close friends all the time, they get caught up in bitter feuds that separate whole families, they decline invitations to parties and other events they'd actually like to attend, they feel they can't make time for what matters, they postpone visiting relatives, they give up on reconnecting with religion, they relegate to the bin of "nice idea but can't do it" the many ideas of reunion and reconnection that come up from day to day.

One of the best lessons I ever learned about overcoming these obstacles to connection was told me by Priscilla Vail, an author and a learning specialist. Priscilla, who is in her sixties, was sitting with three women friends when one of them asked, "I wonder how many years of marriage the four of us have, combined?" They went around and added up the years. It came to 172 years of married life between them. How had they done it? They didn't know. They decided to ask their spouses to see if any of them had any special insights. Priscilla's husband offered an explanation that serves as one of the best answers I have ever heard on how to stay connected. "We have stayed married so long," he said, "out of an abiding determination to do so." I know Priscilla and Donald. They love each other deeply. His words do not mean that every day has been a struggle. Not at all. He simply meant that for any relationship to endure it requires frequent attention. Like a garden, it must be tended or it will fall into disrepair.

To stay connected—to a friend, to a spouse, to an institution, to a team, to whatever—you must be *determined* to do so. Because no matter what the connection may be, no matter how loving or deeply felt, there will be times you feel tempted to walk away from it.

·   ·   ·

I'd like to focus on some of the most common reasons that make connecting so hard: not enough time, not enough money, fear of more responsibility, fear of rejection, and a feeling that people can't be trusted. These are the reasons I encounter most often when I discuss with people why their lives aren't better connected.

TIME

Who has time anymore—for anything?

A woman in New York told me the following story. She said there was a man who stood at her bus stop every morning for years. One day he said hello to her. She said hello back, and they started to talk. It turned out he lived two houses down from her. "Imagine that," she said, and they smiled at each other at the bus stop for another year. Then one day the man said, "We should get together sometime." The woman wholeheartedly agreed. Another six months passed, both people smiling at each other at the bus stop each morning. Then one day the man said to the woman, "Let's not put this off any longer. Why don't you come over tonight after dinner at nine o'clock for dessert?" The woman agreed to come. When she got home from work that evening she said to her husband, "I can't believe I did this, but I told the people who live two doors down that we'll come over for dessert after dinner tonight." All through dinner the woman regretted having made the date, wishing she could just go to bed and read or watch TV instead. But, when nine o'clock came around, she and her husband trudged down the street two doors. As so often happens, they ended up having a great time, staying until midnight, telling stories about the neighborhood, their own past lives, and everything else under the sun. That night began an important friendship. But it almost never happened.

We work so hard that sometimes we lose our priorities.

The same goes for children. One parent wrote,

I feel sorry for my children in today's world. I do not feel they have the total support of the community. We have lived in several different areas, and it is hard to find a true "neighborhood" anywhere. When I was growing up, I was introduced to all my neighbors. I felt comfortable talking to them. I knew my parents had made connections with these people. They had, not knowing it then, formed a support group. In today's world, one feels isolated from the world. People go to work, come home, lock the door, and do not reenter unless they are forced to (e.g., for groceries, entertainment). It is rare to find a neighborhood which also functions as a support group. I truly miss for my children what I had as a child, but I know in my heart that it will probably never be that way again. People today are not brought up to "help thy neighbor." People have to look out for number one. And with what you hear on the news about crime, no wonder people lock their doors from the neighborhood. Trust is not there anymore.

I don't think the country has suffered an attack of misanthropy; indeed, an outgoing nature is part of the American grain. But we have put ourselves on a kind of high-speed merry-go-round that allows us only a quick glimpse or the briefest hello as we circle by.

Not enough time.

Time and money go hand in hand, of course.

MONEY

Lots of us have painted ourselves into a corner. We have set up a lifestyle that requires a certain income that we can maintain only if we continue to work inordinately hard. Whether the reality justifies it or not, we feel that we have to keep working this hard or suffer an economic blow we are not prepared to take.

I know, in my own case, sending our kids to private school is a high priority for Sue and me. We can't think of any investment that matters more. And yet, to earn the extra income required to send three kids to private school in Cambridge, I have to work much harder than I would if my kids did not go to private school. Working harder means I have less time for friends, family, and so forth.

People who make less money than I do might say, "Well, it should be easy for you to make time. Just send your kids to public school. Or live in a smaller house. Or drive a cheaper car. Or cut back on your disability insurance. You're writing a book about how important it is. Why don't you make these changes yourself?"

In fact, I lead a very connected life, at considerable sacrifice of time and money, but it could be more connected, if I had more time and money. I look at people who make more money than I do, and I think to myself, Now, if I had their kind of money, I could really take the time I want to take for all the different kinds of connection I am writing about in this book. If I had their money, I wouldn't feel so pinched to cut a lunch conversation short, or say no when the church asks me to do something, or not go visit relatives who live far away because I can't afford the plane fares.

I would speculate—indeed, I have observed—that those people who have more money than I invoke the very same reasons that I do for not doing the things I just mentioned. They say they do not have enough time or enough money.

My point is that, above a certain subsistence level of income, time and money become psychological quantities much more than most of us realize. No matter how much money you have, you feel that you don't have enough. No matter how much time you have, you feel that time is short. Now more than ever.

The paradox is that the *feeling* of not having enough money, or enough time, is born out of insecurity. Insecurity is the very state that connection improves the most. If we spent more time developing connectedness we wouldn't feel the need to spend so much time making so much money. It is a psychological trick millions of us play on ourselves every day.

Hold on, you say. How will connectedness pay your children's tuition bills? There are financial realities, and if you decide a private education is a high priority, then you have to earn the money to make it possible.

I am not saying there aren't financial realities. I am reminded of them every day. What I am saying, both to myself and to others, is that we should beware of the psychological trap we set for ourselves by constantly insisting we do not have enough time or money.

For I have found—again, both in my own life and in the lives of others—that you can make the time and you can find the money. You can make the time for what matters most, and then you can find the money for what you need. If my finances collapse, then my kids will have to leave private school, or apply for a scholarship. But as my wife reminds me when I worry about this, we would still have each other, plus our kids, our friends, our church, our extended family, our memories, our health, our capacity to work—in other words, all the things we have tried to maintain a strong connection with. Somehow we can usually find the money for what we need.

This is not true for everyone. People who are really poor need more money—period. This is not psychological but real.

However, for most people, time and money keep them from developing connection for irrational reasons.

A woman described to me how she has seen life change along these lines. "I remember as a child, my mother had a knitting club which met weekly, more to eat, chat, tell jokes, and drink wine than to knit. I remember when it was Mom's turn to host, I would sit on the stairs and listen. All my friends report similar stories of 'clubs' their mothers had. Now that I am a mother, I wonder what happened to these groups of neighborhood women who got together on a regular basis, without the kids, to be friends. There are too many pressures to schedule play dates, sports events, et cetera, for the kids. And also, with people working so many hours, the question becomes, if I make time for friendship groups, when will the laundry, dishes, cleaning, et cetera, get done? This is what working parents do with their 'free time' now."

If time and its cohort, money, are so pressed that people just do laundry and dishes in their free time, then it is small wonder there is little left over for developing meaningful connections.

But even if time were abundant and money were no object, the desire to connect would still encounter obstacles.

Two important ones are the fear of responsibility and the fear of rejection.

FEAR OF ADDITIONAL RESPONSIBILITY

Kate Wenner, a dynamic woman who worked hard involving parents to create a connected world at her children's school in New York, told me, "If you're writing about connection, make sure you emphasize that it begins in responsibility." You can't sit back and expect it to be done for you, and you can't complain when someone takes charge and asks you to participate. You—we—have to expect to make some sacrifices, and give up some of our solitude if we want to live connected lives.

The minute you volunteer to be a part of something, you take on a responsibility. Ideally you do your utmost to look out for the welfare of whatever it is you are connecting to—a school, a relationship, a corporation, a baseball team. The truly connected person stays up into the night thinking of ways to make the school or the team or the family or the company *better*. The connected person doesn't whine. He works to improve the situation.

Without responsibility, connection lacks power. If you are connected only as long as the connection pleases you, then this is not true connection. It is merely attendance.

In this sense connection is a burden. You have to be there in bad times as well as good. Sometimes, you can be embarrassed.

For example, I was pulling into a parking space in a mall in Cambridge one day when another car snaked in ahead of me, stealing the space I was headed into. I found another space not too far away, and on my way into the store I saw the woman who had stolen my space. I wasn't going to say anything to her until I noticed the bumper sticker she had on the rear of the car: *Practice Random Acts of Kindness*. Once I saw that, I couldn't contain myself. I jogged up to her and asked, "Was stealing my parking space your random act of kindness for today?" She stopped, opened her mouth, but no words came out, so she quickly turned on her heel and hurried away.

It is one thing to display bumper stickers about being nice to people. It is quite another actually to act that way. Most of us who speak the words of connection don't always live up to them in our own lives.

There is much more I could do if I made the effort, but I don't want to take on more responsibility. Somewhere I have felt I needed to draw the line. As much as I might not like to think so, I am sure my own comfort has come before all else, time and again.

This is why many people opt out altogether. They (we) do not want to take on additional responsibilities. It makes sense not to take on more than you can handle. It makes sense not to put yourself in a position of not being able to live up to your responsibilities. But on the other hand, too much avoidance can leave you in an isolated, disconnected place.

FEAR OF REJECTION

Let's say you are prepared to take on new responsibility. A major obstacle is often the simple fear of rejection. What if I decide to get really involved at school, but no one likes my ideas? What if I decide to organize the neighborhood to do some charity work, but only a pitiful few agree to participate? What if I decide to run for some office, and I lose? What if I invite over the neighbors and they don't like me? Grown-ups don't like to admit it, but we can be just as nervous as a seventh-grader when it comes to our fear of rejection. It can be easier just to hold back.

Whether they share my fear of going to a party, or they can't speak up in groups, most people fear rejection in one way or another, at least once in a while.

We can easily understand the feelings one woman related to me: "The anticipation of going to a larger group activity, like a wedding or a business seminar or what have you, is extremely stressful for me. My family belongs to a skating club that requires us to attend a certain number of dinners on Friday nights. The meals are served buffet style, with rush seating. The fear this creates in me is like being back in junior high school—who will I sit with? what will we talk about? The evening usually ends up being much more tolerable than I imagined, even enjoyable, but my husband and I are still toying with the idea of having a T-shirt printed up that reads, *I survived Friday night dinner at the skating club!*"

Most of us have our versions of the Friday night skating club. It requires effort to go, sometimes, simply because of the stress of dealing with people on a social basis. Who will I sit with? What will we talk about?

We may invoke the other excuses I already mentioned—I don't have the time, I can't afford to do it, I don't want the additional responsibility—when what we actually fear is rejection. What if I make the effort and get rebuffed? What if I come across as boring? Saying I don't have time or I can't afford it is so much cleaner, much less embarrassing. After all, isn't the fear of rejection only for weak people?

There must be adults somewhere who never feel this twinge of insecurity. There must be people who are so confident that they never give a second thought to what anyone else thinks of them. I always imagined my grandfather was like that. The thing is, I can *imagine* such people, but I have never *known* one. Oh sure, I knew my grandfather, but it was more my imagined version of him that I knew. I didn't know the inner workings of his heart. And that is where we tend to carry these kinds of fears.

One step you can take to help yourself is simply to know that such fear is universal, that you are not a weakling if you feel this way, and that the people you imagine never feel this way probably do. All of us feel social fear at one time or another—as we walk into a party, as we stand up to speak in public, as we send in our job proposal.

If it hurts to be rejected, why not play it safe?

The answer, of course, is, nothing ventured, nothing gained. What you can gain in connection is sometimes worth what you must venture—your feelings. Sometimes it's not. The trick is not to let those few times when you get burned turn you off to the whole enterprise.

The dance we grown-ups do around our fear of rejection is truly artful. We sometimes conceal what we are doing even from ourselves. "I don't want to go to that party because those people bore me"—I have used that one. "I won't join that committee because all committees are a waste of time"—I've used that one, too. "I won't accept their invitation because they are just trying to use me"—I've heard that one. "I just can't make time for another friend"—someone said that to me just the other day. All valid excuses, but what lies behind them, often, is a simple fear that rejection lurks at the party, or at the meeting, or wherever.

When I was in high school, I used to feel bad because I didn't think I was in with the in crowd. In retrospect, I am sorry I worried about that, because my feeling was based on an illusion. There were cliques—the brains and the jocks and the artsy crowd, for example—and there were a few golden boys at the top of each clique within the class; but even those golden boys, I suspect, had their own moments of insecurity and loneliness.

Since high school—where being *in* is the ultimate goal—I have come to the conclusion that there really is no in crowd in adult life, there is only the perception of one. Some people just have more confidence than others, and these are usually the ones we designate as in. But the whole idea is a sham. Particularly today, as class structures, clubs, old-boy networks, and other relics have crumbled, the in crowd lies wherever there is confidence. Some would add that it lies wherever there is money—but the in crowd is different from the rich crowd. I have known fabulously wealthy individuals who felt, deep down, very out.

There is a lesson we each should learn, but few of us ever do. You really can make your own in crowd, just by getting together with others and believing in one another. Connectedness creates its own power. Connectedness brings *in* everyone it touches.

MISTRUST OF OTHERS

This is perhaps the most obvious reason people avoid connection. It is summed up in the words of one of my patients: "People? They're all jerks." Many caution that people in general are not to be trusted; certainly they're not to be loved or even liked. "When you come right down to it . . . ," the argument often begins. What you find when you come right down to it, in the opinion of many, is selfishness and meanness at the core of human nature.

It reminds me of a cartoon that depicted a man and a woman looking romantically into each other's eyes as they sat at a bar. Next to each of them sat a lawyer. One lawyer was saying to the other lawyer, "My client would like to buy your client a drink. However, the offer of said drink does not constitute a commitment, nor should its acceptance imply a contract of any kind. My client would also like to make it clear to your client that he takes no responsibility for the content of the drink, nor for its effects. No obligations . . ."

The world of connection has become a paranoid place.

The reason, however, is usually not philosophical but practical. "I got hurt before," the person says, "but I won't get hurt again."

A loving, trusting, bright-eyed three-year-old doesn't stay trusting too long. Life intervenes. Kids can be mean to one another. You learn your lessons young. You learn how to play it safe.

After a while you resolve: *I won't get hurt again.*

One physician described the adult version of this process in telling me about a friendship she had during her training with her chief resident in medicine when she was an intern. "Through sleep deprivation, forced togetherness, and the natural congruency of interests, we somehow became best friends. As the year wound down and I anticipated going on into a psychiatry residency the next year, I had a fearful foreboding this relationship was going to end, because I was going to change. I did change, as I inched toward psychiatry—more introspective, more morose, possibly depressive.

"The last conversation we had was sad," she went on. "I guess I wanted to see if our friendship could survive my transition, so I talked about my feelings in a process of saying good-bye, me off to psychiatry, she to her career in medical intensive care. After that conversation, in which she was mostly nonresponsive, she told mutual friends she was 'very hurt' by me. My phone calls went unanswered. I even showed up at her apartment just to talk. She pulled away from any of my entreaties to talk about what was wrong. Soon she moved away, and inquiries made to her through mutual friends made it clear she never wanted anything to do with me again."

All this happened over a decade ago. "After years of reflecting about what we went through," she concluded, "I realized this cutoff was inevitable, and my foreboding was a realistic expectation. I've had the experience of gradual disengagement from friends—for example, from high school—over the years, gradually wondering what in the dickens we ever had in common. But in medical school and residency we had to become chameleons, and the faster we could change, the better off we'd be. This emotional 'toughening' which accompanies the process of becoming a doctor comes at a great cost. It felt to me like a real loss of innocence."

Most of us experience such a loss of innocence at some time in our lives. Often we experience it several times over. Whether it be in fourth grade, or in high school, or at age thirty, most of us get hurt and respond by pulling back, shutting down a little, covering ourselves up in sophistication and grown-up talk.

The past can hurt us into pulling back, sometimes forever.

This is not always a bad thing. As my old teacher of psychiatry

Leston Havens used to tell us, "The world is full of wolves. You must help your patients learn how not to be sheep."

But my experience as a psychiatrist has been just the opposite. Since I left Dr. Havens's tutelage and went into the world of my own practice I have found that my patients need to learn, or relearn, trust more than caution. They have become highly skilled in mistrust. In their efforts not to be sheep, they have gone into hiding.

Even if they are active in the world, making lots of money, raising a family, going to cultural events, and being good citizens, they do not connect. They don't dare. They play it safe in life. They wait.

I think this is what Thoreau meant by quiet desperation. Most of my patients are quietly desperate to make better connections with other people. But lack of trust holds them back, "lessons" of their past. They don't want to get hurt again.

My response is not to deny that people can be mean, even evil, or to deny that the best of us can betray our friends. After all, it was Peter, the rock of the Christian church, who denied Christ three times. The possibility of betrayal is built into connection.

My response is practical, not theoretical. We are better off with one another than without one another. We're better off putting up with one another than systematically getting rid of each person who disappoints us. The medical data are abundantly clear: people do better with people. Even if we all *are* a bunch of jerks, we're better off dealing with one another, in all our annoying ways, than disconnecting.

You don't have to trust people completely to connect with them. In fact, a little skepticism is probably a good idea. But I have found in the patients I treat that the far greater risk is in being too skeptical. If you always hold back out of fear or mistrust, the next thing you know you have no one to talk to—honestly and openly—except yourself, and maybe a few other frightened, mistrusting people.

If you find that life has hurt you so badly that you simply cannot trust again, try as you might, then it is probably a good idea to see a therapist or some other person with whom you can talk about these feelings. I have seen many times that trust can be regained.

But it doesn't happen in solitude. Indeed, in solitude mistrust only grows and becomes encrusted with cynicism and anger.

It is much better to reach out to *someone,* or to God, and begin a conversation about life. Talk out your pain, talk out your anger, talk out your hurt. It can be done. You can rediscover your faith in people and in life. And doing this can literally *save* your life.

TWENTY-THREE

The Community of Good People

I believe that people have lost the feeling of being connected to family, neighborhood, and community, and that our pace of life has quickened to the point of displacing what is really important in life. Personally, I have been striving to increase my connectedness since the birth of my niece, three years ago. She is the first grandchild for my parents, and it is amazing how she has pulled our family to work on restrengthening our connectedness. I have also been amazed by how my husband and I have become more connected with our golden retriever puppy—two years old and always a constant source of joy, love, affection, and a profound reminder of what is most important: being friendly, carefree, and loving toward family and friends, and greeting everyone with the promise of a good ear rub!

A letter from a woman who attended one of my lectures

I HAVE LEARNED something wonderful about the people in this country from traveling and lecturing over the past five years. I have learned that for the most part, this country is made up of good people. I was surprised by my discovery, given what I see in the media every day; sometimes you can get the impression that the country is full of ignorant, twisted, violent people. But that is the slant the news takes to get our attention. As the media folks say, if it bleeds, it leads. Good news isn't news. So the basic decency of most people in America can go forgotten. But in traveling I see it all the time.

Obviously, this is not a statistically reliable observation, but it has impressed me so constantly that I trust it and believe in it. Wherever I go, I find people who are filled with good intentions and positive energy. They have warm hearts and open minds. Their problem is they often don't know where or how to plug in their positive energy and goodwill. They are looking for better ways to connect.

Bad people make up a tiny minority, but they get a whole lot of publicity. Murders, beatings, white-collar crime—these are the bad deeds that fill the news. But these are *not* the events that fill most people's lives.

Most people are trying to make the best out of life, and it isn't easy for any of us. Most people wish the extremists would quiet down. Most people don't have all the answers, are willing to listen to a new idea, care about people in trouble, aren't consumed with anger and hatred, and want to do the right thing. Most people know they're not perfect and don't expect other people to be. Most people will cut you some slack, as long as you play it straight with them. Most people have been there before, wherever it is, or can imagine being there.

The problem is, this "community of good people," as I like to call it, has gone underground. It isn't out there lining the streets in the Fourth of July parade the way it used to be. It isn't down there at town hall watching over the town budget the way it used to be. It isn't out on front porches watching the neighborhood, keeping an eye on your kids when you're not around. It isn't out there organizing bake sales for families in trouble, or setting up neighborhood picnics, or canvassing for a political candidate. Instead, the community of good people are at their jobs, busy trying to make ends meet, or trying to sustain a certain lifestyle.

The invisible network of connection that used to knit together America's cities and towns has disappeared. The people who made it up are still out there, but the connections among them have frayed. Sure, my region's local Democratic committee still has its meetings the fourth Thursday of the month at a local restaurant in

Kingston, Massachusetts. But ask the average person if they would ever consider running for political office and you will usually get a resounding *"No Way!"* The whole fabric hasn't come undone, it just needs some new stitching and strengthening so it can re-involve the good people it has lost.

You can sometimes see this community of good people rise up magnificently when a crisis strikes. Bob Tobin, rector of Christ Church, defines a true community as a place where, when there is a crisis or difficulty, the people involved know what to do without having to be asked.

For example, a woman in Cambridge, Massachusetts, told me what happened to her when she needed help. "Pregnant with my second child," she wrote,

> I was put on bed rest at home for potentially two and a half months (I made it only one month). My daughter was two years old and had a hard time accepting new baby-sitters into her life. We decided after a few failed attempts at hiring someone wonderful to help out at home that we would make do on our own with family help. My daughter went to day care for a few hours each morning, and then was home with me until dinnertime, when my husband, who had just started a new job, returned.
>
> It was amazing how *quickly* news got around to my web of friends and relatives and neighbors that I was on bed rest. Almost instantly people organized themselves to come and spend the afternoons with us, playing with my daughter, Anna, picking up the toys, and often bringing supper or feeding her with their own kids in our kitchen. My mother organized our baby's room, bringing up all the baby clothes from the basement, and friends organized a shower for me knowing that I needed special clothes, etc., for a premature four-pound baby. People even gave blood for our baby.
>
> I had been part of a mobilized action for other friends and colleagues who needed help, but had never had the efforts directed to me. The power of the friendships and the connections that were so apparent during that period is something I'll never forget.

A community of good people is available to us all. However, it can be like a ship in a bottle, not yet erected. When a craftsperson makes a ship in a bottle he constructs the entire ship flat, outside the bottle. He rigs it so it can be pulled upright by one string. Then he guides the flat ship into the bottle, pulls the string, and, presto, a ship rises up, contained within the bottle.

Connection in a community can be like a ship in a bottle, waiting for the string to be pulled. The next chapter shows how a disaster can pull that string.

TWENTY-FOUR

A Murder Next Door

I DROVE UP to Reading, Massachusetts, to give a lecture about connection in the winter of 1997. After the lecture people came up to me and said that because of a recent tragedy, they knew firsthand what I was talking about.

They then told me about a murder that had recently been committed in the town. As they told me about it, I realized that this incident in Reading demonstrated exactly the powers of connection all cities and towns possess.

On the one hand, this story demonstrates the destructive power of connection: a husband murdered his wife. But it is a redemptive story as well, demonstrating the healing power of connection throughout the town.

The story began when a woman was reported missing. Let me let Sheila Mulroy, who lived through it, tell the rest. Sheila is married to a computer programmer at Harvard, and the couple have three daughters, aged twelve, nine, and six. When this story unfolded, a family named Donahue lived across the street: a mom and a dad, and four children.

"Starting at the very beginning," Sheila said, "one day Elaine Donahue, the mother across the street, was said to be missing. Their daughter was my daughter's best friend. The neighborhood was quite concerned because we are fairly tight, even though we all go in different directions every day."

Sheila had not talked to the media about her experience, because it hurt so much. I could tell as she started to get into this that we were going into painful areas. She wanted to talk to me because she knew I was writing about connection, and she hoped her experience could be helpful to people in other places.

Sheila continued, "We were concerned when Elaine was missing because she was such a responsible person. We were a little put off by the fact that her husband, Ed, was sort of nonchalant about it, but we trusted he knew best."

"How long was she missing?" I asked.

"Weeks. After the first week, everybody got much more worried. The nurses who worked with Elaine were especially concerned. She worked at New England Memorial Hospital in Stoneham, and the nurses there formed a walk for her. Many people in town joined in. The nurses had shirts printed up with Elaine's name on them and her picture, all the vital information about her, and they put yellow ribbons around the town. They got everybody mobilized."

"They did this without anybody asking them to or organizing them?" I asked.

"Yes," Sheila replied. "They wanted to make sure that people remembered Elaine and pushed to find her. I believe there were about three hundred people who joined the walk from the center of Reading to the Redstone Plaza in Stoneham, where her car had been found. They had put yellow ribbons from the Redstone Plaza all the way down my street to right in front of her house. The nurses were very vigilant. They began to feel that her husband had something to do with it. We neighbors felt that that was impossible. We felt that that couldn't be."

"You knew her husband," I said, "and you felt that he just—"

Sheila interrupted. "He was not somebody I always saw eye-to-eye with, but I just could not believe this could happen. It was not something that could even enter my mind."

"Who was saying otherwise?" I asked.

"The nurses Elaine worked with. They absolutely believed that Ed had something to do with her disappearance. As it turned out, he did, but at the time none of us neighbors could believe that he had anything to do with that.

"The nurses also planned a church service for her," Sheila continued. "I keep calling it a memorial service, but at the time it was not a memorial service, it was a prayer service. The church, Saint Ignatius in Reading, which is a fairly good-size church, was filled to capacity with people lighting candles, praying for her healthy return."

"These were just people from around the neighborhood who came to service?" I asked. "People she didn't even know?"

"They were people from the entire town of Reading, all the nurses, the neighborhood, lots of people who didn't know Elaine. It struck such a chord because it was totally out of the realm of possibility that this type of thing would happen in such a quiet little town. Elaine had four children who attended school. They were just regular people. She was a nurse who was always willing to help people. The church was filled with people who were praying for her safe return. As time went on, I actually was speaking quite a bit to the nurses. I was fairly defensive of the husband. It was ironic. I was adamantly defending him and they were insisting that he was the cause of her being missing.

"We started forming tight-knit friendships with each other. I got to know a couple of the nurses quite well, and when they had the walk for Elaine it brought us even closer together. It was a nice feeling, in spite of the fact that it was an awful time. As time went on, the police started obviously watching Ed. They made him nervous. Then the police told him they were going to go into the house with a search warrant. Ed began to panic. That's when things began to unravel for him. He apparently went into the woods with the mattress that had been soaked with her blood. A state police officer confronted Ed in the woods at two in the morning. That was a Friday, I believe around October seventeenth or eighteenth."

"You remember it well," I said.

"I sure do," she replied. "A neighbor of mine called me and said there was something going on at the house. There were a number of unmarked police cars in front of the house. I could see them out my kitchen window. I'm picturing that right now, as I tell you this. I saw Ed talking to his older son, and then I saw him talk to his daughter, who walks to school with mine, and as I was watching, more police cars came up, and we then knew that something was happening. Apparently they went in with the search warrant and they were going to look through the house.

"My kids went off to school, and when I came back to my house at ten, the entire street was filled with cars. We had to show a license when we went down the street to prove that we lived in the neighborhood. This type of thing, I think, brought us even closer together, because only the state police and the Reading police were allowed down the street. No trucks were allowed, no person who lived in Reading who was not a resident of the street could come down, but all of the people who lived on the street had pretty much free rein. We were just watching the scene unfold."

"What did you see? What were you watching?" I asked.

"We were watching the police go in and out. Ed was just standing outside. We were standing on lawns. A couple of us did go up and talk to Ed. We said, 'What about your kids?' We were very concerned about the children, not wanting them to come back to our street and see the police going in and out of the house."

"This was happening all in one afternoon?" I asked.

"Yes, this was all during one day. It started in the morning as we were watching them take evidence out. We were very concerned about his children, but what we didn't know at the time was that DSS (Department of Social Services) had been called. I called each of the principals of the schools to tell them to be aware of the fact that something was happening. And then at some point the police got involved with the schools. The children were taken from the schools and brought to the church. The church was very involved. They were wonderful. They talked to one of the priests there with DSS, and then they went to a relative's house. During the rest of the day the neighbors were just wandering back and forth. Even to this day it still has not really hit me what happened. It was hard to believe. As time went on, even throughout the night, we were watching. The neighbors were gathering, using flashlights, in small groups talking quietly."

"Had they arrested Ed yet?" I asked.

"No, because they had not yet found her body."

"It must have been awful. What were you saying to each other at this point?" I asked.

"I'm trying to remember. I think we were just trying to go through everything that had ever happened—you know, could this be possible? And what about the kids? We kept talking about the kids, and what were the children going to do, and who was going to take care of them, and we had a lot of concern about our own children and what they must be thinking. Some people chose to tell their children quite a bit about the situation, while some of us chose not to say very much.

"We still didn't know what happened until Sunday morning, when her body was found in a storage locker in Lynnfield. Elaine's best friend called me at two-forty-five A.M. to say she had just gotten a call from one of the Reading police detectives. She and I talked a little while on the phone, and of course neither one of us could get back to sleep."

"How had they found her?" I asked.

"In their search in the house they found quite a few things. They had found blood on the wall that had been washed off, but they used some special substance with ultraviolet lights to find it. They found a receipt. Somebody from either HQ or Home Depot had recognized Ed because he had bought a fifty-gallon Rubbermaid container. It turns out Elaine's dead body had been in the house all that time, hidden in the basement, wrapped up. Ed had, at some point, moved her to the Rubbermaid container and then moved her to a storage locker in Lynnfield. They found the receipt to the locker, and that's how they traced it. My daughter was actually in the basement a couple of times when Elaine's body was down there. I just can't stop thinking what could have happened if the two girls were down there and had discovered something."

"You know they had been in the basement with the body?"

"Yes. Of course, neither of them knew that at the time."

"How did Ed keep it from smelling?" I asked. "I hope you don't mind my asking."

"I myself had a big question about that," Sheila replied. "A couple of days after they had found her body I went down to the police station because I wanted to tell the police detectives that they really did a tremendous job, but I did have some questions about her being in the basement for almost a month. They told me that because she was wrapped so tightly in a plastic bedsheet and then blankets and sheets, and then put over into a corner in the basement and not touched for a while, her body wouldn't have decomposed so badly and the smell wouldn't have been so bad. As soon as she was moved, then the smell was horrible. I did ask my daughter, 'Couldn't you smell something in the house?' She said no. I just didn't understand how this could be.

"The next morning a woman told me Ed had been arrested. I went to church and they did announce it at church before the press conference. Of course, everybody was really thrown by that, because our church had been very involved with the prayer service."

"Did you see them arrest Ed?" I asked.

"No, he was at a hotel, I believe, and he was told not to leave. That was done at two o'clock or three o'clock in the morning. He was not allowed back into his house."

"And the kids were taken by DSS?" I asked.

"They wound up going to relatives' houses. They had been very close to these people. So if they had to go anywhere, it was a very good place for them."

"After he was arrested, then you all had to sort of make sense of all of this," I said.

"Right. I don't think any of us have, even now. It's just something that is so impossible to believe, and it hasn't totally sunk in. I think the way we dealt with it, we just kept gathering in small groups, talking about what had happened, how could it happen, and how terrible we felt for these kids, who not only lost their mother but lost their father as well, because he was arrested. They lost their home. They never have come home.

"When they had the wake at the church, it was one of the most beautiful things I have ever been to. It was amazing. It was a coming together of everybody. There were hundreds and hundreds and hundreds of people who came through the church. People who didn't know her. Many of us wanted to ease the burden of the family as much as we could, because we just couldn't imagine what they were going through, Elaine's two brothers and her sisters-in-law.

"A couple of my neighbors were wondering what was going to be done about the food after the funeral. Somebody from my church said that they thought that they would put together some sandwiches and things for people afterwards, and all I could think of was that at the prayer service there were hundreds and hundreds of people, as well as at the wake. All I could imagine was that the funeral was going to be mobbed."

As Sheila unfolded the story it sounded like the feeding of the five thousand from the Bible. She went on, "We asked some people for help, and each of the PTOs of the grammar schools; there are four grammar schools in Reading. We asked if they could bake, and then a couple of us went around to the merchants in Reading, which is not a big town. But there are some pizza places and sandwich places, and we asked each merchant if they would mind donating some food. They couldn't do enough for us. For some, the food that they had wasn't appropriate, for example, the pizza place, but that guy said, 'Well, I'll put some calzones together. I don't make them, but I'll make them for you.' And there were bakeries that said they would do things, supermarkets said that they would put together fruit and vegetable trays and crackers.

"People started the night before bringing in food. Soon they had so much food in the downstairs of the church that there was no place to put it. The food just kept coming in and coming in. Somebody else donated paper goods, and there was just not enough room to put it all.

"The day of the funeral it was just beautiful. The service was so touching. It pulled together the entire community. They had her casket draped in white with her nurse's cap on top. At one point the priest was talking about Elaine when all of a sudden a light came in through the window and lit up the white nurse's cap. It lit it up so bright that a couple of us who saw it talked about it afterwards and said it was as if Elaine was there. I had never seen anything like that. I don't believe in signs, but whatever this was, it was amazing. The cap turned a brilliant bright white as the priest was talking about Elaine, and then the priest talked about something else, and the light very slowly moved away. Even though I don't believe in signs, it seemed like one.

"After the Mass many people went downstairs. People were talking and even laughing a little bit. The situation brought so many people together. At the end of the funeral there was so much food left over we decided we would do a bake sale. Well, just on the baked goods alone we made fifteen hundred dollars that went toward a fund for the Donahue children. I've been involved in bake sales before, and we were happy if we made three hundred—and this one made fifteen hundred. One of the youth groups at the

church did a bottle drive. Again, I've been involved in bottle drives, and six hundred dollars would be considered amazing. They
made two thousand in this bottle drive. The nurses had a raffle. I
don't remember how much money that made, but it was thousands
of dollars, with all the proceeds benefiting the Donahue children. I
don't know how much the final total was of funds raised, but it was
at least thirty thousand dollars, if not more—just from raffles, bake
sales, and little things like that."

"People did what they could," I said.

"Yes," Sheila said. "It gave us, I believe, some control when we
felt like everything was out of our control. It was something solid
that we could do and have a little bit of control over, where everything else had just gone crazy."

One of the most powerful benefits of connection is this feeling of
power and control it gives the participants. Even if you do not have
total control—and who does?—feeling connected to a larger effort
that you believe in gives you a feeling of having some power. It may
be a political cause, or a local zoning issue, or a blood drive for a sick
friend, or as in the case of the people of Reading, a traumatic event.
Whatever the issue may be, people feel stronger when they connect.

One of the things that impressed me about how the people of
Reading reacted was how spontaneous their response was. I asked
Sheila specifically, "Did all this happen without a coordinator?"

"There was *nobody* in charge, no coordinator," she replied. "We all
just felt that we had to do something. We really didn't know what,
but it snowballed. I don't believe much laundry or dishes got done
during that time."

"Are you still closer as a neighborhood now," I asked, "almost a
year later?"

"Definitely we're still close," Sheila replied. "My family lives in
a fairly small house, and we're wanting to find a new house, but I'm
very hesitant about leaving this neighborhood because we bonded
in a way that probably won't happen again. I could be friendly and
be on very good terms with people in another neighborhood. I'm
extroverted, I like talking with people, I like doing things with
people. But . . . I don't even know how to describe it, that real bonding that we had, not all of our neighbors, but some of the neighbors. I don't think I would find that in a new neighborhood."

"Who lives in that house across the street now?" I asked.

"Nobody, not right now. I don't know what they're going to do with it. I believe Elaine's father is keeping up the maintenance of the house, and then her best friend, Janice, and Janice's son have been mowing the lawn recently."

"It must obviously feel weird to have this empty house sitting there," I remarked.

"It's disconcerting," Sheila agreed. "The police brought Elaine's car back and they put it in the driveway, and when you go by, for a second you think the whole thing was a bad dream. But of course it wasn't."

"Why did Ed do it?" I asked.

Sheila took a deep breath. "Well, apparently, unbeknownst to most people, he had had a gambling problem. I remember quite a few years ago that Elaine and Ed had separated. I didn't know the reason why. Elaine just told me that Ed wasn't living at the house. I thought it had something to do with depression. He always seemed to be down. He lost his job many times. I thought maybe he had a drinking problem, but apparently it was gambling. I do know that he had gone through their savings, and I believe he had stolen some of her jewelry. She had put the house and cars in her name alone, and I believe she had changed her will to state that if anything were to happen to her, everything would go to the children. Not knowing any of this, many of us neighbors just couldn't believe that Ed had anything to do with her death. Now, the one question I would like to ask him is, 'What were you thinking?' "

"He's in jail now?" I asked.

Sheila nodded. "He's in jail. He went to trial and was convicted of first degree murder. In Massachusetts there is no death penalty, which I am glad of because I think that would be even more devastating to the children. He's got a life sentence with no parole."

"What a tragic story," I said.

"It is, it's terrible. But as I was saying before, there were some very good things that came of it."

"It brought people together?"

"Like you'd never imagine. One day I came home," Sheila went on, "and there were a dozen long-stemmed roses with the most beautiful note on my front porch that said, 'I've been thinking about you and how terrible everything must have been to be part of the whole situation.' Just to know that the sender was thinking of me meant so much. Another friend dropped off a gift certificate to a restaurant so we could take the kids out of the neighborhood and have someplace to go. It was things like that. People treated you in ways that you wouldn't normally think of. They were so helpful and so incredibly kind. People just wanted to do anything they possibly could to help anybody.

"Now," Sheila said, "we look out across the street, and the house is still there, and the car is still there, and maybe until somebody moves in, it will be a constant reminder, but it gets a little easier as time goes on."

Each time I think of this story it makes me wince. The details of the murder drive home the fact that, at times, connection leads to disaster. Ed went after the person closest to him. Why? No one can say for sure, but we can say for sure that Elaine would have been safer if she had never got involved with Ed. At times, a close connection leads to death.

But at the same time the story points up the power of the community of good people to help out in a time of crisis, or, as the Reverend Bob Tobin says, to do what needs to be done without being told.

At Christmas time in 1997, the year of the murder, and again at Christmas time in 1998, members of the neighborhood put candles in plastic milk bottles filled with sand, set six or eight of them in their front yards at night, and lit the candles in memory of Elaine. One evening, a group of neighbors walked from house to house caroling. Sheila told me this is a tradition they plan to continue each year both to commemorate Elaine and to remind each other of their strong connection.

Sheila's daughter has kept up her relationship with Elaine's daughter, who now lives in another city with Elaine's brother and sister-in-law. Sheila spent some time with all four of the Donahue children when they got together Christmas of 1998. She told me that all the kids are doing well now.

~~~~~

TWENTY-FIVE

Be a Hero, or a Star?

WHICH DO YOU WANT FOR YOUR CHILDREN?

DO YOU WANT your child to be a star? Or is being a hero what matters most? I'd choose hero for my children. If they become stars, that's fine, too. But if we're not careful, a whole generation of children will grow up believing stardom is the *only* way to happiness. It is already happening in some areas. People who single-mindedly pursue stardom often make a deal with the devil. "Grant me the prize," the deal goes, "and I'll do anything you want me to do to get there."

A survey from *Who's Who Among American High School Students* reported that 80 percent of top students admit to cheating in school. Apparently cheating is so common that it is taken for granted in many places.

I had the following conversation with a teacher from an affluent suburb of New York. He was telling me how distressed he was that school had become such a cynical game of achievement for achievement's sake. The kids believed in absolutely nothing except success. They would cut one another's throats in a heartbeat if they thought it would get them another point on the chemistry test.

"It's the times we live in," he said. "The kids are terrified they won't make it up the ladder. And this is one of the most affluent school systems in the country. The fact is, these kids will have to work hard *not* to succeed. Most of them have it made already. But they behave as if they have to kill their friends or get killed themselves! They'll cheat whenever they think they won't get caught, they'll do anything that advances them. Their only guiding principle, if you want to call it that, is success."

"Do they have any fun?" I asked.

"Are you kidding? They have drugs as an outlet, but they don't have fun. They can't even enjoy their successes, because the pressure is always on. Their goal is many, many years away. The only way these kids would have fun is if 'fun' could be put on their college application. You know, 'Andrew is gifted at fun. Shows remarkable talent. We should keep an eye on him. Is the cover of *Time* too much to imagine? I don't think so.' No, these kids do not have fun, at least what I consider to be fun. What they do is work. I suppose that's a good thing, isn't it? It's *why* they work, and *the way* they work, that bothers me. For example, it's not unusual for a kid to be going to bed at midnight and getting up at five-thirty the next morning."

"Really?" I asked, astonished, thinking back to my days at Exeter, certainly a high-pressure school. I worked hard then, or so I thought, but I *never* worked hours like that! "These are high school kids?"

"It happens all the time," the teacher replied. "We hear about it frequently. By Friday, the kids are so tired it's a joke around school, they're so worn out. Kids are falling asleep in class, falling asleep on their plate of spaghetti in the cafeteria, falling asleep on benches in the locker room, even falling asleep on the floor in the shower. On the weekends they try to catch up, but they can't during the week. By Friday they're just dead. Their bodies shut down. It's worrisome. All the kids can see is success, but at what cost?"

"It's like the tail wagging the dog," I said.

"And they're not getting an education, because they're not thinking about learning, they're only thinking about their grades," he said.

"So, it's not as if they're on their way to becoming lifelong learners," I added. "They probably hate what they're doing and can't wait until they don't have to do it anymore."

"Exactly, exactly," the teacher agreed. "The smarter ones fake it better. They pretend to be genuinely interested, because they know that's what the teacher wants. I don't know, maybe it's the way we're teaching them. Whatever the cause, it is a problem."

It is a problem for sure. Maybe it is more severe in this man's school, but I see it in various forms wherever I go across the country, and I see it in the young people I treat.

In my opinion as a child psychiatrist, the problem all comes back to a lack of connectedness in modern life, particularly in the lives of children. They feel completely on their own. Dog eat dog.

Now, some people, especially dads, say to me, "Well, that's good preparation, because that is the way life is." But it *isn't* the way life is, and these dads know better, if they only take a moment to think about it. We all have *some* supports available, if we choose to use them. Far from preparing a person for life, it ultimately disables an individual if you tell him there is no help to be found in life, that he is entirely on his own.

Success in life depends more on your ability to work with others than it does on your ability to work alone. More and more, the ability to be *effectively interdependent,* as opposed to independent, is the key to success. In a world of specialization and knowledge overflow, success depends upon knowing how to choose the right partners and employees, knowing how to inspire others, to command loyalty, and to motivate groups.

This kind of skill is learned in childhood. Indeed, childhood is like a laboratory of social connection. Sharing, negotiating, sticking up for the one who is being excluded, finding something good to say, playing by the rules—these simple tasks of childhood can become life skills of the highest order.

Connection breeds security. And disconnection breeds cynical, amoral opportunism. In the affluent suburb of New York the teacher described, where the most privileged children live, school has become a frenzied cauldron of insecure, ambitious adolescents who fake sincerity to get a good recommendation and cheat when they won't get caught.

Well-meaning parents tell me that they need to scare their children so they won't get complacent. They tell me they want their kids to know how tough it is out there, so the child will be ready to deal with the harsh realities of adult life.

This is exactly the wrong approach! Well meaning as it is, it runs the risk of producing precisely the opposite of the results intended.

The study I did at Exeter, mentioned in Chapter 1, gave concrete evidence of how this approach can backfire. Exeter is a high-powered school, a kind of proving ground for tomorrow's achievers. If any school is dog-eat-dog, you would imagine it to be Exeter.

But what the study showed was that the kids who bought into the dog-eat-dog mythology, as evidenced by their feeling driven to do well, were the very kids who were most likely to suffer depression, abuse drugs and alcohol, feel pessimistic about the future, and get low grades!

On the other hand, the kids who got the best grades, were the least depressed, were the least likely to abuse drugs and alcohol, and reported optimistic feelings about the future were the very kids who reported the lowest scores of feeling driven.

When I was a student at Exeter, the myth had always been, "The more it hurts, the better it is." Yet my study and others like it, such as the National Longitudinal Study on Adolescent Health, point in the opposite direction. The recent studies give strong evidence that it is connection that matters, not pressure to achieve. Give a child a feeling of connection at home and at school, and achievement will come.

That is not to say every connected child will become a superstar. Indeed, few will. By definition, there can't be many superstars. But the measure of life should not be becoming a superstar. If we think about it for a moment, all of us parents will realize that what we want for our children is not fame and riches, necessarily, but happiness and fulfillment.

We also want them to become good people. Sure, we want them to get ahead, to earn plenty of money, to have material success. But we don't want them to become amoral opportunists in the process.

There is no reason they cannot succeed materially and also become decent people. We just have to show them how.

The way to do it is to develop in them a strong sense of connection early on—not just to success, however that word is defined, but also to the community of good people, to the ideal of doing the right thing, to their fellowman.

A lot of very bright kids are growing up sneering at these ideas. They believe that the only way to live is to live for themselves. I give lectures often to audiences of adolescents, from grade school through high school. I'll never forget an exchange I had with one twelfth-grader. I'll have to reconstruct it from memory, but this is basically how it went.

I was giving a talk about connectedness to a group of two hundred high school students. At the end of my presentation, I had a period of discussion. One young man raised his hand and stated, "I just don't buy it."

"Tell me why," I replied.

"Because you are saying we should all connect to something larger than ourselves and be good to each other, but that is not the way life is. I mean, *don't you get it?*"

He was a big kid, with dark curly hair and black glasses. He looked sort of like a teddy bear, not a cutthroat type. I chuckled at his words. "Maybe I don't get it. Would you explain it to me?"

"Sure," he said, with a grin. The other kids laughed, as if they had heard him give explanations on various topics before. "I mean, I wish we could all be nice, like you say, but that is just not the way the world works. If you want to do well (like me—I want to have nice cars and a swimming pool), if you want to have money, you have got to make sacrifices. You can't just spend your time playing around, being nice. You have to get serious."

I could almost hear some adult's script running through his brain. "But I never said you shouldn't get serious," I interjected. "And I certainly didn't say you have to be nice to everyone. I just said I think you'll be happiest if you lead a connected life. The fact is, you'll probably also make more money that way, as well."

"As long as it's money I'm connected to, I'm all for it," the kid replied, and everyone laughed.

"But do you think money can take care of *everything?*" I asked.

"Pretty much," he replied, and everyone laughed again.

"It can't make you live forever," I said.

"No," he replied, "but it can make you happy while you live!" he replied, and everyone laughed again.

We debated back and forth for a while, always with a humorous tone. Finally I said, "Just look at this conversation. We are connecting, you and I. I think you are enjoying talking to me, and I know I am enjoying talking to you. This is what makes life worthwhile."

The kid started to speak, but then he stopped and smiled. "You *like* talking to me?" he asked. Everyone laughed.

"I love talking to you," I said. "You have totally made my day. In fact, I want to put you in my next book, is that OK?"

"Will I get royalties?" he asked.

"No," I said. "They all go to my children." .

"You see? You proved my point," the kid said, and everyone laughed again.

We left it at that. I have not forgotten him, and I have put him in my book, but not just because I told him I would. It is because our exchange pointed up the problem so perfectly. Here was this great kid, a born connector, espousing a philosophy of selfishness because I presume, that is what he had absorbed from his culture—his home, his peers, his school, the media.

There are millions of young people today who are starting out life with the wrong idea. They are starting out life believing that the way to happiness is through stardom, being Bill Gates or Michael Jordan or Tiger Woods.

But not everyone can be a star. And certainly, not all stars are happy! However, *everyone* can be connected.

With connection comes moral development. If you feel a part of something larger than yourself, you will not want to let that something larger down, you will not want to disappoint it, you will want to please it. Whether that something larger be your family, your school, your Little League team, or the kingdom of God, if you feel connected to it, you will want to please it, and you will not want to let it down.

This is how moral education happens at its best—through connection. Moral instruction—do this, don't do that, this is right, that is wrong—is fine, but it is ineffective unless it is combined with connection. Connection provides the emotional punch. Connection is what makes the child—or adult—*want* to do what's right.

Rick Lavoie, the head of the Riverview School, told me the following story, which captures in a single moment what connection can do.

"I spent a significant part of my career in Greenwich, Connecticut," Rick wrote to me.

Greenwich is a wonderful town that is populated by many of the movers and shakers in our society. There is a sense of competition that pervades this town, and the concept of connection is often sacrificed at the altar of competition.

One day I was sitting at a counter at a downtown Greenwich pizza parlor. I was splitting a small pepperoni pizza with my five-year-old son, Christian. As we sat there, I could not help but overhear the conversation among three teenage boys who were sitting in the booth directly behind us. They were dressed in tennis whites and had obviously just returned from a morning at their fancy local tennis club. Two of the boys were discussing the faults and foibles of another boy, who was not in attendance. They criticized his tennis play, his mode of dress, and every aspect of his personality. The boy obviously suffered tremendous social isolation and rejection. They laughed as they regaled each other with stories of his various faults and failures.

At one point, one of the boys turned to the third boy, who had been silent during the discussion, and said, "None of us *ever* wants to play with Mike. He's such a *nerd*. But whenever the coach asks us to choose a partner for doubles, *you* always choose to play with Mike. *Nobody* likes Mike. *Nobody* will play with Mike. Why do *you* play with him?"

The third boy responded quietly, "That's *why* I play with him."

I looked over my shoulder at that courageous young man, and then I looked at my own son. My fondest hope at that moment was that my son would develop the strength of character and courage that that boy possessed. I hope that young man's father knows how proud he should be of his son.

Be a hero, not a star.

~⌒~

TWENTY-SIX

Breaking a Connection

JUST AS YOU have to weed a garden, sometimes you have to re-move a connection in order to make others strong. Sometimes one bad connection weakens all your others or demands so much energy that you have no time for any others. Sometimes the most impor-tant step you can take in tending your garden of connections is to get rid of one or two bad ones, the ones that are choking the growth of the others. This is usually difficult, sometimes painful, but once it is done, your other connections can flourish.

I'll give an example. One day a lovely woman in her forties walked into my office to get a consultation regarding her son's learning disabilities. She gave off a simple radiance. As she talked, I felt a special quality about her, a kind of confidence with vulnera-bility. I have learned that this trait is typical of the connected per-son; confidence embedded in a willingness to show vulnerability comes with being connected.

Let me name her Sophie. She was forty-nine, a single mom, and a professor of special education at a college in New York. She wore no makeup, had short-cut sandy blond hair, and wore a simple dress and a beige cardigan sweater. After we talked about her son for a while, I asked, "What's happened with *your* life in the past few years?"

"Well, somehow or other I have arrived at a place I'm really glad to be at, and I feel very fortunate," she replied. "At this point, almost on a daily basis, I think of how fortunate I am. Looking back over the last six years, there has been a lot of change." When she said "a lot of change," I didn't anticipate all that she would tell me next. She had been diagnosed with breast cancer six years previously, had had one mastectomy, and now faced having a second. She had also been divorced during that period. But she said she was happier now than she'd ever been. I wondered how this could possibly be, so I asked her to tell me more.

"I was married in nineteen seventy-seven. It wasn't the best selection of a spouse, but I put a lot of effort in, as I tend to be tenacious and try to think, What else could I do to make things better? I put years into trying whatever I could to get this relationship to work. By nineteen ninety, there had been some separations and getting back together—it had been a rocky course.

"Then in nineteen ninety-two came the diagnosis of breast cancer. My then husband rallied to the situation and was supportive and made going through mastectomy and chemotherapy easier. I thought there might have been a silver lining to this experience of cancer, that a new focus on what was important in our marriage may have been identified by my illness and that maybe we could have a future together. We did, and do, have two fantastic children. My son is now eleven and my daughter is now twenty-one. At that time he was four and she was fourteen. They responded differently to the illness, but it was hard for both of them. As my chemotherapy was coming to a close it became apparent that the changes in behavior on my husband's part had only been temporary and had been fostered by the crisis. He then started training for a second career and became unavailable, self-absorbed, and angry again."

"What was he angry about?" I asked.

"I think he was worried about trying to juggle a new career with the rest of his life, and his anxiety just came out in impatience and a short temper."

"His career shift was from what to what?" I asked.

"It was from geology to being a stockbroker," Sophie replied.

"Quite a change!" I commented.

"That's for sure. He started off OK but I lost him to it. After about another year I decided that I had survived cancer and cancer treatment, but I didn't feel glad about the relationship that I was in. It wasn't the kind of connecting with a person that I wanted, and I felt that I had settled for a partner who wasn't a good match for me. I was giving up on the opportunity to embrace life the way you want to. So I took responsibility for that."

"Why do you think you had settled for less?" I asked.

"Oh, some history of self-doubt and lack of confidence about whether I was worthy of more. But those feelings had lessened as I grew older. Cancer helped me look beyond where I had been uncertain before. It made it apparent that I might not live a long time. My mother died at fifty-five from breast cancer and my grandfather died in his early fifties from prostate cancer, so there were lots of reasons to question my longevity. I wanted to make a life that I would be happy with.

"I had to be brave enough to give it a try. I thought that some integrity would come from that. I used to squirm writing Christmas cards to people I didn't see often because I didn't want to reveal just how disappointing day-to-day life was on the home front. I was ashamed reporting cheerfully what we were all doing. To some people I did share the reality, but one doesn't broadcast that. So, I made the decision to get out. It took more courage than I knew I had."

"How do you suppose you got the courage to do it?" I asked.

"My thought was, I would be disappointed if this was all I tried for. I wanted to at least try for the brass ring. Now I feel so much better about myself and so much more at peace, even though I had cancer. Yes, it would be nice if I were involved with someone, but I think my real goal is to be at peace with myself and to feel good about what I'm doing. The happiness comes in because I feel as though I'm a good parent and a good teacher and a good friend. You know, I have heard you talk about connection with causes, and I'm absolutely passionate about the reading field and helping to improve how children are taught to read. I've been doing research for twenty to twenty-five years in that area. I find it a source of joy to share that with other people."

"So, through the papers that you write," I said, "and the teaching that you do—"

"Yes," she enthusiastically interrupted, "the teaching, the conferences, and now I'm being called on to take the fight before legislative bodies, or I'm being consulted by other experts, and so there's a sense that a lot of work over a long time with a lot of dedication is really coming together. It's satisfying to see that making a difference. I feel very fortunate."

"There's your connection to that cause, as well as—what are the other connections that you found sustaining? To friends, students?"

"My children," she immediately replied, "are a big connection. I'm a very committed parent. However much you give, you get more back, and I give a lot to parenting. One feels the love back. You are doing the best for them. I find their love almost unexpected but extremely wonderful. Another place is with teaching. I give a lot to students and I'm available a lot to them and my grad students are awesome. They work so hard and are so earnest and so intelligent and so receptive. After teaching for a number of years I was surprised to find that not only is parenting a very nurturing activity, but teaching is too, and I enjoy that. Again, you give and give because you want to give, and then you get things back.

"In terms of friends, that's been building more slowly for me. I have friends that go way back who mean a lot to me, but when I was in my marriage I tended to isolate myself in my marriage and put my efforts there. Since getting out I have more tentatively tried to reach out for people. I know that they're there if I need them. At least my confidence in that is gradually growing. It's going to be a process over more years. It's still easier for me to give help than to ask for help," Sophie said.

"What is the fear in connecting with friends?" I asked.

"I guess it's being rejected," she replied.

"And since you broke up with your husband, have you dated people?" I asked.

"Only a little," she replied. "Nothing much. I don't meet many people that I'm interested in dating. I'm wistfully hopeful that that might happen. I am recognizing that love comes in a lot of forms and that I'm fortunate to have it in as many ways as I do."

"It was quite a change," I reflected, "in terms of how you feel within yourself between when the diagnosis of the cancer was made and today."

"I think so. It was growing over the years. I was not happy with myself for staying in a relationship that was not good for me."

"It wasn't good from the start?" I asked.

"It was bad from the start. He was self-absorbed and not ready to be in a mature relationship. I found it hurtful. There were horrible arguments. He was sometimes violent. It became a relationship where I took on too much responsibility and he abdicated responsibility—so, that was my fault as much as his. But it wasn't a relationship of equals, it wasn't a relationship of real friends. He had some tremendous strengths, though. There certainly were parts of the relationship I enjoyed. I would think about those, and then there would be promises, and there would be heartfelt talks. I was just incredibly gullible. How often I would try it one more time."

"And he would promise what?" I asked. "To . . ."

"To be there," she replied. "To interact more, to be more reliable. He was good on vacation, when there was nothing else going on. We had great vacations. But day-to-day life seemed to be overwhelming for him. He would not take care of personal relationships—of course, that included me and the children—and there was just a lot of wear and tear."

"So he would just work?"

"He would go to work, he would stay there until two in the morning, he wouldn't get up with the family the next day. It would get so that he would be storming around with a frown on his face and he would be angry all the time. When he was driving a car, he would be swearing at other drivers. There was just too much anger. Too often. I didn't have the environment I wanted to live in."

"What was he so angry about?" I wondered.

"I don't think he felt good about himself," Sophie answered after a moment's thought. "He is extremely smart and he is capable of doing a lot of things, and to his credit he taught himself a lot of different skills. I admire that. But he would get himself into situations that he wasn't prepared for. For example, he worked in geology with a B.A. in English, and he was working with Ph.D.'s in geology, so he was often trying to play catch-up and was unsure of himself. He was disorganized and would start one project before he finished another one, and it always seemed like there was a crisis. There was a deadline, there was something due. He wasn't going to get it done on time. He wasn't sure if it was going to be done right. There was a lot of self-doubt in there, which contributed to the problems he was facing in our relationship. I think the self-doubt made him say things to me that no one should say. He didn't mean them, but they were incredibly damaging. Things that no one should take."

"Like what?" I asked.

"Things like, 'I'd like to beat your face into a bloody pulp,' or 'I don't care about you.' Things like that."

"Yes," I said with a wince. "And it's been how long since the divorce?"

Sophie paused. "I forget, which is amazing. I had cancer in nineteen ninety-two. Two years later I asked for a divorce. It took two years to get the divorce."

"How do your kids feel about it all?" I asked.

"Well, my daughter's comment was, 'I wish you had done this a long time ago.' My son asked what would happen if I died, and I said, 'Well, I guess you would go live with your father,' and he said, 'Do I have to?' And I said, 'Well, does that mean you wouldn't want to?' And he said he would rather live with somebody like me. And I said, 'What does that mean?' And he said, 'Well, you're both nice. I like him and I enjoy my time with him. But you're more cuddly.' And I laughed and said, 'Really? Even though I'm the one who makes you do your homework and makes you do chores and stays on your back?' He said, 'Yes.' "

"You'd known all along you weren't happy," I remarked, "but you stayed because you didn't know that you could do any better?"

"Yes, or I feared that I would do worse or I feared the effects of divorce on the kids."

"It wasn't finances?" I asked.

"I had a job, so that was not it. It was more at an emotional level, dealing with it in my head, weighing the pros and cons for way too long. I didn't listen to my gut. My gut knew it wasn't right for me. My gut knew, and I kept trying to talk my gut out of it. I tried to think about what his qualities were that were good, and whether there was anything else I could do to change the situation. All that thinking wasted a lot of time."

"And now you've discovered within yourself . . . what?" I asked.

"Listen to your gut," Sophie replied.

"Now you feel stronger, you feel better about who you are?"

"Yes. Also, I know the sky didn't fall down. You know, my plate is rather full with ongoing cancer worries, and I got my teenager through her teenage years on my own, and my son has academic challenges that take a lot of time, and yet I feel buoyant. I feel that there are two wonderful people in my life and I'm lucky to have a job that is so satisfying, and I'm even indulging now in things I enjoy. I put in a perennial garden last year with help from knowledgeable friends, and that has been fantastic. So, when I thought I might have a cancer recurrence recently, I was really surprised to reflect on the difference between now and six years ago. I'm really enjoying life. There are areas I would love to improve, there is no doubt about it, but it's a fine life. I'm not in a state of indecision where I'm holding back."

"Being in a state of indecision, of ambivalence, is . . ." I paused, looking for a word.

"Ambivalence is horrible," she jumped in. "And being sensitive takes a lot of effort. Whereas, once you decide what direction you really want to go in, you get a lot more energy. Does that make sense to you?"

"It sure does. Did God or spirituality play a part in it at all?" I asked.

"No, not for me," she replied. "I'm not religious, and that makes it harder. You have your own belief system. Talking to therapists helped. That might have backfired, too. I think that when you go to therapists for marriage counseling, the presumption is that this marriage should be saved. And so, you know, you put a lot of time in doing what you can to save it. It would be nice if there was some written test you could take to see if two people would really be better off without each other. On the other hand, I had peace of mind that I tried everything. I grew during those difficult years. You get compassion, and you get insight, and you get wisdom, so it's not all bad, even though it was pretty painful."

"The turning point was getting the cancer?"

"It seems to have been. One could also look at my career and say it certainly has been taking off, so that helped. The turning point might also have been just getting out of the marriage. I had been debating that before I got cancer and then went back to the marriage when I was diagnosed. As I say, he was quite lovely then, but I didn't want to have to have a fatal illness to get the good side of him."

"And your health status now, you're thinking about a second mastectomy versus not?"

"Right. After the first mastectomy I had thought intellectually that I didn't identify myself with my breast and I'd be fine. I was surprised how much I grieved for this breast that had been a nice part of my body and had nursed my babies, and I was just surprised that one has to grieve a body part as if it were a lost relationship or something. I suppose I was again trying to use my head and also not to buy into the culture's overemphasis on body image for women. It took a while. It's a bit harder on the single scene to tell someone you're going out with that you're missing a breast. It just sort of complicates life."

"Yes," I said. "Yet you told me your chances are ninety-five percent you won't get a recurrence of the cancer if you have the second operation, but sixty-five percent if you don't have the operation. Is that correct?"

"Right. I have had three biopsies now in my remaining breast, and the mammograms keep looking suspicious. The pathology reports indicate a sort of in-between state between totally healthy breast versus malignant breast tissue, which elevates your risk likelihood. Part of you just wants to go on being busy and doing things you enjoy, and hope for the best; and part of me wants to reduce the anxiety and the fear. My kids would both immediately say, 'Off with that breast!'—they would rather have me around. And whenever the specter of cancer comes up again, it's very clear what the priority is. That life is dear, and even without two breasts, it's a blessing, and it's well worth having and sustaining as long as possible. So that's clear.

"Where it gets hard is with the math of, *Well, do I have to go through another operation?* And do I have to lose another body part, and do I have to now yet be a stronger person to have a good relationship with a man? So I'm checking out information. I'll talk to my oncologist later this month about other ways to reduce risks, and I'm toying with talking to a plastic surgeon. I tend to be very much be-who-you-are, don't-be-phony, so reconstruction makes me a bit uncomfortable, but I've been thinking, Well, does one have to accept what cancer dishes out? If you were in a car accident and lost your arm, of course you would get a prosthetic arm. Those are decisions to be made."

"And you're at a great place in your work now," I added.

"Excellent. I'm thriving," she said, smiling.

"Well," I said, "if I may say so, I think you are a beautiful woman both on the outside and on the inside. I think men would line up if they knew where you were. It's a very moving story, one I think that a lot of people can identify with. It took so much courage. It's not like you left into the arms of another man. You went into the arms of uncertainty and cancer."

"At one point," Sophie said, "there had been a colleague who was interested in me and whom I respected a lot. But I did not get involved with him. I wanted to sort out what my relationship was with my husband before moving on. In the meantime he got involved with someone else, and we're friends. I think all of that was the right choice. I felt better trying to sort myself out, even though in my fantasy life it would be nice if someone had come along while I was going through the divorce and had been supportive. But I think it's more important for me to have reached this sense of well-being that I have myself and to know that that feeling can come from me. But it's certainly not coming from me alone, because I'm supported by children and colleagues and students and friends, and yet there is more of a sense of being responsible for myself. I think as that solidifies I will have a better chance of being in a good relationship and of being at peace with me. I'm about ready for a relationship now, but it's probably been for the best that I haven't had one. How's that for rationalizing?" she said with a laugh.

TWENTY-SEVEN

When the Worst Happens

THE DEATH OF A CHILD

DAVID NUNES WAS born in December 1982, and he died in May 1993. His death was sudden and totally unexpected, resulting from an extremely rare parasitic infection that silently surrounded his heart and finally stopped it.

His dad, Tony Nunes, and his mom, Gail Nunes, still live near Cambridge, Massachusetts, where David lived his whole life. David's sister, Mariel, was five when David died. Gail and Tony have since had another child, Akacia, who is now three.

David had been adopted by Gail and Tony when he was six months old. His biological mother was Tony's sister, but she was unable to care for him because she had schizophrenia.

Tony, whose parents were both of West Indian descent, had an abusive dad who was a cop in the Bronx. Tony's mother left his dad when Tony was ten. She moved Tony and his four siblings to Cambridge, where she raised them by herself. Tony went through various phases of rebellion and hell-raising, but he ended up getting his college degree at Wheelock at age thirty-two, and then getting a master's by going to Wheelock at night. He has had a fifteen-year career as a teacher in the Boston area, starting at Shady Hill, moving to the Cambridge Public School system, and now being assistant head of the Neighborhood House Charter School in Dorchester. He is widely respected.

As is Gail. Gail is of Sicilian descent. Tony laughs as he says that because Gail is dark and Tony is light, most people don't know "what race we are." Gail has worked many jobs. Now she works as a school counselor and play therapist. She is superb at what she does.

I know the Nuneses because our children attend the same school, Shady Hill in Cambridge, we attend the same church, Christ Church in Cambridge, and for a short period of time David was my patient. His parents brought David to see me when he was eight because of some behavioral problems. Luckily, I was able to help him and his parents, and for the last few years of his life he was doing great in school and in life in general. He always seemed to be in excellent physical health.

David was a special kid. Which kid isn't, I guess, but still, David had a special something about him, an energy, a joie de vivre. At times some would say he was *impossible*, but always everyone would say he was lovable. People naturally felt drawn to him.

Now there is a park in Cambridge that bears his name, the David Nunes Park. David's class just graduated last spring from Shady Hill, and the school dedicated the yearbook to him. The anniversary of his death is remembered each year in church. His last gift to the world was to strengthen the connection of these communities.

I asked Gail and Tony to talk to me about his life and death.

"The day David died," Tony told me, "I came home from work late, about five. I was teaching school, and I was in a meeting after school. When I came in, he was watching TV on the floor with the baby-sitter and Mariel. I was in a real nice place mentally. The day before, Sunday, was like one of the best days. All the puzzle pieces of life felt secure. Life felt complete. It really did. I remember that. When I came home I was still carrying that feeling. So I came home, and I just kicked the kids on the foot lightly, and asked, 'Did you do your homework?'

" 'No.'

" 'Well, come on, get up and go do your homework.'

" 'Well, I don't feel good.'

" 'Oh go on, do your homework and you'll feel better.'

"He said, 'Well, I'm not going to do it at the kitchen table.'

"I was going in to cook, and that was the nineteen fifties image in my head of parent cooking dinner with kid doing homework at the table in case he needed some help. His bedroom was the dining room, next to the kitchen. He had to assert himself and say, 'I'm going to do it in my room.' I said fine.

"The last time I saw him really alive I looked from the kitchen into the dining room and I saw his face didn't look right. I said, 'You really are sick.'

"He said, 'Yeah.'

"I said, 'Forget the homework. It's the end of the year. You can either do it after dinner when your mother comes home, or I'll write a note.'

"He went to the refrigerator, gulped some juice, ran into the living room, where Mariel was sitting, put his head into her lap, and he expired.

"Mariel came into the kitchen and told me that David went to sleep and she couldn't wake him. Gail always said that she would sit and rock with him, and if he fell asleep, he'd feel better, so I said let him sleep. Mariel knew something was wrong. She saw his life sputter out of his body. She stood on his stomach and tried to wake him up, and she couldn't. She came back in and she told me. Kathy, the baby-sitter, came into the kitchen to help with dinner, and the dog started to lick David's face. I thought David was sleeping. When the dog licked his face I said something isn't right.

"I immediately started some CPR, and I told Kathy to take Mariel out to the kitchen and to feed her, and I called nine-one-one. I said, 'Kathy, I need your presence. I need you with me for Mariel. I need to be in there. I'm not leaving him alone.' When the emergency people came, the cops came in and one cop lost it. The cop saw what was going on and the cop started to shake and tear. And I grabbed him and said, 'Hold on, buddy, he's going to be OK,' trying to convince myself. I remember them asking me, when I blew into his mouth doing mouth-to-mouth resuscitation, what he gurgled up. I said he choked. So they were going to do a tracheotomy. And they pulled out a scalpel and they were going to cut his throat and I remember grabbing the man, saying, 'Don't destroy the body.'

"Gail called when I took them in the kitchen to eat, and I said to myself, Let me be as calm as I can. What was I going to tell her, he's dead? I said, 'Gail, come home, it's an emergency. David is very sick.' "

Gail, who had been listening to Tony's account of that awful night, then spoke: "I said, 'Is he throwing up again?' And he said, 'No, just come home.' I put the phone down, and I knew right then. I knew.

"I turned to the person I was working with, and I said, 'I have to go.' I got in my car, and I had to go down the Mass. Pike. I remember going like eighty-five miles an hour. I pulled up and there were two ambulances, a police car, a fire engine, and Tony pacing back and forth."

"I saw her pull up," Tony said. "They were ready; they had him strapped down on the gurney on the stretcher taking him out. And I said, no way am I going to let my wife come into the house while they're taking him out. He was dead. I said hold up. I stopped them from carrying him out."

Gail broke in. "And then Tony crossed the street to me and said, 'I think we've lost David.' I just flipped out. I said, 'What do you mean?' A number of things went through my head. I'm very unclear about a lot of it. The first image I saw was trying to go by the cop to get to David, and him holding me back, and I said, 'I need to get to my son. What are you doing? I need to get to my son. Let me get to my son.' He said, 'No, you can't.' I said, 'What do you mean, I can't?' So that was the first thing I remembered.

"The second thing is that Tony then said, 'You need to see Mariel,' and boom, it kicked in, I've got to get upstairs. I had been working in hospitals for a long time and knew what a code scene looked like, and this was a code scene, and I said, 'Oh, my God.' That's when I really saw what had happened in my living room. I ran in to Mariel and I said to her, 'I'm going to bring your brother home, don't worry.' She already knew. I could see it in her face that she already knew.

"I went down to the ambulance and talked to the guard in the other ambulance, and the other image I remember seeing is the four people across the street staring at me, not saying a word. We got in the backup ambulance and I turned to the EMT and said, 'Talk to me, I work in hospitals, I want to know about it. Did you code him? Have you tried to resuscitate him? Have you used paddles? Is he able to come back?' Tony looked at me and said, 'I don't know. I think he choked.' " The truth is the granuloma was so large by this time that a team of cardiologists couldn't have saved him.

Gail went on, "The doctors told us later that even if a team of cardiologists had been in the room with David, it was too late. He could not have been saved, no matter what anyone did. This was important for us to know, obviously."

Both Tony and Gail were calm as they told me all this. They sat next to each other on the couch, touching now and then, and simply spoke what they recalled from four years ago.

"When we got to the hospital it was pretty much as you can imagine," Gail said. "It was nuts. Everybody came running from everywhere."

"Children's Hospital in Boston?" I asked.

"Yes," Gail replied. "Everybody came running from everywhere. They didn't tend to us, but left us standing in the hallway."

"This was actually kind of funny," Tony added. "I said, 'I want some place that's quiet.' I guess I really am some sort of a believer because all this came forth. The only place I could think of that I wanted to be was someplace quiet, in a church. And I said, 'Is there a chapel where we can sit? I don't want to be in the middle of all this chaos.' So they put us in a room. They asked, 'Do you want a chaplain?' I said, 'Not a bad idea. Let's get the last rites.' So they found this drunk Irish Catholic priest who came to me reeking of alcohol. He asked me what my name was, and I said Nunes. He said, 'Oh, you're Portuguese. I've got some good friends that are Portuguese.' I said, 'Look, my son is in another room in a code, and I'd like the last rites.' He said, 'You want the last rites for yourself?' 'No, for my son,' I said. So he went in there with David, and he came back out and he wanted to keep talking to me about did I know this family from New Bedford. I said leave me alone.

"Then I had to go out to call to get a ride home. I called Bob Tobin (the rector of Christ Church in Cambridge). I'm in the middle of an open room full of people, I didn't have a quarter in my pocket. I would have appreciated the privacy of a phone booth, or a private phone, but they plugged in a phone on a counter, thinking they were doing me some help. I had to call Maurine Tobin (Bob's wife) and tell her that my son died, with a room full of people listening. That was, to me, so insensitive. Not only did I have to endure the worst, but I had to do it publicly. The same way Gail has her memories, I remember that."

Gail then interjected, "They were doing a lot of work on David, and then they just came in at one point and said, 'We don't think David's going to make it. We need to ask your permission to pull the plugs.' And then they asked for his organs. And you know, we thought—"

"I said, 'Take what you want,' " Tony said.

"But because it was an unknown death," Gail added, "they had to keep everything. When they let us go into the room, I went over to David and held him. He was cold. I remember trying to warm his arms up. I was saying, 'You're too cold and you have to be warm,' and I was rubbing his arms. All I wanted to do was hold him. I wanted to put him in my lap and hold him. I knew he was dead."

Then Bob Tobin arrived at the emergency room. "Bob came into the room," Gail recalled, "and all of a sudden out of all the cold I felt this big warm hug, his arms coming around me. I looked at Bob, and the first thing I said to him was, 'You know, we did a lot of work, don't you?' And he said, 'Yes.' There was a part of me that was feeling that we failed David. Right in that moment I thought, no matter how much work we did, it wasn't enough.

"Then there was the awful time of waiting. We went home, and I had to tell Mariel. I brought her into the room and I told her, and she wanted to just sit there and watch *Snow White*. So the Tobins, myself, and Mariel watched *Snow White*. I was hoping she would go to sleep so I could just let go, but she wasn't doing that. And Tony was on the phone."

Tony said, "Bob and Maurine stayed until our family came over. We tried calling my brother-in-law, but he had a teenage daughter who was on the phone. Finally they interrupted the call."

"The police came to their house," Gail said. "The phone was busy and the police went to the house. That's how they found out. Ronnie said that the policeman came to his door and told him his nephew died."

Tony looked puzzled. "I still don't understand how the policeman came to the door. We're calling the house, the phones were busy. Did we call the police?"

"No, the operator," Gail replied. "You called the operator, and the operator called the police. You said you wanted to cut into the line, and they said they couldn't."

Gail sighed. "Anyway," she said, "a couple of things about connection I think are really important in this. I was working two jobs that year, and on the second job a black woman and I became very close friends. She had lost a child, an eight-year-old, about twenty years before. Once when David was sick with the flu I said to her, 'Mary, you know, I don't think I could live if I lost one of my children. I really don't think I could live.' And she told me in that moment what I would do. She said, 'You would live, you would make it through the funeral,' and then she gave me sort of instructions about how I would do this.

"I remember her coming through the receiving line after David's funeral. Tony had taught a child at Shady Hill that had a soft tissue cancer, and he had died. We had seen Stephanie, that child's mother, one day in the parking lot when I was pregnant with Mariel. Her son was really sick. She said to Tony, 'I think we have to let him go.' I turned from her and I couldn't help but cry. I was just a wreck. Here I was coming from having an ultrasound on my new baby, and she's losing her child.

"Well, those two people, Stephanie and Mary, came through the funeral line together. Next to each other. They didn't know each other, but they were standing there next to each other. And they came to me at the same time. I said, 'If it wasn't for the two of you, I don't think I could be here right now.' And they didn't even know each other.

"'The other thing that happened,' Gail continued, "was the dream I had the week before David died. I called you about it, actually."

"I remember," I said.

"There was an incident where David was being baby-sat and he went around the house and pulled all the curtains down. Remember, I called you about that. The baby-sitter was very freaked out by this. He got up from his sleep, went and pulled every curtain in the house down. In the dream that I had, all the shades popped open, and this white light came flashing through. Everyone at my job was in a circle in this dream, and the white light had a piercing siren sound to it. I kept saying, 'I have to get out of here, I have to get out of here.' This was a week before David died. So that was another message to me.

"Then, the Saturday before he died he came to me just like he did when he was three, and he put his hand on the couch, and he said,

'You know, there's a little boy who died, a fifteen-year-old who died at the W.E.B. Du Bois Academy.' And I said, 'Well, David, that's really strange. Kids don't usually die.' I was sort of freaked out about it, so I did what we all do when we're freaked out. We don't answer. He then asked to put on the movie *All Dogs Go to Heaven.* We put on the movie, and he, his sister, and her best friend watched it. They had the best afternoon. We all sat there, eating popcorn and ice cream. This was Saturday. Saturday night we were still hanging on to that very good feeling. I remember we were cracking up because David used to make fun of the way Chinese people talked. He would do this singsong thing. We were all doing it, and he was cracking up."

Tony started to laugh, and he interjected, "They were cracking up and I was trying to say, 'This is not right, this is not cool, you are being disrespectful.' But they were laughing so much that my PC went out the window, and I had to join them in the laughter. They were having such a good time."

"We all played games that night," Gail went on. "We played board games, which we had actually never done as a family. Scrabble, I think it was, and the very next day David was in the church play. That night we were at a barbecue and the kids were watching the little neighbor's boy from next door, and I said to David, 'You're really good with this kid. We should have another child.' And he said, 'Yeah, yeah, let's do it.'

"The next morning I went into school with him. Mariel's class was having a breakfast. I left him at his door at fourth grade and I went down to the breakfast, and he showed up. He said, 'Can we crash this breakfast?' and I said, 'Sure, why not?' That's the last time I saw him alive. That was five years ago."

At this point some tension between Tony and Gail surfaced a little bit. Often when a couple loses a child, they split up. Gail and Tony did not, and from what I can see, never will—they love each other a lot—but there is some residual tension, which only makes sense. Gail said, "The thing that stands out most of all was that I was having a very, very hard time the year after his death. Mariel and I went to a seminar, a hospice seminar run by a group. They took bereaved kids and parents. But Tony didn't want to go."

"I *couldn't* go," Tony protested.

"Whatever," Gail said, "but you didn't go."

Tony replied, "I'll tell you why I couldn't go. It was the same weekend as the vestry retreat. Don't say I didn't want to go."

"Right," Gail said. "But you could have come with us. Anyway, I met some people there who had lost family in a fishing accident on Martha's Vineyard. Two women had each lost a husband and a son. I met the mothers and daughters of the two families at that weekend and we have been friends ever since. It was the first time that Mariel felt she met somebody who was like her."

"She had asked to go," Tony added. Gail and Tony make up fast.

"When parents need support after a tragedy like this and they don't know how to ask for help anymore, other people sometimes just disappear."

"They don't know what to say to you and so they stay away," I guessed.

Gail and Tony nodded. Gail said, "I think they're just so afraid. They think it could happen to them, and that maybe just even knowing somebody that it happened to could, you know, make it happen.

"I had so many people say to me after David died that that was their worst nightmare. And it had never crossed my mind that it could ever happen. Until I met that woman, Stephanie.

"David and I were so connected. I wouldn't let other people take care of him as a toddler because I felt they couldn't. They didn't know how to talk to him and treat him well, because the more you became negative with him, the more he would react. And so I wouldn't let many people take care of him, because I was afraid of the damage they might do.

"I remember David when he was three and four. At three he sat on the back of the couch looking at me, and I said, 'You want to know about your mom, don't you?' And he said, 'Yes I do.' He said, 'Did she break her leg?' That's because we would tell him that she was sick, and she wasn't well, and that's why she couldn't take care of him. So I said to him, 'Well, kind of like that, but it's like you really didn't break your leg, but it's your mind that doesn't work well. Someday when you're older you'll understand this, but right now it's too hard, so just know that she loves you very, very much.' One image I'll always remember is how he looked at me then.

"The next image was of him not being able to get to sleep. I especially remembered this story of white light and how he loved horses. Our nightly going-to-bed story was how a little boy carried a shield of armor in one hand and white light in another. He would be riding a horse on the beach in the story. Nothing could ever harm him. He would carry the white light with him wherever he went. David would then fall asleep and he would sleep through the night. We would do this every night. And you know, I really do believe that that white light was with him when he died. I think that he was peaceful when he died. I think it was like him falling asleep, the way Mariel explains it to me."

There was a pause as Gail looked away. Then she continued. "I want to say a little bit about David and his spirit. The year after he died, when I was having a very hard time on Martha's Vineyard, a friend of mine saw an ad in the paper and said somebody here on the Vineyard does psychic life-reading work. I said, 'I have to go see this lady because I can't get this out of my head.' I was really reeling at that time, not being able to figure out what I did, and what I should have done.

"So I went to see this lady. She told me over the phone, 'This is what I would like you to do. I'd like you to meditate and think about whoever you're coming to talk to me about, or whatever you're coming to talk to me about, throughout the night. And then I want you to come and visit me in the morning.' And she set a time. Well, I pulled up and it was at a place where there were stables. One white horse was there with a woman nearby. I went over to talk to her. I don't know why I did this. I was supposed to go inside, but I went over to talk to this woman instead. And she said to me, 'See that horse over there? He's been rearing all night long.' I said, 'Oh really.' She said, 'We have not been able to contain him. It hasn't been raining, there hasn't been lightning, so I don't know what's going on with this horse.' And I said, 'Well, I think I do.' And I told her the story about David, and how connected he was to horses, and how much I thought his spirit was probably here. And she said, 'Wow, it makes so much sense. You stopped to talk to me. What made that happen, if not him?'

"Then I went in for my appointment, and the psychic lady did some imagery work with me. It was about putting myself in an imaginary bubble with David. We were pretty much crying through the whole thing. She said to me, 'Can you see David? He's right here. I see him, he's surrounded in light.' For that moment I was trying, but I couldn't see him. She said, 'He's right with you. He's here. What do you want to say to him?' I said, 'I want to tell him how much I love him, and how much I miss him, and I'm so, so sorry.' Then she said, 'Now I want you to picture yourself, and I want you to hug David just like you used to when he was little. You know how you hold somebody, you know how you do that.' And I said yes. She said, 'Picture that. Then, when you're ready, I want you to let the bubble go.' And I said, 'How many bubbles do I get?' She said, as many as I need.

"I was afraid if I let the bubble go I would never get it back again. The thing that helped me let go of the bubble was when the woman said, 'You don't want to hold David back.' That's all she had to say, because a parent doesn't want to hold a child back no matter where they are. When she said that, she said, 'He has work to do.' And I said, 'Yes. I mean, look at all the work he did here.' I still get numerous letters from people who he had met. He had done a lot of work here.

"And in my own work he goes on helping me, because I work with children who are like him. Often, when I'm feeling out of focus and off center with these kids, I shut my eyes for a quick minute and I say, *David, help me.* And something happens. He shows up. It's really, really amazing, because he literally shows up in all the little kids. Those little boys who I'm trying to work with who are just as lively and spirited as David. One of the things I hope for parents who have children like this is that they don't kill that spirit, because they can.

"After my visit with the psychic lady, I was doing some meditation later, and I actually saw David as pure light. Pure golden light. He was sitting right in front of me. That was the first time and the only time that I had an actual vision of him.

"Another vivid memory was when I viewed the body after they got it to the funeral home. The funeral director wanted me to fix him because he had a suit on. I started fixing him like he was getting ready for school. There was a song I used to sing to him, a Pentecostal Baptist lullaby that I sang to him every night, and for some reason I just broke out in song and sang, and all the people there sang, too. It was the last lullaby that I ever sang to him. Nobody could soothe David the way I could soothe him. We were so connected."

"Do you feel connected to him still?" I asked.

"Oh, very," Gail immediately replied. "There are times now when I say, oh yeah, David's here. You sense the presence, the sense of him, you know. I do say a prayer to him every night. I say that I love him, just like he was with me, and that I miss him.

"David was eight," Gail said, "when I recognized what society does to little boys. That helps me in my work today. I think the message parents need to hear is that we need to help each other. We need to support each other no matter who we are, especially in death. When we lose a child, in our heads you can intellectualize, I can say to you that David did everything he came here to do. I can tell you that intellectually, and that makes me go on. But I can also tell you that there's moments when there's deep, deep, deep anger, and deep, deep, deep sadness."

"How do you get through?" I asked.

"I don't know that I have gotten through it," Gail replied. "In the first three years I was able to sit with my sadness. I sang to myself a lot. I remember telling boys at the camp where I work—the ten-year-olds who came into my office totally in tears the first week of camp. I'd be doing administrative work, and they'd come into this office and say, 'We want to go home.' Part of my heart would break because I wanted to hug these little boys whose mom has sent them to camp and I've lost mine.

"This is what I do. I tell myself that if I can make it through breakfast, then I'm OK. But then if I need to cry, it's OK. So I can go and cry whenever I need to, and then I can make it to lunch. And then if I need to cry again, it's OK, because then I can make it to dinner. That's literally how I made it through the first few months after David's death.

"We needed to be surrounded by other people, but I also think that we needed to be able to sit with our own sadness. I needed to help Mariel, too."

"How about God?" I asked.

"I sang the same song about God, the song of Isaiah. 'Surely it is God who saves me. I will trust in him and not be afraid.' I sang that to myself over and over again, for at least three months.

"I worked with Mariel. She would draw pictures and I would write and try to help her to go through her memories. I'll never forget when I finally did go back to work—I do play therapy with children. Mariel was five, and she was playing in my office. It was really then that I discovered what happened that night David died. Mariel played the entire scene out for me. She didn't know I was listening. I was working at my desk trying to finish my reports, when all of a sudden I tuned in to what she was saying and I heard the entire thing. That was my first clear picture of what happened that night because between the two of them it had been sketchy."

Gail now talked a little about how her connection to Tony had been jeopardized. "I think that marriages can fall apart in those times. We came close, just before we moved into this house, to losing everything."

Tony and Gail looked at each other, and I could see that they had climbed way back up. "Do you still believe in God?" I asked.

"Oh, definitely," Gail immediately replied. "Now more than I ever did. I believe in the God that exists in every living thing."

"Do you believe in immortality?" I asked.

"Absolutely. I do believe that if we look for the real God, it is the goodness in people. It's not even just the goodness, its both. It's in the good and the bad."

"How do you explain the injustice of David being taken so young?" I asked.

"It's not about the length of time we have, but what we come here to do. I believe we come here knowing what we're going to do and if the people who raise us nurture that, it will come true.

"I also believe that we need angels all around us. I'll never forget one day walking in Cambridge, I was really bummed out. Out of nowhere, this guy appears who was white haired, young, no shirt, no shoes, and a pair of dungaree shorts on. He starts talking to me. I don't know how this conversation happens, but he tells me everything I need to hear. And then he just disappears and I never see him again. Now, in Cambridge I know everybody, but I never saw this man again. My mother used to say that God walks the earth in different forms. I believe that. I do believe that each of us has God within us."

Gail continued, "I studied with Native Americans, who talk

about the circle of death. For them, that is the connection that we all have. They believe that if the Hopi stop their dancing, the earth stops spinning. It's metaphorical. There is where I think David exists. Out there, in that splendor that we really can't have until we get there."

I V

SELF-ASSESSMENT

and

PRACTICAL

TIPS

How Connected Is Your Life?

A SELF-ASSESSMENT QUIZ

AS YOU BEGIN to understand the power of connection, you may also want some way of assessing how connected your own life is. This way you can see more clearly the areas in which you might want to develop deeper connections, and also see the areas in which you already have a solidly connected life.

In my practice, I have found that people benefit from organizing their thoughts about this. They quickly agree that connection matters, but they do not know how, specifically, to deepen the connections in their lives.

That is where this chapter, on self-assessment, and the next chapter, on how to connect, can help. This chapter lays out the twelve areas of connection and asks questions to help you decide whether each is an area you want to work on or not. You can gauge for yourself how connected you feel in each area.

Give yourself *one point* for each question to which you answer "yes" in the set of questions below. Although you'll come out with a score, the final number you generate is not very important. What matters is how this quiz can help you determine *which areas* you want to work on. One reason the final number doesn't mean much is that for some people one kind of connection means a great deal more than it does for other people, yet the final score is not weighted to reflect that fact. For example, family, friends, and work may be all that really matters to you. Your final score will be low, and yet you are quite connected. Still, you can use the information from this self-assessment to guide you to deepen other areas, but you certainly do not need to feel bad that your score is low, because it is high in the areas that matter the most to you.

So, rather than focusing on a score, just review these questions, then ask yourself, section by section, *Is this an area I would like to improve?*

FAMILY OF ORIGIN

Are you as emotionally close to your family of origin as you'd like to be?

Have you made peace with all the members of your family of origin?

Are you in communication as often as you'd like with all the members of your family of origin?

Do you make time, even if it means giving up some activity you might enjoy, to be with members of your family of origin?

Do you feel comfortably connected to your family of origin?

IMMEDIATE FAMILY: FAMILY YOU'VE CREATED OR JOINED

(If you live alone, skip this section.)

Do you feel comfortably connected to your immediate family?

Do you eat family dinner together whenever you can, or spend time together each day in some other way?

Do you treat one another with love and respect?

Do you feel your family is fair?

Does your family strengthen your feeling of security as much as you'd like it to?

FRIENDS AND COMMUNITY

Do you have friends you see on a regular basis?

Do you keep up with your friends as much as you'd like to?

Is your neighborhood as connected as you'd like?

Do you know the people who live next to you well enough to ask them to do you a favor?

Is your neighborhood safe enough for your children to go out and play without supervision?

WORK, MISSION, ACTIVITY

Do you feel connected at work, at school? For example, do you feel that you are treated fairly there, you are appreciated for what you do, and that people like you?

Do you feel a sense of mission at work? For example, do you feel a purpose larger than just taking home a paycheck?

Do you derive satisfaction from work?

Do you sometimes get so interested in your work that you forget what time it is or where you are?

Would you continue with your work even if you were independently wealthy?

BEAUTY

Is there a form of art that you particularly like (such as music, painting, literature, dance, photography, film, drawing)?

Do you make time for enjoying whatever forms of art you like?

Do you pause and notice beauty in nature from time to time?

Do you encourage an interest in beauty in others, like your children or friends?

Do you have experiences every week in which some form of beauty catches your attention and makes you feel better inside?

THE PAST

Do you feel the power of the past in your daily life? (Do you visit the graveside of deceased relatives now and then? Are you aware of your family's or your company's or your school's traditions? Do you look to the past for guidance?)

Do you feel connected to the history of your country?

Do you know details about your parents' lives and your grandparents' lives?

Do you feel connected to your family's past?

Do you feel you have an adequate knowledge of history in general?

NATURE AND SPECIAL PLACES

Do you feel a connection to the world of nature?

Do you spend as much time in nature—however you define that term—as you'd like to?

Are there special places that speak to you in ways no other place can?

Do you visit these special places as much as you'd like?

Do you explore new parts of the world of nature from time to time?

PETS AND OTHER ANIMALS

Do you own a pet?

Do you enjoy having your pet?

Do you like animals in general?

Can you understand intuitively why it is that old people do better if they have pets around?

Did you have a pet as a child?

IDEAS AND INFORMATION

Do you feel comfortable that you know how to gain access to whatever information you may need?

Are you as organized as you'd like to be?

Have you put up sufficient barriers so that unimportant messages, random data, and useless information are not overwhelming you?

Do you feel that you know how to get the most out of your brainpower?

Do you feel at ease in the world of ideas?

INSTITUTIONS AND ORGANIZATIONS

Do you belong to at least one institution or organization in which you take pride?

Do you regularly attend meetings of at least one institution or organization?

Do you vote in all elections in which you are eligible to vote?

Is there at least one institution or organization on whose board you would be willing to serve if you were asked?

Would you be willing to serve in a political office if you felt you were qualified and would do a good job, and you didn't have to campaign?

THAT WHICH IS BEYOND KNOWLEDGE

Do you feel a connection to whatever is beyond knowledge, whether you call it God, the cosmos, or by some other name?

Do you pray or in some other way interact on a regular basis with this being, power, or God?

Do you continue to seek after the truth by whatever means make sense to you?

Do you keep alive within yourself the big questions, like the meaning of life and the reason for suffering?

Is it important to you to deepen your connection to whatever is beyond knowledge?

YOURSELF

Do you feel comfortable being who you are?

Even though you may be different with different people, do you feel you can relax and be genuine in most relationships?

Do you feel OK about your body?

Do you feel OK about your mind? For example, do you feel smart enough, creative enough, skilled in as many areas as you'd like to be?

Are there parts of yourself you'd really like to change?

Remember, this quiz is *not* intended to give you a passing or a failing grade, but rather to point out areas where you may want to put more energy into developing a stronger connection.

The more "yes" answers you have in each section, the more connected you are in that area. Obviously, there could be hundreds of questions in each area, and the quiz could be thousands of questions long! The point in this brief self-assessment is to give you a framework for looking at how connected you are in each area.

The next chapter proposes practical steps you can take to deepen your connections in each area.

TWENTY-NINE

Practically Speaking

TIPS ON CREATING A MORE CONNECTED LIFE

CONNECTIONS AT THEIR best involve your whole soul.

Not every connection, of course, will draw upon all of you, but if you give yourself honestly in all your interactions, you will lead a connected life for sure. If, each day, you resolve to make contact; if you resolve to reach out, no matter what the response, in a genuine way; and if you resist the urge to pull back, then you will connect. In short, if you try to draw pleasure from connecting, you will.

But first, you have to make time. As much as I recommend connecting throughout this book, the only way you can make time for the connections that matter is to get rid of the connections that don't. You can't get rid of all the connections that aren't rewarding, but you can try to get rid of those you control. It is sort of like losing weight. Once you shed the pounds of excess connections, the ones that weigh you down, you'll find you have new energy to put into the connections that really matter to you.

This is one major change most people need to make to create a balanced and connected life. They need to *cut back*.

Easier said than done, of course. But it is not written into the laws of physics that all human beings must juggle one or two more balls than they can. We *choose* to do this. Therefore, we can choose not to.

I'm not recommending a boring life. I'm not even opposing the rapid-fire, frenzied pace so many people crave. I'm simply saying that to enjoy that kind of life, or any kind of life, you must also make time for the connections that really matter to you. You will probably not be satisfied in life unless you do this, no matter how fast you go or how much you achieve.

Making cuts is hard, but once you do it, the time you free up can give you new energy, just as if you had lost twenty-five pounds! You can cut back on your commitments the way you might cut back on your budget, or on eating fat. Maybe decline a certain membership, or back out of a group that your heart really isn't in anymore, or put off that new project that might be exciting but will consume a chunk of your time, or stop staying up that extra hour just watching mindless TV or surfing the Net, or stop seeing that friend who makes you feel bad each time you see her, or eliminate those "obligatory" phone calls to people you don't care about, or decline the flattering or prestigious offer to serve on a committee that will end up costing you time.

As you do this, your pleasure in other connections will start to grow.

You sit across from an old friend over lunch, and as you talk about even a trivial topic, in the back of your mind you are saying to yourself, *This person means so much to me.* Or you walk into the corner store where you've picked up your newspaper and coffee for ten years now, and you feel contentment the minute you see the proprietor's friendly smile. Or you sit in a symphony hall listening to a piece of music you know well; you feel a unique pleasure as you take in this wonderful piece of music once again.

There is a common shape to the process of connection.

It is a circle. You reach out, then whoever or whatever it is you are connecting with responds. You listen to the music, it answers back to you, you respond to it, and a circle grows. You speak to your friend, she replies, you speak again, and the conversation draws each of you in. You pour out your energy, and it is returned to you, changed. It has been added to, deepened, expanded.

Even if you say nothing to a person, you can connect. Two men fishing together can be totally silent, yet connected. Two kids playing catch in the backyard can say nothing, but feel very close. They can enjoy their bond in silence; indeed, they may prefer it that way. On the other hand two people talking rapid-fire at a cocktail party can be totally disconnected. Words, or the absence of words, are not what count. What counts is the give-and-take of energy.

It impresses me every day how available this tool is, and yet how underused. As the psychologists Miller and Stiver said, "Mutual empathy is the great unsung human gift."

For most people, the question is not whether to connect, but how to connect. Often people say to me, "OK, I agree that I want to be connected. But practically speaking, how can I do it? Can you give me some specifics? Some practical tips?"

One of the big problems these days is balance. How can we balance just family and work? And how can *anyone* balance all twelve kinds of connection in one life? Certainly, for most of us, there will not be perfect balance, but there does not need to be. If you work for a living, you will put many more hours into work than into your connection, say, to pets. My only point in mentioning many categories is to allow you to survey the variety of connections in your life, then decide what you want to deepen or change.

I offer here a set of concrete suggestions to get you thinking in practical terms on how better to connect. One reason people lead disconnected lives is that they give up too soon. They assume they can't make changes that matter. Use these suggestions as a springboard for adding your own practical steps you can take to develop a more fully connected life.

I offer five suggestions for improving each of the twelve areas of connection. Of course you can make up others that are tailored to fit your own life.

FAMILY OF ORIGIN

Make sure you see everyone in your family of origin at least once a year.

Speak to everyone at least once a month, or use E-mail or snail mail to stay in touch.

Try to make up with family members from whom you are estranged. Don't take no for an answer, either from them or from yourself!

Discuss with family members how they feel about the family. Then try to change whatever is wrong, if possible. Just naming the problem can set in motion a process of repair. Often there is an elephant in the room and no one is talking about it. If you start talking, the elephant begins to disappear.

Don't let anyone drift too far away.

IMMEDIATE FAMILY

Eat family dinner as often as possible.

Read aloud to children every day, if you can.

Have family meetings from time to time to discuss plans, problems, solutions, and goals.

Make peace before you go to sleep.

Limit TV, video, and computer time so that you still have time to talk to one another in person and do things together.

FRIENDS AND COMMUNITY

Make a regular date to see a friend once a week. Put it in your calendar, and never cancel unless you absolutely must.

Try to get to know one neighbor you don't already know.

Use E-mail to stay in touch with friends if you can't see them.

Volunteer for some community organization, even if it only means doing something once or twice a year.

Call one friend you have been meaning to get in touch with. Call today.

WORK, MISSION, ACTIVITY

Resolve to make your workplace more connected. Then do what seems appropriate. Speak to your boss if that seems right, speak to coworkers, or simply take steps—like asking how things are going, or putting up pictures of the last staff party—that can create a more friendly atmosphere.

Take trivial contact seriously. Smile in the elevator, don't just stare up at the floor numbers or look at your shoes. Say hello at the water cooler. Make eye contact and give a nod as you pass someone in the corridor. Be pleasant even to those people you don't know.

Try to think of what you could do to increase human moments among coworkers: for example, organize a pizza lunch now and then, or an exercise group, or a trip to a ball game or a play.

Make time, even only a half hour a week, for a nonwork activity you love but neglect—like playing an instrument, growing a garden, reading a novel, or cooking a new recipe.

Go speak to people at work in person, rather than using E-mail, now and then. Human moments, though less efficient, create much more positive feelings than electronic ones.

BEAUTY

First, identify which kinds of beauty you would like to connect with more fully. Music? Fine Arts? Literature? Dance? Theater? Movies? A few of these?

See if someone would like to join you in this pursuit.

Take a course, if one is available and you want to.

Put aside feelings of intimidation.

Engage as much as you can with whatever form of beauty you want to develop a connection with. This is the most important step. Go to museums, go to concerts, read books, go to movies—whatever you choose. Just do it. The beauty will work its magic on you, once you are in its presence.

THE PAST

Get to know as much of your family's history as you can. Talk to grandparents or other family historians, read any books that might be relevant, develop a family tree (you can find services that do this on the Internet).

Visit the gravesides of loved ones every year. This provides a time and place for remembering and reconnecting with the past.

If you have big gaps in your knowledge of world history, try to read a book or two on that area. Ask your librarian or bookstore owner to guide you to the most *interesting* such books, as getting bored will only disconnect you further.

Talk to old people. They are natural historians. They are usually extremely interesting when you get them talking.

Talk to your children about current events in terms of their historical meaning. For example, on voting day, talk about the wars we fought to preserve democracy, or talk about women's fight for their right to vote, or talk about places where literacy tests were used to prevent people from voting. Or use the Fourth of July not only for a barbecue and fireworks but for discussion of some exciting part of American history. There are hundreds of opportunities throughout the year to use a current event or holiday as a springboard for historical discussion with your children.

NATURE AND SPECIAL PLACES

Make it a point to stop and notice nature every day. Even if you live in the city, there are plenty of chances to do this. It takes only a second or two, it's free, and it feels good.

Keep in your mind, as possible things to do in free time, walking the beach, or just strolling down the road. If you have a regular route that you walk, not only will you connect with nature, you will start noticing all kinds of details on the walk, from the animals you meet to the state of the vegetation to the amount of moss on a rock to the people you usually encounter.

Adopt a small local store or restaurant as yours. Go in often, get to know the owners. Pretty soon this will become a special place for you, an oasis of welcome.

Visit the places that have meaning to you as often as you can—your old school, a reading room in a certain library, the coffee shop that has the special easy chair where you can read the newspaper, a bench in the park.

Try to experience one new form of nature every year or so. For example, if you've never been to a canyon, try to visit the Grand Canyon, or for a waterfall, head to Niagara (it really is amazing!), or if you've never climbed a mountain, try climbing a small one in summer, or if you've never seen a wheat field, take a drive through Kansas, or if you've never seen and felt snow, find a reason to come up north some winter, or if you've never seen a brook trout, see if you can't find some brook and a fisherman who'd like your company, and maybe your kids' as well.

PETS AND OTHER ANIMALS

Not everyone can do this, but if you can, try to own a pet. Studies have shown that people who do, of all ages, feel happier.

If you can't own a pet, try to make a friendly relationship with the pets you encounter. This may sound ridiculous, but pets bring out important parts of us. There is physiological evidence that people who are inhibited, for example, can bond with an animal but can't with a person.

Try to support public agencies, like the SPCA and the agencies that help control overpopulation among stray cats.

Take your children to zoos and petting farms, especially if you can't have pets at home.

Read books about animals, both for yourself and for your kids. Just look in the animal section of any big bookstore. You'll be amazed at how large and varied the selection is.

IDEAS AND INFORMATION

Above all, recognize that fear is the worst problem when it comes to developing a solid connection to ideas and information. Work within yourself, or with a friend, teacher, or counselor, to put aside fear. Remember, the only stupid question is the one you don't ask.

Try to become computer literate and gain access to the Internet.

Limit how much information you try to digest each week. If you try to take in everything, you will get overwhelmed.

Consult with experts in areas where you feel unqualified.

Let yourself play with ideas. Important ideas often start off as impractical notions or even whims.

INSTITUTIONS AND ORGANIZATIONS

Join one volunteer organization you believe in and attend its meetings regularly. The MacArthur Foundation study showed that this is one of the main factors that is associated with a long life. The organization may be your church, or it may be the Boys' Club, or it may be the Elks. It doesn't matter what it is, as long as it matters to you and you attend its meetings.

Find out the names, addresses, and telephone numbers of your elected representatives, local, state, and national. If you call the reference desk of your local library, the person there can help you in finding this information. Once you have the names of these people, get in the habit of contacting them when you have a concern.

If you have children or grandchildren in school, get to know their teachers. Spend a few minutes just chatting with the teachers now and then, and give them your thanks. Teachers, along with parents, do our society's most important job, but they get little support or credit.

Take your children down to city hall. Explain to them how your town or city works. On different outings, take them to the fire department, the police station, the local library, the hospital, and maybe on a tour of a large business if there is one in your area.

Speak up in the institutions and organizations that matter to you. Try to encourage others to do the same. Apathy and disengagement are the great enemies of democracy and of connection. Support a political candidate, if you like one. Vote in the elections in your professional organization. You might even consider running for office yourself!

THAT WHICH IS BEYOND KNOWLEDGE

The key here is to pursue the connection, rather than ignore it.

Meditate or pray on a regular basis, every day. Many studies have shown that people who do this are happier and healthier than those who do not.

Talk about this connection with your children or grandchildren.

Exercise your faith, if you have one, on a regular basis by attending services or observing other rituals that have meaning to you.

Come to terms, in your own mind, with how you make sense of death, unnecessary suffering, evil deeds, and unexpected losses, so that when these things happen you will have the foundation of a response.

YOURSELF

"To thine own self be true" and "To thine own self be enough." These are the two cornerstones of a healthy connection with yourself. Try to be a hero, and don't feel you must become a star. Remember that success and failure are both, to quote Rudyard Kipling, "imposters."

Practice being good to yourself. This starts with giving yourself permission to do so. Remember, being good to yourself is not the same thing as being selfish. Indeed, if you are good to yourself, you will be better equipped to help others.

If there is a part of yourself you would like to change, make a plan to do so. Often consulting with a specialist— like a good psychotherapist, or a diet specialist, or a hair stylist, or an experienced salesperson in your favorite clothes store, or a fitness expert —can start you off in a positive direction.

Try to keep in touch with your creative side. You can do this by taking a creative writing or painting class, or reading a book on lateral thinking, or attending some creativity workshops, or just by giving yourself time to play.

Be real. You are not the same person with everyone, but you can always be genuine in a given context. Being fake is a sure way to disconnect from yourself. Pretty soon you don't know who you are. On the other hand, genuine connection is the greatest pleasure life has to offer.

V

FINDING

the

HEART

of

YOUR LIFE

THIRTY

"If You Want to Be Happy . . ."

WHEN I WAS a little boy, my father used to say to me, "If you want to be happy, then make sure you always have one or two true friends." He said this many times. "The amount of money you make doesn't matter," he would say. "Fame doesn't matter. How much you achieve doesn't matter. What matters most is close friends. If someone will stand by you even at risk to themselves, then you have made a good life."

Science has proved my father right. As a psychiatrist, if I have seen one change make people feel better most often, it is finding a meaningful connection—to a person, to a job, to a club or team, to an institution, to God. Once you feel a part of something larger than yourself, the dread of isolation lifts, and you start to find joy and confidence in life. You achieve more, too!

The power of connection is vastly underrated by many people. It is thought of as window dressing, or a frill for the well off and wealthy.

But nothing could be further from the truth. Science has proven over and over again that connection is good for your health. The medical evidence is beyond question now: connection makes you live longer. It is no frill. It is of core importance to any plan for a long and healthy life.

As the authors of the MacArthur Foundation Study on Aging, which was cited in Chapter 1, wrote,

Loneliness breeds both illness and early death. And as a rule, people whose connections with others are relatively strong—through family (including marriage), friendships, and organizational memberships— live longer. And for people whose relationships to others are fewer and weaker, the risk of death is two to four times as great, irrespective of age and other factors such as race, socioeconomic status, physical health, smoking, use of alcohol, physical activity, obesity, and use of health services. The bottom line is we do not outgrow our need for others. The life-giving effect of close social relations holds throughout the life course.

My father would be glad to know his advice has been proven true. He is gone now. He died when I was in medical school, twenty years ago. But I think about his advice often. He was a crusty, skeptical New Englander, not one you'd expect to extol friendship as the secret to a good life. When he died—a respected public school teacher in New Hampshire—a busload of admirers came down from his school to his funeral, but I think Dad had long since lost touch with the people he would have called his closest friends. I think his trials in life—divorce from my mother when I was four, his battle with manic-depressive illness, his ongoing feud with his own brother and one of his sons—had cost him whatever it is that keeps a person open to deep friendship, or close connections of any kind.

I remember his last days. He wrote me a letter telling me, in his characteristically blunt fashion, that he had been diagnosed with lung cancer of a type so bad that the doctors couldn't identify it precisely. "It has them all buffaloed," was how he put it, almost with pride, as if to say, if he was going to get cancer, he was not going to get your average identifiable cancer, but instead a real stumper. I was a fourth-year medical student when I received the letter. I remember wondering what news Dad would have to offer, as I tore open the envelope while riding an elevator up to ward rounds one November morning. Then I read the news, written in blue ink in Dad's instantly identifiable slanting script. I remember thinking, *This can't be. He's too young.* He was only sixty-four. I stuck the letter back in my pocket knowing my life would never be the same.

The ancient elevator doors (I was at Charity Hospital in New Orleans, a vast city hospital) rattled open onto the ward where I was to meet my group to make rounds. Attending physicians do the teaching in the third and fourth years of medical school by conducting Socratic dialogues in hospital corridors and at patients' bedsides. I recall the attending physician asking me a question that morning—and my going blank as he spoke. "Ned," he said, "are you with us today?"

It wasn't in the style of the times to say, "No, I'm not with you, I've just had word that my father is dying," so I asked the attending please to repeat his question. I somehow mustered an answer good enough to move us down the corridor. *This is how life goes,* I remember thinking as we walked into the next patient's room. The river just keeps running, the bad things keep happening, and you have to keep on doing your work, because the current pulls you. You can't buck it. There didn't seem to be a choice. The world doesn't stop.

My group of four med students plus the attending had no way of knowing it, but they formed my life raft in those stark moments, my link to safety, my connection to useful work. I tried to steady myself by studying the eyes of the patient at whose bedside we were standing, as my Dad's phrase *"It has them all buffaloed"* rattled through my mind. I didn't know what to do, so I tried to listen, as if the words I heard the attending speak made a railing I could grip. As emotion started to well up inside me I suddenly volunteered a response to a question that a vigilant part of my brain must have heard, comprehended, and answered, without my noticing the process. "Aortic stenosis," I stated.

"Very good, Hallowell," the attending replied. "Welcome back."

I booked a flight that night and I was in my dad's hospital room in Derry, New Hampshire, the next day. A no-nonsense primary care doctor told me it was just a matter of days before he would die, and that my father was currently "in and out of his senses," a warning I was glad he gave me.

When I entered his room he was spitting into a Styrofoam cup. I looked at him and he looked at me, and in half a second his mind did a trick that I guess it needed to do. "John!" he bellowed. "Thanks for coming!" Dad had decided that I was my brother John. John and he had been feuding for years, and he must have known that this was his last chance to make up. Since he and I had always got along well, he didn't need to make up with me, so his compromised brain played its little trick, which I was adroit enough not to disagree with, thanks to the warning I had received from his doctor.

We talked for a few minutes, me as John, Dad as Dad, and then he softly fell asleep. I went over and gave him a kiss on his forehead. I think that must have been the only time I ever kissed him when he was asleep, a fit response to all the times he had kissed me good night after a bedtime story, usually one he would make up about his favorite character, Johnny Creepmouse.

I later found out that my mother also came up to see Dad that day. She told me that he asked her to fluff up his pillows, something my mother always did well. She told me they had talked for a while, and that, yes, he had been glad to see her. Although they had divorced twenty-five years before and had had only minimal contact in the ensuing years, they had never fallen out of love, if you ask me. Dad sent her pink roses every June 26, her birthday, and she fluffed up his pillows as he lay dying. The connection never completely broke.

The day after my visit I was back at medical school making rounds in the hospital. Two weeks after that, Dad died. I think of him often now. It especially makes me sad that he never met my wife, Sue, or our three kids. He loved kids, and kids loved him.

He died without the presence of what he said was most important in life—one or two close friends—but he had me and his second wife, Betty, and my oldest brother, Ben, and other members of the family. He had all his colleagues and students from school. And as I learned at the funeral, he had a raft of people who had been his close friends long ago—line mates, like Dunny Holmes, from the hockey team he starred on at Harvard back in the 1930s; a fellow from the boatyard where he worked for a couple of years; another man who told me he knew Dad from some business or other, and then proclaimed, "He was the finest man I ever met." I wonder if there is someone out there who thinks that about each of us, but doesn't say it until he or she shows up at our funeral.

Sadness attended my father's death, too, of course. His needing to call me John, my mother's coming up only at the very end, Betty being left alone, all this was sad.

But I think he got it basically right about life, in his advice to me. What matters is not all the money, fame, and trophies we accumulate, but the connections we make along the way.

Yet Dad—like so many people—had trouble following his own advice. How many fathers tell their children the sort of thing Dad told me, but still don't carry it out in their own lives? Life's bruises made Dad pull back, instead of staying close to people, so that when he died he was more alone than he should have been.

I think Dad should have told me—and reminded himself—that making and keeping friends takes effort and patience, but most of all it takes a strong desire to do so. Sustaining connections of all kinds, not just to people but to institutions and groups and ideals as well, requires determination. The older you get, the more pain you see others endure and you suffer yourself, the greater the temptation grows to shut down, pull back, and disconnect from anyone or anything that can hurt you. I believe this is a great mistake.

But how can you know for sure? Maybe it *is* better to pull back and find safety in your own personal bunker. Since it's so hard to sustain connections, a person may sensibly ask, why bother? Why connect and get disappointed, betrayed, abandoned, or any of the other bad things that can happen once you put your trust in something outside of yourself? Why get into relationships at all, or become a committed member of an organization, or put your heart into the place where you work? Even my Dad, who had professed the value of friendships, gave up on them by the end, or so it seemed to me. You have to wonder why any of us should connect to anything at all when connecting is so predictably difficult.

The reason is that we are better off doing it than not.

In championing the value of connection, to combat whatever life dishes up, I can pay a kind of homage to my Dad by completing, or at least extending, what he wanted me to do. "If you must be a psychiatrist," he said to me, slightly disappointed when I told him psychiatry was to be my field, "at least try to be a useful one."

Now, at the age of fifty, I hope I can be useful in bringing to life the single most valuable lesson I have learned in my years of doing this job: if you want to lead a good and happy life, you should try to connect passionately to things larger than yourself.

It doesn't matter what you connect to, as long as it is not destructive. If you bring your true self into the connection, and you nourish it with your best energy, it will sustain you over time like nothing else can.

One woman, now a fifty-three-year-old social worker, mother, and wife of thirty-two years, wrote to me,

Without connection throughout my traumatic life, I would not be the successful, resilient person that I am. Key people, starting with day care providers, extended family, and teachers, were there for me at key times. One person in particular was my grade 9 homeroom teacher, who was also my biology and science teacher. This led to a forty-year relationship, including his being my mentor and his family taking care of my daughter when I returned to work. This key teacher, and my wonderful mother-in-law that I modeled myself after, have been essential to my successful journey in life.

In my work as a psychiatrist, I've heard of the depths of misery, and I have seen the many ways people become unhappy, as well as the ways they find happiness. I have seen the same mistakes made over and over, but I have also seen certain solutions that seem to work most of the time.

The solution I have seen that works best is an epigraph of this book: "Only connect . . ."

There is an ancient Middle Eastern fable that John O'Hara used in his novel *Appointment in Samara*. In the fable, a man sitting in a bar on a warm afternoon in Constantinople overhears a rumor that Death is looking for him. The man goes into a cold sweat and bolts out of the bar, telling the bartender that he is going to ride his horse as fast as he can to Samara to escape the hands of Death. Later that day, Death comes into the bar and asks the bartender about the man who had fled hours ago. The bartender replies he has no idea where the man could be, adding that he hasn't seen him in weeks. "Really?" Death says with a sly smile. "If you do happen to see him, would you kindly tell him I have an appointment with him tonight . . . in Samara?"

The closest thing we've got to an insurance policy against the bad things that can happen in life is not trying to pull back. That is like galloping off to Samara.

In connection, we stand a better chance. We do not have to flee. We can hold our ground against the tide that always wants to wash us away. In connecting to other people, to great causes or small moments, we can sink our ankles into the sand against the constant undertow of loss and pain.

I don't know where I'll be when I die. I might die tomorrow while I'm playing with my kids. It might happen forty years from now in a nursing home while I'm watching the Red Sox on TV. It might happen driving home from work next week. How can I get ready? How can any of us? My answer is the refrain of this book: only connect.

I didn't know when my dad would be taken out of my life, and he was taken quite suddenly. I don't know when I will be taken from my children's lives, but even if I did, I don't know what I'd do, other than tell them that I love them. Isn't that the best way for us all to prepare? To love well now what we must leave someday.

Sometimes someone will say, "These big questions are too heavy. Just forget about them and live your life." The problem with that is, we all will face moments of desperation in which we *must* deal with big questions and extreme emotional pain, one of these days. As humans, we think and reflect. We anticipate and remember. It is worth developing an idea *now* of what you'll do when bad things happen, because they will happen. It isn't a matter of whether we'll face such moments, it's only a matter of when.

Life jolts us into addressing the big questions in strange ways. A man once walked into my office, sat down, wiped his brow, and told me, "I just made twenty-five million dollars in a real estate deal today, and I walked over here to see you wondering to myself, What does life mean?" His windfall had thrown him into a quandary of big questions. A quandary we'd all no doubt enjoy!

But more often the big questions come up in times of distress. The father of a baby that had just died in childbirth once demanded of me, as if I could answer, "Why did this happen? Why did our baby die?"

And I recall, as an intern fresh out of medical school, on one of my first nights on duty, admitting a young man who was scheduled for surgery soon. He suffered from aortic stenosis and needed one of his heart valves replaced. I took his history, did a physical examination, drew some blood, and wished him good night. His wife was sitting at his bedside when I left and went back to the on-call room. A few hours later a code blue was called in the man's room. The nurse had found the man pulseless, his wife sleeping in the chair next to his bed with her hand entwined in his hand. Death took him without even waking his wife. Resuscitation failed, as the man had totally blown out his aortic valves. I can still remember his wife searching into my face, as if maybe I had an answer, and asking, simply, "Why him?"

And I remember only too well seeing a baby, Sue's and my baby, on a fetal ultrasound screen. I remember our being told that the baby didn't have a heart that could work, and I remember our being told that the baby could not survive, that the pregnancy had to end. I remember watching Sue cry, and I remember not wanting to believe what I was seeing and being told.

I didn't know what to say to these people. I didn't know what to say to the father of the baby who had died. I didn't know what to say to the wife of the man whose heart had given out. I didn't even know what to tell myself when I found out we'd lose our own baby. I didn't, and don't, have the answers.

You might wonder where I turned. I turned to my connections. To Sue, to our relatives and friends, to God. I didn't find an answer to why it happened, but I found a *means of getting through the pain* and of dealing with the loss. In connection we find not so much answers as support, a life raft on the waves.

The time given us to make and strengthen our connections is brief. It is here one moment and taken away a phone call later. We have to make the most of each day.

Sue and I lost one child, but we have three others. Now and then I think of the baby we lost. I wonder what the baby would have looked like. I love our three children so much. I wish that fourth one could be with us, too.

I wonder why these things happen. Sometimes I say a prayer for the dead baby's soul. Then I look at my nine-year-old daughter, Lucy, doing cartwheels in the park, and I want to make time stop. But of course I can't. And my six-year-old, Jack, and my three-year-old, Tucker, both smile up at me with a twinkle in their eyes that urges me to hold on to the moment for all that it's worth.

Make the connections live. Tell your friend you love her. Make peace with the relative you're mad at. The next time you go into the drugstore, ask the pharmacist how he likes his job. At your New Year's Eve party, speak to an old friend in a new way. Breathe life into the connections you make. Every day. Now.

ACKNOWLEDGMENTS

SINCE I HAVE been writing this book for most of my adult life, a complete list of acknowledgments would include thousands of people. I wish I had the space—and memory—to offer that, but of course, I do not. Nonetheless, I would like to thank all those people who have crossed my path, who have connected with me in one way or another, and offered their help.

More specifically, I thank Linda Healey, editor and friend, for her faith in this project from its inception, and for her help and encouragement on my other books. She was always there when I needed her, which was often. Thank you, Linda, thank you so very much.

Also, my agent, Jill Kneerim, has been a wise counsel as well as faithful friend. More mentor than agent, Jill has guided me through the mysteries and insecurities of the writer's life like a fairy godmother. Thank you, Jill.

Dan Frank, Jennifer Weh, and the whole group at Pantheon were immensely helpful, as was my office staff in Cambridge, particularly Christine DeCamillis and Tricia Walsh.

Lisa Berkman was especially helpful in sharing her research with me, and I am most grateful. My teachers Charles Magraw and Ed Khantzian as usual helped dispel my doubts.

I also wish to thank Irene Pierce Stiver and Jean Baker Miller for their wonderful book, *The Healing Connection,* and Judith Jordan for her marvelously helpful work in the area on connectedness.

I dedicated this book to my parents, who always did their best, and to the many people who gave me their stories for this book. I thank them again, and hope they feel pleased with what I have done.

My friends and family have proven the truth of what I claim in this book: that connections are what make life good. Susan Grace Galassi, Jon Galassi, Peter Metz, Phyllis Pollack, John Ratey, Michael Thompson, Theresa McNally, Bart Herskovitz, Jeff Sutton, Alex Packer, Paul Sorgi, Susan Downing, Sharon Wohlmuth, Bill and Valerie Grace, Ken Duckworth, Mary McCarthy, Sara and Eric Meyers, Priscilla and Donald Vail, Kim Rawlins and David Pilgrim, Suzy and Eric Wetlaufer, Alan Brown and Linda Foxworthy, Anna Fels and Jim Atlas, Maggie and Herb Scarf, Kate Wenner and Gil Eisner are just some of the friends who have helped me with this book, and with my life. If I left anyone out, please forgive me and read into it only what is there: I have a brain that makes mistakes!

I am also blessed to have a wonderfully supportive extended family: Josselyn and Tom Bliss make my life easier every day, as does my cousin Jamie. Their love means so much to me. My brothers Ben and John paved the way for me. My nieces and nephews, Molly, Ned, Tim, Jake, and Anna on one side, and David, Chelse, Corey, Audrey, and Sally on the other fill me full of gladness whenever I think of them, which is all the time. Bill and Pat George, my mother and father in law, and LouAnn and Phillip and Terry and John and Christopher and Leslie and Richard, my brothers and sisters in law are super people whom I love a lot. My aunt, whom I call Duckie, is like a substitute mother to me. And my Aunt Janet and Aunt Roz both gave me great doses of warmth and affection.

Finally, my immediate family I thank now and forever. Sue, my wife, is simply the love of my life. And my kids, Lucy, Jack, and Tucker are the stars in my sky. They shine every day. Loving them is the best thing I ever do.

INDEX

abuse, child, 72–74, 78–79,
93–94, 95, 148–49
Academy of American Poets,
220
achievement, connection vs., xii,
3, 9–13, 14, 21, 62, 84,
120, 144, 206–9, 210,
220, 253 59, 299, 303
acquaintances, 10
Adams, Scott, 116
adolescents, 6–8, 186–87, 234
heroism vs. stardom in,
253–59
adoption, 54, 55, 150–51
agnosticism, 203–4
Alameda County Study, 5
alcoholism, 22–24, 28, 172
Alfred, William, 26, 27
algebra, 166–67
All Dogs Go to Heaven, 276
Alzheimer's disease, xviii, 59
ambivalence, 266

Anderson, Jim, 117–19
angels, 281
anger, 12, 36, 65, 67, 92, 94,
96, 238, 261, 264
animals, 58–59, 156, 161–64,
288, 297
anomie, 133
anxiety, 58, 95, 125, 206, 267
Appointment in Samara (O'Hara),
308
Arnheim, Rudolf, 143
art, 56–57, 141–46, 221, 222,
287, 295
assembly line, 117, 126
ATMs, 135
attention, 125–26
attention deficit disorder
(ADD), 19, 94–95,
98–101, 167, 185
automotive industry, 137
avoidance, 227–28, 232, 235,
307–9

baby boomers, 22
banishment, xvii, 70–71
banks, 135
beauty, 56–57, 141–46, 222, 287, 295
Berkman, Lisa, 5
Bernabe, Franco, 213–14
Berra, Yogi, 202
betrayal, 209, 237
Bible, 200, 201, 249, 280
bird-watching, 160
Bishop, Elizabeth, 218, 219
block parties, xii–xiv
boarding schools, 6–7, 26–27, 35–36, 71, 147–48, 183, 254, 255–56
body memories, 94
body therapy, 108
Bok, Derek, 180
bonding, 134, 292–93
Borger, Tex., 173
Boston Globe, 60, 162
Boston Partners in Education, 170
breast cancer, xvii, 260–68
    mastectomies and, 261, 267
Brothers Karamazov, The (Dostoyevsky), 147, 151
Brown, Alan, 82
Browning, Robert, 61
business, xvii, 114–15, 213–14

cancer, 116, 197, 275
    breast, xvii, 260–68
    colon, 67–68
    lung, 304–7
    testicular, 191
careers, 67, 261, 262–63, 264

caretakers, 59, 78, 209–12
Carnegie Mellon University, 20, 122, 133
case studies:
    Alex, 130–31
    Alice, 66–69
    background of, xvii–xviii
    Chris, 106
    David P., 136–39
    Diane T., 182, 190
    Dr. L., 17–18
    Dr. P., 209–12
    Fred, 85–102
    Hank, 116–17
    Harry, 128
    Jack W., 135–36
    Jann, 106–11
    Jason, 207–9
    Jay, 70–71, 78–79
    Justin, 193–95, 196
    Maeve, 106–11
    Marie, 85–102
    Mr. G., 10–13, 14, 16, 17, 18
    Mr. S., 37–49, 192, 196
    Molly, 75–79
    Ray, 131–32
    Sarah (doctor), 106–11
    Sarah (patient), 148–49
    Sophie, 260–68
    Susan (curator), 141–46
    Susan (therapist), 106–11
    Tibo, 72–74, 78–79
    Zack, 129–30
Cathcart, Noble, 22–26, 28, 29, 30, 32–33, 35, 36, 147, 157
cell phones, 19
central subject, 187–88, 189

change:
  managerial, 118–19, 138
  personal, 212–14, 229–30,
    236, 261
  technological, 16–21
cheating, 253–54
children, 80–83
  abuse of, 72–74, 78–79,
    93–94, 95, 148–49
  adopted, 54, 55, 150–51
  creativity of, 215–18
  cruelty of, 182–83, 190,
    235–36
  death of, 269–82
  divorce and, 70, 265
  fears of, 169–70
  as heroes vs. stars, 253–59
  history and, 153–55, 296
  needs of, 80
  in neighborhoods, 228–29,
    248, 249–50, 251, 252,
    256
  parents' connection to,
    42–48, 80–83, 89, 263,
    265, 269–82
  pets for, 59
  social exclusion of, 186–87,
    234–35
  tasks of, 255
  traditions and, 153–55
Children's Hospital, 273–74
Christ Church, 171–81, 270
churches, 171–81
  as communities, 14–15,
    171–81
  connections in, 5–6, 171–81
  as families, 23–24
  as special places, 158
  see also religion

"circle of death," 281–82
class size, 190
cliques, 186–87, 234–35
clozapine, 40, 48, 197
Cohen, Sheldon, 8
colds, 8–9
colon cancer, 67–68
communities, 239–52
  breakdown of, 13–15
  churches as, 14–15, 171–81
  connections in, 55–56,
    228–29, 239–42
  crisis and, 177, 241, 243–52
  definition of, 177, 241, 252
  ersatz, 14
  of good people, 239–42, 256
  local, xii–xiv, 228–29, 233,
    243–52, 256
  practical tips for, 294
  self-assessment quiz for, 287
  sense of, 115
  support from, 228–29,
    243–52
companies, 114–15, 136–39,
    213–14
competition, 104, 117
  children and, 182–83,
    253–59
  in companies, 136–39
  feelings and, 130
  in marriage, 102
complaining, 123
Conant, Louise, 15, 175
conformity, 216–18
connection:
  achievement vs., xii, 3,
    9–13, 14, 21, 62, 84,
    120, 144, 206–9, 210,
    220, 253–59, 299, 303

connection (*cont.*)
  author's experience of, 22–36
  avoidance of, 227–28, 232,
    235, 307–9
  balance in, 291–93
  breaking of, 260–68,
    291–92
  change and, 16–21, 118–19,
    138, 212–14, 229–30,
    236, 261
  as connectedness, xvi–xviii
  creation of, 53–222, 285
  in crises, 81–82, 95–101,
    177, 241, 243–52,
    274–75
  dangers of, 252
  death and, 5–6, 64–65,
    269–82, 309–10
  difficulty of, 225–28
  dis-, *see* disconnection
  diversity of, 9
  electronic, 4, 16, 18–21,
    122, 124–32, 133, 134,
    139–40, 227, 292, 293,
    294, 297
  endurance of, xviii, 48–49
  energy from, 84–85, 102,
    114, 126, 127–28, 260,
    307–8
  face-to-face, 124–40, 227
  as garden, 53–54, 74, 104,
    205–6, 209, 222, 227,
    260
  grass-roots, 180–81
  happiness and, xii, 62,
    133–34, 262, 303–11
  language of, 173, 232,
    292–93

  maintenance of, 41, 53–54,
    225–38, 291–99, 307–11
  need for, xi–xx, 3–21
  networking vs., 4
  networks of, 16–17, 239–42
  obstacles to, 225–38
  with oneself, 62–63, 84–85,
    87, 205–22, 289–90,
    299, 307–8
  as past and present, 27–36,
    57, 145–55, 288, 295–96
  persistence in, 41, 227
  power of, xvi–xviii, 3–49,
    78–79, 111, 138, 175–76,
    181, 184, 191–92, 232,
    235, 243, 250, 285, 303
  practical tips for, 291–99
  rebuilding of, xix–xx, 64–79,
    97–101, 227, 237, 291–99
  research on, 5–9, 20, 114–15,
    134, 255–56, 298, 303–4
  self-assessment quiz on,
    285–90
  self-growth and, 205–14
  self-interest vs., xix–xx,
    13–14, 89, 235–36,
    257–58
  stabilizing, 17–18
  time for, xiv, xviii, 225,
    228–30, 233, 291–92
  transportability of, 26–27
  trust and, xviii–xix, 79, 134,
    135, 197, 228, 235–38
  twelve points of, 54–63
  types of, xiv–xvi, 5–6, 9,
    53–63
  values of, 182–90
Conrad, Joseph, 205

control, xii, 95, 250, 291
cooperation, 182
cortisol, 133–34
courage, 262, 268
creativity, 62, 120, 121, 126,
    127–28, 299
  of children, 215–18
  fear of, 215–22
crises, 81–82, 95–101, 177,
    241, 243–52, 274–75
cruelty, 182–83, 190, 235–36
Culture of Narcissism, The
    (Lasch), 13
curiosity, 165
custody, child, 70
cynicism, xix–xx, 9, 11–12, 14,
    120, 135, 238, 255

dating, 107, 263
death, 5–6, 64–65, 269–82,
    309–10
death risk, 5–6
decision making, 206–7,
    213–14, 262, 266
de Geus, Arie, 114–15
depression, 3, 7, 9, 13, 20, 58,
    75, 76, 116, 122, 133,
    207, 251, 256
Dexedrine, 98–101
Diamonti, Michael, 6
Dickinson, Emily, 221–22
Dilbert, 61, 116
disassociation, 95
disconnection, 225–82
  causes of, 225–38
  education and, 189–90,
    253–58

fear and, 176–77, 225
freedom of, 15–16
health impaired by, xii, xvii,
    3–9, 11, 134, 303–4
human contact lost by,
    xi–xii, xvii, 5–6, 13, 14,
    133, 231, 232, 238, 255,
    259, 263, 303
illness of, 197–98
institutional, 175–77
memory and, 148–49
of self, 205–14
technology and, 18–21
as "vitamin deficiency," 3–4,
    11
divorce, 91, 108, 260–68, 304,
    306
  children and, 70, 265
doctors, 115–16, 135, 144, 209
domination, 74
Donahue, Ed and Elaine, 243–52
Dostoyevsky, Fyodor, 147, 151
doubt, 202, 209, 210, 262,
    264–65
dress codes, 188
drug abuse, 7, 254, 256
Duckworth, Ken, 191–98
Dunlap, "Chainsaw Al," 115
Durkheim, Emil, 133
dyslexia, 167, 168–69, 185

echocardiograms, 81
economic diversity, 185, 189
education, 6–7, 15, 117–23,
    165–70, 182–90, 229,
    230, 253–58
  see also schools

Eldredge, Mrs., 168–70
Eliot, T. S., 209
E-mail, 20, 60, 76, 109, 121,
    124–32, 134, 139, 293,
    294
emotions, 10, 12–13, 106,
    120, 123, 126, 193,
    210–12, 234, 265
empathy, 183, 208, 209–11,
    293
employment, 167
Eni, 213–14
entrepreneurs, 10–13, 56,
    87–88, 129–30
epinephrine, 133–34
Episcopal Church, 174–75,
    176, 177
evil, 182–83, 190, 203
exercise, 121, 122
eye contact, 134

face-to-face meetings, 124–40,
    227
families, 64–79
    connections in, 5–6, 7, 20,
        54–55, 64–79
    disconnection in, 74–77,
        227
    disputes in, 70–71, 213, 227
    distance and, 75–76
    endurance of, 64–66
    extended, xv, 14, 23, 55,
        75–76
    immediate, xv, 55, 286, 294
    of origin, 54–55, 109, 286,
        293–94
    practical tips for, 293–94

relationships in, 5–6, 7, 20,
    64–79
relocations and, 76–77,
    97–101
self-assessment quiz for,
    286
separation from, 75–77
substitute, 23–24, 71–74
successful, 71, 74, 78
traditional, 71
traditions of, 153–55
values of, 183
Farrar, Straus & Giroux, 218,
    220
fashion, 16
fatigue, 3, 120
fear:
    in children, 169–70
    of creativity, 215–22
    disconnection and, 176–77,
        225
    of information, 167–70
    of rejection, 228, 233–35,
        263
    of responsibility, 228,
        231–32, 233
Fessenden school, 26, 27,
    147–48
Ford, Henry, 117, 126
Fortune 500, 115
Frick, Henry Clay, 56–57
Frick Collection, 144
friendships, 103–11
    acquaintances vs., 10
    bad, 103–4
    connection in, 55–56,
        103–11, 303–4, 307
    disengagement in, 236

female, 106–11
as gift, 110–11
maintenance of, xiv–xv,
    104–11, 227, 236
male, 104–6
marriage and, 108–9, 110,
    111, 263
practical tips for, 294
rituals of, 107–8
self-assessment quiz for,
    287
support from, 6, 106–11,
    121
time for, 104, 121, 228–29,
    234
trust and, 109, 121
visits and, 8, 134
frustration, 126

Galassi, Jonathan, 218–22
gambling, 251
Gaud, Henny, 28
Gaud School, 30
genealogy, 153, 154–55, 295
genius loci, 58, 156
"girls' talk," 186–87
goals, 149, 226, 254
God, 23, 62, 81, 156,
    199–204, 213, 238, 266,
    280, 281, 289, 303, 310
golf, 56
grade head system, 186–87,
    189
graduate students, 117–23
grandparents, 77
granuloma, 269–82
gratitude, 211

Greater Boston Interfaith Orga-
    nization (GBIO), 180–81
Greece, ancient, 187–88
Green, Phil, 60

Haldol, 40
Hallowell, Ben, 306
Hallowell, Betty, 65, 306
Hallowell, Edward M.:
    childhood of, 22–36,
        147–48, 157–58, 168–69,
        183, 185, 306
    parents of, 22–26, 64–65,
        151–52, 202, 303–9
    as psychiatrist, xv, xvii–xviii,
        xix, 9, 16, 37–49, 61,
        72–74, 161–62, 191–98,
        206, 208, 213, 303, 307,
        308
Hallowell, Gammy, 25
Hallowell, Jack, 64–65, 183,
    201, 310
Hallowell, John, 53, 202,
    305–6
Hallowell, Lucy, 80–83, 104,
    154–55, 183, 184–85,
    187–88, 201, 216, 310
Hallowell, Sue, 53, 62, 64, 80,
    81, 83, 174–75, 201,
    229, 230, 310
Hallowell, Tucker, 62, 64–65,
    201, 310
hallucinations, 133, 194, 202
happiness, xii, 62, 133–34,
    262, 303–11
Harvard Business Review, 115,
    213–14

Harvard Medical School, xvii
Harvard University, 26,
    117–23, 174
Havens, Leston, 236–37
health, xii, xvii, 3–9, 11,
    115–16, 118, 134, 197,
    303–4
health care, 115–16, 118, 197
heroes, 253–59
Herskovitz, Bart, 105
Hewat, Christopher, 221
history, 57, 153–55, 295–96
Hitt, Bobby, 28
"H-line," 152
HMOs, 116, 118
Holmes, Dunbar, 152, 306
Hopi, 281–82
hormones, 89, 90, 133–34
hospices, 276–77
Houck, Mr., 29
Houghton Mifflin, 219
Hugh, Uncle, 27–28, 30–31
human moment, xi–xii, xv,
    3–21, 124–40, 226, 295
Hutchins, Merrill, 172

"I Am Here Because They
    Were There" (Hallowell),
    36
ideas, 59–60, 165–70, 218,
    288–89, 297
imagination, 217–19
Impressionism, 145
impressions, 144–45
independence, 255
individualized education plan
    (IEP), 168

individuation, 77
Industrial Areas Foundation
    (IAF), 180
infants, 132
information, 165–70
    access to, 4, 20, 60, 165–70
    as connection, 59–60,
        165–70
    electronic, 4, 20, 122, 133,
        139, 227, 292, 293, 294,
        297
    fear of, 167–70
    practical tips for, 297
    self-assessment quiz for,
        288–89
    see also knowledge
Ingres, Jean-Auguste-
    Dominique, 145
innocence, loss of, 235–36
insecurity, 225, 226, 230,
    233–35, 255
instincts, 130
institutions, 60–61, 171–81,
    289, 298
integrity, 262
interdependence, 255
Internet, 4, 14, 20, 122, 133,
    139, 227, 292, 293, 294,
    297
interruptions, 19
Irving, John, 166
Isaiah, 280
isolation, xi–xii, 231, 232,
    238, 255, 259, 263, 303
    depression and, 9–10,
        13–14
    longevity and, xvii, 5–6
    stress and, 121, 131–35

Jesus Christ, 73, 237
"Jesus game," 73
Jews, Orthodox, 20–21
Journal of the American Medical Association, 7, 8

Kelly, James, 91–96
Kennedy, John F., 173
Kenney, Murray, 176
King, Martin Luther, Jr., 173–74
Kipling, Rudyard, 299
Klein, Calvin, 16
knowledge, 117, 139–40, 166
    questions beyond, 61–62,
        199–204, 289, 298–99
    self-, 205–14, 265–66
    see also information
Kraut, Robert, 20*n*
Kublicki, Joe, 53

language:
    ability in, 133, 167
    of connection, 173, 232,
        292–93
Lasch, Christopher, 13
"latrine ministry," 179
Lavoie, Rick, 258–59
lawyers, 112–13
leadership, 114
learning disabilities, 80,
    82–83, 133, 166,
    167–69, 185, 260
Lee, John, 179
life skills, 255
listening, 110
loneliness, 3, 20, 133, 303–4

love:
    capacity for, 10, 12, 14,
        78–79, 162
    power of, 55, 102, 144, 193,
        201, 263
    romantic, 86–87, 101–2
    unconditional, 59, 162
Lowell, Robert, 218
lung cancer, 304–7

MacArthur Foundation Study
    on Aging in America, 8,
    134, 298, 303–4
McClain, Frank, 34, 35
McGill University, 133, 142
manic-depressive illness, 22, 304
marriage, 84–102
    commitment in, 88, 102,
        227
    connection in, 84–102,
        276–77, 281
    counseling for, 91–96, 266
    feelings in, 10, 12–13
    friendship and, 108–9, 110,
        111, 263
    intimacy in, 84–102
    needs in, 96–97
    relocations and, 97–101
    respect in, 102
    responsibility in, 262,
        264–65
    teamwork in, 88–89, 102
    see also divorce
Massachusetts Mental Health
    Center, 37–49, 104,
    191–98
mastectomies, 261, 267

material simplicity, 188–89
Matisse, Henri, 145–46
Matthews, Olivia, 170
Maynard, Mr., 26
"Meaning of Life, The" (Wald), 202–3
media, mass, 122, 239–40, 244
Meisel, Steven, 16
memories, 27–35, 57, 94, 96–97, 130, 147–50, 155
mental efficiency, 120, 122, 130–31
mental illness, 37–49, 179, 191–98, 202
mental management, 117–23
mentors, 17–18, 143–44
Merrill, James, 218
metaphysics, 61–62, 199–204, 289, 298–99
Metz, Peter, 81, 104–5
middle age, 8, 9
mission, sense of, 56, 113, 144, 287, 294–95
Mr. Fenwood (cat), 161–62
mistrust, xviii–xix, 135, 228, 235–38
Mitchell, Christine, xii–xiv
Monet, Claude, 145
money, 113, 115, 207–9, 228, 229–31, 233, 257–58, 303
Montale, Eugenio, 220
moral values, 182–90, 206, 210, 255, 258
motivation, 87–88, 120, 149
Mott, Lucretia, 154–55
Mount Auburn Cemetery, 64–65

Mozart, Wolfgang Amadeus, 122
Mulroy, Sheila, 243–52
murder, 243–52
Museum of Modern Art, 142
music, 122, 123

Nannicelli, Linda, 195
narcissism, 13–14
National Longitudinal Study on Adolescent Health, 7, 256
Native Americans, 281–82
nature, 57–58, 156–60, 288, 296–97
  beauty in, 141–42
  religion and, 156, 159, 202–3
neighborhoods, xii–xiv, 228–29, 233, 243–52, 256
Nell, Aunt, 169
networking, 4
neurological development, 132
New England Journal of Medicine, 113
New England Memorial Hospital, 244–45
New York Times, 16, 133
norepinephrine, 133–34
normalcy, 217–22
Nunes, Akacia, 269
Nunes, David, 269–82
Nunes, Gail and Tony, 269–82
Nunes, Mariel, 269, 270, 271, 272, 274, 275, 276–77, 278, 280, 281
nursing mothers, 134
nurturing, 59, 78, 209–12

O'Donnell, Kendra, 6
O'Hara, John, 308
old age, 8, 134, 296
One Flew over the Cuckoo's Nest,
    192
opportunism, 255, 256
organizations, 8, 60–61, 134,
    171–81, 289, 298, 307
Overworked American, The
    (Schor), 112
oxytocin, 88, 134

pain, sharing of, 83
paranoia, 197, 235
parents:
    abusive, 72–74, 78–79,
        93–94, 95, 148–49
    biological, 54–55, 150–51
    children's connection to,
        42–48, 80–83, 89, 263,
        265, 269–82
    separation from, 66–69
    substitute, 73
    values instilled by, 182–83,
        210, 255
Paris Review, 220
Paul (homeless man), 178–79
perception, 143–45
performance groups, 136–39
Perry, Dewolfe, 24
Perry, Tinka, 23
persistence, 41, 227
Peter, Saint, 237
pets, 58–59, 156, 161–64,
    288, 297
Phillips, J.C., 173
Phillips Exeter Academy, 6–7,

26–27, 35–36, 183, 254,
    255–56
physical presence, 125–26
Picasso, Pablo, 142, 143, 144,
    145–46
places, special, 57–58, 156,
    157–59, 288, 296–97
Plato, 216
play, 216–17
poetry, 41–48, 218–22
politics, 14, 61, 240–41, 298
Pollack, Phyllis, 81, 82
Poulnott, Miss, 29
poverty, 231
Power Lunch, 170
praying, 23, 24–25, 81,
    199–200, 298
Presumed Innocent (Turow), 220
principal investigators (PIs),
    17, 113–14
privacy, 213–14
probability, 166
problem solving, 131–32, 211
productivity, 21, 117, 120, 121
progress, 216
Prozac, 75
psychics, 278–79
psychosis, 39–40, 72, 86, 193
publishing, 218, 219–20,
    222

racism, 173
Random House, 219–20
Ratey, John, 105
reaching out, 79, 138
reading, 168–70, 262–63
Reading, Mass., 243–52

rejection, 228, 233–35, 259, 263

relationships:
 commitment in, 88, 102, 227
 in families, 5–6, 7, 20, 64–79
 healing and, 192
 intimate, 84–102
 limits of, 161, 261–62
 work, xv, xvii, 112–40
 see also friendships; marriage

relatives, xiv, 70–71

religion, 69, 134, 174, 199–204, 211, 266, 289, 298–99
 nature and, 156, 159, 202–3

relocations, 76–77, 97–101

Rembrandt, 57, 144, 200

resentment, 66–67, 68, 92

Resnick, Michael, 7

respect, 102, 112–13, 116–17, 129–30, 182, 184–87

responsibility, 216, 217–22, 228, 231–32, 233, 262, 264–65

Rich, Frank, 60

Ropes and Gray, 170

Rotary Club, 173

sacrifices, personal, 85, 87, 257

Saint Michael's Church, 23–24, 34, 35, 174

schizophrenia, 37–49, 179, 197–98, 202, 269

schools, 165–70, 229, 230
 boarding, 6–7, 26–27,
  35–36, 71, 147–48, 183, 254, 255–56
 class size in, 190
 colleges and universities, 117–23
 elementary, 15, 182–90
 secondary, 15, 253–58

Schor, Juliet, 112

Selby, Mrs., 24, 27

self-assessment quiz, 285–90

self-condemnation, 11–12, 209–12

self-esteem, 7, 15, 87, 92, 94, 170, 225, 226, 234–35, 260, 262, 263, 264–65

self-identity, 77, 84–85, 187–88, 205–14

selfishness, xix–xx, 13–14, 89, 235–36, 257–58

self-knowledge, 205–14, 265–66

Semrad, Elvin, 193

sensory deprivation, 133

Shady Hill School, 182–90, 269, 270, 275

Shakespeare, William, 205

Shaw, Bishop, 181

Shaw, Bruce, 185–90

situs inversus, 81–82

situs inversus totalis, 81–82

skepticism, 237

Smith, Alan, 32

solitudine, 213–14

Southern Baptists, 73

Spiegel, David, xvii

Spielberg, Steven, 216

Spindler, Amy, 16

Spitz, Rene, 133

sports, 10, 56, 60, 104–5, 258–59
Stanton, Elizabeth Cady, 155
stars, heroes vs., 253–59
stress management, 117–23, 130–31, 133–35
Strivers, 138–39
success, xii, 3, 9–13, 14, 21, 62, 84, 120, 144, 206–9, 210, 220, 253–59, 299, 303
suicide, 117–18, 119, 133
summer camp, 71–72
Sunbeam, 115
Sutton, Jeff, 105

talent, 62–63, 206, 221
talking, 124–40
"talking cure," 192, 197–98, 237–38
teachers, 26–27, 35–36, 56, 253–54, 262–63, 298
teamwork, 88–89, 102, 135–40
technology, technological change, 16–21
teddy bears, 58, 59
telephones, 19, 128
television, 14, 20, 122, 167, 227, 292
Terry, Charlie, 35
testicular cancer, 191
Texas, University of, 172
therapeutic environment, 72–73
therapy, 72–73, 118, 122, 123, 192, 197–98, 208, 210, 237–38, 266
Thoreau, Henry David, 237

Tobin, Bess, 172
Tobin, Bob, 171–81, 241, 252, 273, 274
Tobin, Maurine, 171, 175, 176, 178, 273
tradition, 146, 153–55
transitional objects, 58
trapezius muscle, 122
Tremallo, Ellie, 35, 36
Tremallo, Fred, 35–36
trust, xviii–xix, 79, 109, 121, 134, 135, 197, 228, 235–38
Turow, Scott, 220
twenty groups, 137

underachievement, 3, 120
University of Texas, 172

Vail, Priscilla, 227
values, moral, 182–90, 206, 210, 255, 258
vasopressin, 134
Vietnam War, 14, 61
Vittone, Bernard, 159–60
volunteer work, 56, 231–32
vulnerability, 102, 138, 260

Wald, George, 202–3
Washington, George, 173
Watergate scandal, 14, 61
Webster (horse), 163–64
Wenner, Kate, 231
Who's Who Among American High School Students, 253

Williams, Ted, xv
Winnicott, D. W., 58
Wolfe, Tom, 220
women's clubs, 231
work, workplace, 112–40
  change in, 16–18, 118–19,
    138
  communication at, 118, 122,
    124–32, 133, 134,
    139–40
  connection at, xv, xvii,
    16–18, 56, 112–40
  disconnection at, 112–19,
    124–35
  financial rewards of, 113,
    115
  good chemistry at, 112–23
  human moment at, 124–40
  isolation at, 9–10, 121,
    131–35

practical tips for, 294–95
relationships at, xv, xvii,
  112–40
relocations for, 76–77,
  97–101
satisfaction from, 56,
  112–23
self-assessment quiz for, 287
sense of mission in, 56, 113,
  144, 287, 294–95
support at, 118–19
worry, 81–82, 118, 120, 121,
  123, 129, 131, 132, 135,
  168
*Worry: Controlling It and Using
  It Wisely* (Hallowell), 118,
  132, 168

Yeats, William Butler, 55